Global Issues in the
Context of Space

Global Issues in the Context of Space

Jean Kachiga

LEXINGTON BOOKS
Lanham • Boulder • New York • London

Published by Lexington Books
An imprint of The Rowman & Littlefield Publishing Group, Inc.
4501 Forbes Boulevard, Suite 200, Lanham, Maryland 20706
www.rowman.com

Unit A, Whitacre Mews, 26-34 Stannary Street, London SE11 4AB

British Library Cataloguing in Publication Information Available

Library of Congress Cataloging-in-Publication Data

Insert CIP data

∞™ The paper used in this publication meets the minimum requirements of
American National Standard for Information Sciences—Permanence of Paper
for Printed Library Materials, ANSI/NISO Z39.48-1992.

Printed in the United States of America

Contents

Introduction

To embark on an exploration of global issues, we must start by defining what we call global issues. Starting with the term *issue*, we generally define *issue* as an emerging reality or subject, or existing status quo that is unsettling in and by itself or through its consequence, and therefore invites a discussion for more clarity, or solution and settlement. In this work, in which we look at global issues, we narrow the definition to mean simply developing challenges to which solutions are needed.

To explore global issues we use the context of space. This means that we need to provide a definition of the notion of space and provide a justification for its use to explain global issues.

WHAT IS SPACE?

The notion of space can be understood from a geometrical sense, from a geospatial sense, from a metaphysical or philosophical sense, etc. It is often used in conjunction with time, leading to the concept of geo-temporal or geo-historical sense, namely of time and space. It is this conjunction of time and space that often allows us to contextualize a number of subjects or issues of interest. This conjunction of time and space appears like two sides of the same coin, namely, head and tail. History itself is written within the context of time and space, to which we add human activity. We pay less attention here on the notion of time. The time we have in mind is *now*. We pay more attention to the notion of space to understand global issues for reasons we explain in the following segment. Therefore, we understand the notion of space here, primarily, in its generic sense, as any surface, an area or a zone, implying a canvas in which the activity or life can take place. This, of course, is a definition from a social sciences perspective, as there may be spaces in which there is neither life nor human activity taking place. We understand space as a theater of human activity. Secondarily, from this generic definition derives the fact that there are many kinds of space in which activity occurs, and therefore issues associated with such activities emerge. In the end we count a number of different kinds of space, which have one thing in common, namely to host human activity.

> As such a space can be abstract. *Abstract spaces are intangible zones.*
> Example: mental space, cyber space (virtual)
> A space can also be concrete (physical). *Concrete spaces are tangible zones.*
> Example: a supermarket, a city
> A space can be neither abstract nor tangible. *The outer space (extraterrestrial space)*
> Example: the universe

In addition, there is a category of spaces that we call *structured spaces*. They are organized spaces that may very well be tangible and physical, such as schools or supermarkets or banks, but also abstract and intangible, such as constitutions, religions, or civilizations. Structured spaces, physical or abstract, have in common the articulation of a purpose, or claim, as there is a reason why they are created; they articulate demands and expectations designed to help them meet the purpose for which they are created.

There are different kinds of space. They are mental space—personal space—private space—public space (with different scales: local, national, international, and global)—structured space—cyber space—outer space. The various kinds of spaces are distinguishable from one another. This is to argue that human activity and the issues it engenders do not proceed from space to space without the realization of boundaries separating the various spaces. Such boundaries dictate the adjustments we make when we act in different spaces. The adjustments are necessary because spaces are distinct and distinguishable through their nature. For example, we act differently when in church versus when in a supermarket. Spaces are also distinguishable through the respective purposes they serve and for the different forms of activity that any given space allows, prescribes, facilitates, or invites. For example, a fertile land in a valley of a semi-arid climate, propitious for agriculture, invites farming, settlement, and maybe the development of a town as opposed to a dry land in a desert. In these two spaces, different activities will take place and, as a result, different issues will arise.

Finally, spaces are distinguishable from one another through structure. Structure is the result of a combination of the nature of any space, the activity that space invites, and the patterned processes of such activity induced by the need for efficiency, productivity, effectiveness, or just functionality. Spaces are functional because activities take place within them. Their functionality is patterned to facilitate the purpose they serve.

WHY THE USE OF THE CONTEXT OF SPACE?

We use the context of space to organize the analysis of global issues for the following reasons. First, spaces are the theaters, the canvases of human activity. Spaces lend themselves to all kinds of activity. They are hospitable to human existence: they provide resources and host and support life. They constitute the habitat of the human species and its activity. The variety of spaces offers a diversity of ways through which human beings, individually or collectively, materialize their interests, visions, goals, hopes, etc. While pursuing these things through their activities, human beings display a multiplicity of preferences, leading to different attitudes, choices, decisions, and actions, many of which may diverge, collide, and cause prejudice or harm, thus creating the issues that are inherent to societies. Human activity, which does not occur in a vacuum but rather in a spatial context, engenders issues that are better understood primarily from that context.

Second, spaces are attractive simply because of their ability to host human activity and facilitate and service human needs. A coastal town with a long, clean beach attracts tourists, hoteliers, and retirees, and the activities they prefer. The vibrant economy of a nation, which is a space, attracts immigrants in their quest for labor. Other nations enjoy the availability of natural resources, which can spark industrial activity. In the international realm, the attraction is international trade and relations. The world's superpowers have enjoyed the attractiveness of spaces with access to the sea, engendering their naval activity. A religion can attract new followers, as in the case of Buddhism attracting followers from the West. The cyber space has made our lives much easier because of what we can accomplish through it such as in the field of communication.

These examples show the various theaters, or spaces, of specific activities, commensurate with their ability to facilitate and host given activities, which explains their attractiveness. The attractiveness of a space explains a series of activities around the notion of spaces and, therefore, a series of issues around the notion of spaces. Such a series of activities include the need to seek new spaces, to access spaces, to control spaces, to use spaces, to organize spaces, to protect or secure spaces, and even to expand spaces.

The Need to Seek New Spaces

There are two main reasons for why people seek new spaces. The first reason is simply human intellectual curiosity, which explains the existence of space science, stimulated by our need to explore more of our universe after we had discovered all the spaces on our planet. Second, spaces already occupied on our planet may be deficient or limited, as a result triggering the need to seek new ones to remedy such limitations. Every discovery of new space brings both opportunities and consequentially, new issues. There may be, for instance, benefits associated with human exploration of the universe, but such exploration engenders competition in the space race among nations, which appropriate technology and programs. The interest in space and the constantly improving engineering science and technology that produce materials that bring us closer to mastering the challenges of planetary exploration, will certainly, as in the time of the Columbian era explorations of new territories, bring a new set of issues relative to whatever we find out there.

The Need to Access Spaces

The need to access spaces by humans, since the beginning of mankind, has produced the activities of conquest, colonization, commerce, and immigration, and also those of human trafficking and the trafficking of sex, organs, children, and labor. With such activities also emerge a new set of issues: abuses, crimes, black market activity, illegal use of drugs, prostitution, sex slavery, etc. The need to access new spaces, therefore, comes with a set of new issues.

The Need to Control Spaces

The need to control spaces is associated with the notion of property, ownership of what is valuable. To ensure ownership we acquire titles, through which we claim ownership. The need to control space has justified the activity of establishing borders, frontiers, and boundaries, which can be natural or artificially designed. Such activity has produced a number of issues both in the past and the present.

The activity of control of spaces occurs through the design of mechanisms to order and regulate the lives of citizens. This necessity has produced issues such as border conflicts, political power and resource conflicts, and other geo-politically driven conflicts. The conflict in Darfur, Sudan, for instance, would not exist if there were no oil in the region nor if the region were not occupied by the Sudanese of African descent, who clash with the Sudanese of Arab descent from Khartoum, both seeking control of the region and, therefore, access to it. The 1994 conflict in Ruanda was about political power before it turned into an ethnic conflict.

The Need to Organize Spaces

The need to organize spaces occurs after a space has been claimed, or taken under control. Organizing spaces consists of the activity of establishing a structural framework in which value systems, norms, customs, and laws are expressed to order and channel the variety of streams of activity in a society to safeguard public peace. This need justifies the existence of structured spaces such as governments and religions, and governing people sharing the space through interactions. It produces in the process shared ethnicity, nationality, culture, and civilizations. The process justifies and explains the existence of political societies. It also explains the issues associated with changing consciousness as values and norms change and as societies experience changes in ideas and ideologies, or negotiate new technologies, etc. The result is emerging issues such as the use of marijuana in the United States, the acceptance of same-sex marriages, or the redefinition of the notion of gender, etc. Issues around cultural identity, ethnic conflicts, religious differences, and value discords, etc., also fall into this realm.

The Need to Use Spaces

The need to use spaces occurs through the exploitation of natural resources, the development of land for production, and other economic activities. Here, as well, such activities have produced, historically and today, a number of benefits but also prejudice and grievances affecting a number of peoples in different spaces around the world and harm to the environment.

The Need to Protect or Defend Spaces

The need to protect or defend spaces is fundamental, mostly when the spaces are coveted because of their riches, resources, strategic value, or simply as spaces in which to live, as a *lebensraum* (German: "living space"). Ensuring the physical safety of people is paramount. Ensuring safety leads to recurrent wars, against which one must defend. But such a need to defend oneself may very well be in itself the expression of malaise or the consequence of a dormant or existing conflict. It leads to military and national security activity. It explains the many wars in history, ane even the war on terror.

The Need to Expand and Extend Spaces

The need to expand spaces can be explained by the need to not be confined, to be able to maneuver, to enjoy the benefit of spaces, to increase control, etc. The same reason we seek to access new spaces explains the need to expand and extend. It leads to activity designed to achieving just that. Since the end of the nineteenth century, the modern world has abandoned the imperialistic tendency of seeking expansion through conquest. Today, expansion of spaces occurs not through settling new spaces but rather through gaining influence, even from a distance. It is done by those nations and actors that have influencing capabilities. It is exercised in the realm, or the space, of international relations. It is also about expanding market share in a global economy or about expanding the space of cultural or religious supremacy. There are, however, other spaces, beyond our planet, that have engendered a fascination with and the need to expand our current world space, which is the basis for our interest in outer space. The activity of such interest is that of the exploration of outer space, which may possibly lead to accessing, settling, exploiting, and using it in whatever way is beneficial to hosting human life. Such activity is already under way, as the National Aeronautics and Space Administration (NASA) constantly feeds us with images and proof of the progress it makes in that regard. Here, as well, such activity carries the potential to create new sets of issues, some of which are already imaginable and others not yet foreseen.

The need to access, control, use, organize, protect, and even expand spaces, and the activity they induce may happen all at once or in any combination, producing a specific issue as a result. Such is the case, for instance, with the conflict in the Middle East between the Palestinians and the Israelis, which is about controlling land. It is grounded in differences of ethnicity, culture, religion, civilization, etc.

Third, we use the concept and the context of space because spaces come in different kinds, in the various categories we have identified. And because in their own kinds they are specifically attractive, they are theaters of specific activity, and therefore produce specific issues. Issues are specific to spaces. Indeed, the variety of spaces that exist, attract a diverse range of activities and their sets of issues. Indeed, an abstract and intangible space such as mental space is a canvas for the activity we call thinking. It is also the space of specific issues we call mental issues, such as mental dysfunctions, pathologies, psychoses, etc. The cyber space hosts a specific kind of activity of communication and exchange of sound, images, words, etc., but it is also a space where we find specific kinds of issues such as cyber bullying, cyber piracy, identity theft, computer hacking, and other Internet-related crime. Intangible, abstract, and structured spaces such as government, religions, civilizations, and even a state's constitution are theaters of activities that are not without their sets of issues. Indeed, in government we constantly negotiate political issues; for example, we argue whether abortion should be legal or not. Religions' teachings cause issues, as there are people who kill in the name of religion. In civilizations, there are issues around value systems that emerge among and between civilizations.

Human issues are engendered by specific activities dictated by the nature and the demands of a specific space within which they occur. As a result, every type of space breeds its own set of issues.

We argue that the variety of issues to be analyzed, their specificity and complexity, or the lack thereof, are comprehensively better explained from a spatial perspective, without which any other explanation, even though insightful in its scope, may lack the necessary scale to analyze global issues. It is this importance of scale that justifies approaching global issues from a spatial perspective. Indeed, issues that qualify as global issues emerge from specific spaces, but their dynamic scales are what render them global. The ability of global issues to transcend their spatial scales is indeed the main characteristic of a globalized world because of the growing interconnectedness of the scope and scale of human activities today.

What this book is about is to highlight the relevance, and therefore the pertinence, of the role of space in the analysis and explanation of global issues. The notion of space therefore serves as the thread in guiding the examination of global issues. We argue that the issues examined here are better explained through the lense of space.

The subject of this book is about the exploration and analysis of global issues in a space context, without consideration of time. Here, we consider only space because the issues we explore pertain only to the globalization era, which means issues that have emerged during the past thirty years. The globalization era has intensified the scale and urgency of some issues, which we call global issues. What this approach of using the concept of space does differently is that it organizes its analysis around the concept of space rather than around a random issue and discussing it ad hoc. Such an approach leaves the feeling of picking up a passenger on the side of the road and taking him or her to a destination, but he or she has not been at the start of the journey.

The need to provide a context to analyzing global issues has led to the need to conceptualize the entire project gradually following the role and impact of space in global issues in their various categories. The content of the book examines the most relevant ones, beginning with the role of space in issues of identity, ethnicity, and nationalist conflicts, and on a larger scale, the role of space in issues involving culture, religion, and civilization and those created by the dominance of structures they produce over individuals. The content of the book also examines the expanding notion of space since the European expansion and the integration process that led to the internationalization of space and the integration of various spaces, which Halford Mackinder (1904)[1] has called "the Columbian Epoch." Such internationalization of space produced a world economy and issues related to access and control of new space, colonialism, markets, and resources. The sustained integration process has led to an intensification of exchange and activity on a global scale and produced a globalized economy. We have since expanded the scale of human activity to reach the entire global space. In the process we have intensified a number of issues including immigration, global health, human trafficking, and environmental destruction.

The above-mentioned issues related to the globalization era have existed before the paradigm of globalization. They have not been caused, nor have they been produced by, globalization—they have only been intensified and accelerated by increased mobility and the extended space of exchanges and actions of people and goods around the world.

This new globalized world is shifting the center of gravity from the West to the East, which are spaces of influencing global world issues. The interest in this new space of influence is justified by the fact that global issues have been ignited, tamed, driven, or controlled by the rising of superpowers. If China is to become a superpower, it will have to be relevant in its quest for finding answers to global issues, as it has already been shown to be in China's interest to tackle the issues of climate change. The center of gravity of world affairs indeed had a spatial locality, beginning with Western Europe during the Columbian Epoch to the United States and its competitor, the Soviet Union. It seems that China has been growing to become a power that is expected to help forge a way out of some of the most pressing global issues. It is this changing hierarchy of influencing capabilities in world affairs and global issues that justifies the concept of changing geopolitical codes.

Changing geopolitical codes examines how little by little, rising centers of economic activity induce an adjustment on behalf of other world nation-states around the world. China is particularly in focus. Geopolitical codes are defined by Flint (2012, p. 44) as a set of parameters through which nation-states determine their position among others by taking stock of their friends, existing and potential, and their foes, real and probable. In the process, they consider options to nurture friends and counter threats. Because of the changes brought about by globalization and its newly induced shape and implications, the traditional constellation of friends and allies needs to be reconfigured. The chapter, therefore, looks at the current picture of how nation-states are nurturing their relationships, defining their competition, and identifying their foes in light of today's imperatives.

In the end, we examine the newest space invented by digital technology: the cyber space. The cyber space is examined as another issue area that has emerged as a result of a newly created space, the virtual space. As a space it is a canvas on which human activity takes place, even when virtually. And as in society, everywhere human activity takes place issues arise. These issues are those of control, conflict, crime, status, identity of actors, regulation, etc. Therefore, this new space and the issues it raises are also subject to examination.

In conclusion, the approach taken in this book consists of linking a variety of issues that we discuss, from their diverse origins as we have categorized them, with the fact that they are the result of specific activity that is induced, stimulated, or explained through a specific spatial context. The approach establishes a causal or consequential continuum between specific spaces with specific activity and specific issues. The intent and benefit of the approach, we hope, is to gain some degree of control over a multiplicity of issues and the variety of fields from where they emerge.

The book, therefore, is designed to provide an inventory of global issues emerging from the most immediate of spaces, namely issues about identity— gender identity, ethnic identity, and national identity. Here is where specific issues such as ethnic tensions and conflicts, and ethno-national conflicts and wars will be discussed, as well as gender issues such as gender-bending, and same-sex marriages.

The next spatial level is the national and international level, where we explore issues resulting from our affiliation to structured spaces, and among them, religions and civilizations, which have a way of telling us what to do through their demands and expectations and cause some of the global issues we face today. Here we discuss issues associated with freedom and the role of church in public space in light of issues such as abortion, sharia law, the display of religious signs, separation of church and state, the tension between religion and politics, and even terrorism in so far as it is justified by religions.

The next spatial level is the global level. Here, we examine issues that have been exacerbated by the advent of globalization. They are issues that affect different countries around the globe, in different ways, and are fueled by the context of globalization. Among them we include immigration, terrorism, the environment, global health, human trafficking of organs, sex, labor, and children.

The next level is that of the new space created by the new technology, the cyber, or the virtual space. This new space, like any other space, is a canvas for human activity. And here, such activity is producing new sets of issues to grapple with. Among such issues we include cyber crime, cyber bullying, cyber spying, cyber piracy, identity theft, and the beginning of the possibility for a cyber war and cyber warfare. All these new issues bring about challenges to lawmakers, users (personal and corporate), and service providers.

The book, therefore, is organized to discuss these issues, which are global in their respective ways from the smallest spaces in which they appear, for instance, identity issues, ethnic issues, and gender issues in communities, to the next set of issues in the next spatial level in which they appear, for instance, the national scale and issues there, followed by the international scale, the global, and the cyber space with the respective issues found in those spatial scales.

NOTE

1. Halford J. Mackinder, "The Geographical Pivot of History,"ß *The Geographic Journal*, April 1904.

Chapter One

Space-Related Concepts as the Primary Locus of Human Activities and Issues

In the introduction, we defined space in its geopolitical sense, which means in its physical spatial sense, which serves as the canvas of human activity and which over time produces human history. As stated in the introduction, human activity engenders issues. Such activity proceeds within specific spaces. Of these spaces the most immediate are those within which we take our first steps into life, into social life. They are spaces of our socialization. They are spaces that range from family to schools to churches. They are our towns and cities and beyond. This perspective compels us in this first chapter to explore such spaces in which our individual, social, and cultural identity is first formed and shaped, because the first set of global issues we subsequently discuss deal with cultural identity issues.

These immediate spaces in which our cultural identity is formed and shaped are specific and come with their own definitions and content. They are spaces we call locales, locations, and places.

Next to space, they are geographic terms with historical and sociological implications. They are space-related terms that we use, sometimes interchangeably if we do not need to be precise. To be precise here we define and explore their meaning and implication to human activities and issues. This step is a necessary one, as these terms will be referred to throughout the text. Following are their definitions and implications to human activity and to global issues.

A *locale* is an institution that organizes an activity within a space (Flint 2012, p. 21). Examples of locales are stores, homes, schools, and churches.

Social beings are involved in a variety of activities, many of which occur in specific locales. Different activities, therefore, require different locales. As a result, the activities of locales are complementary. Indeed, locales complement each other as follows:

- Homes, schools, churches, playgrounds, etc., complement each other, as homes have children who need schools and families often have a faith that invites believers to gather for services in churches, mosques, or synagogues.
- Casinos, hotels, banks, strip clubs, etc., complement each other, as casinos have licenses in specific geographic areas and therefore hotels are needed to accommodate those who come to play/gamble and stay. The environment often attracts prostitution, which justifies the strip club business.

Instead of complementing each other, locales may also be exclusive, simply because the activities they organize and/or promote logically and consequently so impose or require.

- Churches and casinos are not an ideal combination, as churches essentially promote values that are not best served and observed in establishments of gambling such as casinos and their environments. The consequence is that there is a higher degree of probability that we would not see a casino built next to a church. Should there be a situation where such a combination exists, as it is indeed the case in Las Vegas, it is due to the very character of the place, which is purposefully designed to accommodate, facilitate, and even encourage entertainment—some of which ends up being spontaneous impulses but also mature decisions such as getting married.
- Brothels and residential homes are also another combination that has a high probability of not being in the same locale, as residents in typical residential locations would not tolerate brothels, and therefore their elected officials would not allow it to happen.

A *location* is a space with a specific function. Location is the function of a space. It is the role that a space plays in any given situation/case. In other words, it is the purpose that a specific space serves. A business is an example.

What Impact Does a Given Space Have on a Business?

Opening a store on Fifth Avenue in New York City carries very different implications than having the same store in Pierre, South Dakota. The decision of having a store in New York City or in Pierre, South Dakota, can potentially or surely boost or depress the business. Of course, such a decision will depend as well on the nature of the business.

Having a snow removal company in South Dakota makes more sense than having one in Miami. The key parameter is obviously the implication or role of the location to your business.

A *place* is a combination of location and locales. Every place is a location with many locales. This combination gives a place its character. Such an example is Las Vegas.

Obviously, Las Vegas, Nevada, has a different character than Des Moines, Iowa. Every place develops its unique culture based on the combination of location and locales, and the type of activities predominantly found: the culture of Las Vegas versus the culture of Des Moines. In the end, living in Las Vegas conveys a different experience than living in Des Moines. Growing up in Boston allows a different experience than growing up in Brooklyn, New York. Living in Rochester, New York, offers a different set of experiences than living in Pittsford, New York. Places therefore, are unique spaces.

There are many such places throughout the world. They all exude their own characteristics, which ultimately convey to each their character. Obviously, traditionally, such character was even more distinctively striking when places were located far apart by geography, culture, and politics. Although modern life styles tend to reduce such striking distinctiveness of places' characters, they remain vivid. Life in Jerusalem, Israel, is strikingly different from that in Tokyo, Japan. Each place has its own set of attractive features and worries, and therefore impregnating the character of these places. Jerusalem has worries such as national security issues, settlement issues, the tension between Palestinians and Israelis, and absorption of the immigrant population and its attractive features such as the climate, the sacred and holy sites for believers of Judaism, Christianity, and Islam. Tokyo has worries such as fear of earthquakes, scarce real estate, scarcity of agricultural land and its attractive features such as its magnificent parks, restaurants, and food. The same variation of character between places can be identified between Nairobi, Kenya, and Helsinki, Finland, or Mexico City, Mexico, and Atlanta, Georgia.

IMPLICATIONS TO GLOBAL ISSUES

The attractiveness of a place anywhere on the globe may have a global reach. If Paris is attractive as a city to the people of France, it may as well be attractive to the rest of Europeans and to the rest of the world. The number and influx of tourists around the world visiting Paris is proof, namely 28.9 million in 2011. The same thing can be said about Las Vegas and many other places around the world. The world benefits from specific character of specific places around the world.

The worries of any given place around the world may easily become the worries of the rest of the world. If and when the fundamentalists of Boko Haram in the North East Hausa region of Nigeria strike Christians and expatriates, other Christians and the nations of origins of these expatriates are affected. A training camp of Al Qaeda in Islamabad, Pakistan, or a narcotrafficking organization in Ciudad Juarez in North Mexico can be linked to terrorism around the world and crimes in the United States, or to drug import and death in Spain or Italy.

These notions of locales, location, and places that are linked to that of space are relevant to global issues, as they help provide a venue or serve as lenses through which to scrutinize the dynamics of global issues. The most immediate of human issues emerge in these spatial venues. And issues emerging from such venues can be exported into other venues, as spaces are interconnected. There is a natural hierarchy of spatial scales, allowing us to move from one to the next, and that is the case since our activities are not limited to just one locale, or location, or place.

The following chapter examines the first global issue in our table of contents that is best explained through the lens of the existence of space boundaries that give to different places their character, and such character, as it reveals the good things about a place, may also explain or drive conflicts. We do mean cultural identity conflicts or simply cultural identity issues as a global issue.

Chapter Two

Space, Identity, and Global Issues

This chapter discusses the following aspects: how space is organized and structured for the purpose of regulating activity, and how such activity within people sharing a given space accounts for the formation of our identity and the crystallization of shared cultural identity. Indeed there are different identity levels. They start with the existence of human beings, who become aware of their existence as self. Human beings become reflective and in charge of their existence, and start speaking for themselves using the subject "I." Through the process they become individuals with a private identity, or private self, to use the expression of Baumeister (1986). The private self therefore, is the product of a conscious awareness of self in its environment through biographical experiences reinforcing that awareness. Such experiences are cultural and sociological in nature, which produces another level of identity, that of gender identity, professional identity, ethnic identity, national identity, and many others, called the public or social self. Except for the biological self, whose existence before socialization is at first unaffected by sociological processes, other levels of identity have in common that they emerge through an interplay between the biological being that we are initially and the effects of experiences, perceptions, or attributions from our immediate environments. The notion of identity acquisition, both private and social, therefore is a culmination of a social process. For the individual, identity is a continuity or a composite of the life experiences of the self. But such continuity and composite experiences occurs in society. Society shapes even our most individual identity. For our social identity, it is the sociocultural context that determines the process in creating and shaping identity (Baumeister and Muraden 1996). In both cases, society plays a role. The scope of such a role depends on that sociocultural context, as in some, there is more latitude for individual input, and in others less latitude. Trandis (1989) therefore distinguishes between loose and tight societies. Loose societies are those in which such a latitude for personal input in the shaping of identity is large, and we count, on one hand, among them essentially Western nations that have gone through the influence of the Enlightenment and liberalism and their consequences of pluralism and diversity. Tight societies are those in which such latitude is narrow. Among them, we generally count non-Western cultures. The role society plays is justified by the fact that we are social beings and society tends to claim us, to absorb and weave us into its fabric. To do that society has molds or *gestalt*, as German philosophers would say, which is filled by attributes of us, what others see in us, for instance, our body mass; our personality, temperament, and traits; our talents, our sex, etc., and based on which image of us is projected into society and society projects back to us with ascribed roles, assignments, and expectations. In this process, society is interested in whatever features we have that it can use to enhance the tapestry of the social fabric. We acquire the sense of self through the reflection of ourselves from society. And sometimes we have a hard time identifying with that reflection of self from society when we fail to recognize ourselves in the expectations society has of us. It is the case when the individual or private self is in misalignment with the social self. There are also cases where the private self has a hard time identifying with self (the biological self). The risk of disagreement between the private self and the social self, and for that matter between the private self and the self, exists. There is therefore a need for a meeting point, or a point of joining. Speaking of meeting points, Du Gray and Hall (2005, p. 6) write: "the point of suture between on one hand the discourses and practices which attempt to "interpelate," speak to us to hail us into place as the social subjects of particular discourses, and on the other hand, the processes which produce subjectivities, which construct us as subjects which can be spoken." Our identity, both individual and social, is construed in a social, spatial environment. "To have a sense of self is to have a sense of one's location, as a person, in each of several arrays of other beings, relevant to personhood" (Weinreich and Saunderson 1998, p. 34). The role of society in the establishment of our identity ought not to be either total or suffocating or subjugating of the individual, who, after all, has a right to self-determination. It proceeds through a negotiating interplay between society and the individual, as both must adapt to changing circumstances. In the end, in this process of acquisition of identity, the key word in determining the role of society and the individual is adaptation (Baumeister and Muraden 1996, p. 1), as the process "does not imply mere passive acquisition of identity by individuals but it also does not overstate the scope of self-determination." In any case, identity has societal or cultural marks as it emerges and is shaped within a spatial context. The chapter therefore examines how such cultural marking shapes the collective identity of a community to produce what we call *ethnicity*. It examines as well the collective identity of a nation, which we call *nationality*. It finally examines some of the global issues revolving around ethnicity and ethno-nationalism as cultural identity issues, while establishing the relevance of the notion of space.

SPACE AND CULTURAL IDENTITY ISSUES

About borders, Popescu (2012, p. 7) writes: "Humans erect borders as a way to mediate between the familiar of here and the unfamiliar from there."

Our identity is formed, shaped, and more or less firmly established within specific spaces. These spaces are places of our upbringing, anywhere from hometowns to nations. They are organized and structured through norm providers such as values, customs, laws, religions, and institutions. These norm providers regulate activity. Norm providers are instruments of space organization. They order our activity in society through roles and assignments expected or attributed to individuals. They delineate our place in society. We identify with such spaces in which we have found a place, role, and assignments. Who we are, our cultural identity, is shaped through our role, assignments, and places. We affect and are affected by the fate of such space we call communities, in which we pay taxes, find employment, and establish relations and affinity. We become shareholders of the communities in which we live. The issues of such communities become our issues. Among such issues are conflicts arising within and with other communities. Just as issues arise within spaces we call communities, they may arise with other communities. Indeed, communities of people inhabit, occupy, settle, and claim specific spaces that are circumscribed by either environmental conditions (mountains, seas, inhospitable terrain such as deserts, etc.) or by other communities that claim the space nearby (neighboring communities or nations). Although nomadic people are the exceptions to this rule, generally communities and nations have spatial *boundaries*. Boundaries are expressions of delineation of space claimed from space, unclaimed by any given community or a national people. Other interchangeably used terms are *borders* and *frontier*. Borders are defined by Flint (2012, p. 128) as "a region contiguous with the boundary" and frontier as "the process of territorial expansion." While borders emphasize the separating lines between two regions and frontiers the farthest limits expansion can go, boundary, in our understanding, focuses on the conditions of existence within a space as a result of being kept separated from another. Although generally describing similar notions, these terms entail nuances, which is the reason we use one term, *boundary*, rather than the others, *border* or *frontier*. The notion of boundary is of significance, as it allows the process of cultural identity formation. Among such cultural identities that are built within boundaries, we have ethnicity and nationality.

ETHNICITY

It is characteristic of human beings, unlike any other animal, not to have particular proprieties. We are endowed with the ability to reason, adapt, evolve, and be molded and structured to reflect the relevant forces of our existence such as values we subscribe to and laws that shape our behavior. This means that we are born without a cultural identity; it is determined by factors after to our birth. Our cultural identity is construed. In fact, even our culture is construed. At birth, our identity is yet to emerge and here is where space is relevant. Space is here relevant, as it helps explain ethnicity as it constitutes the first source of content that will gradually and over time fill the empty reservoir of our undetermined propriety as human beings. This is not to be underestimated simply because who we are culturally is not predetermined and therefore who we are is the product of acculturation. Let us consider the case of any young people from the Basque region in Southwest France and others from a hill in Saudi Arabia. Chances are they have different ethnicity, religion, value systems, customs, folklore, tastes, etc. There is nothing natural that justifies or explains their difference in culture other than their respective cultural venues that happen to be spaces far apart. Moreover, the same young people would be just the opposite, meaning the young people of Saudi Arabia would culturally be Basque and the others from the Basque regions would now be Arab had they been brought up and lived in each other's cultural venue.

The process explains the centrality of the role played by cultural environments in the constitution of both identity and ethnicity. And if for a moment one considers the content that such identity and ethnicity brings, such cultural differences become more than just differences. They account for a variety of differences of sensibilities, behaviors, preferences, and tastes, which explain and justify their differences of choices, decisions, and behaviors. And let us assume for a second that such choices, decisions, and behaviors are not only different but also contradictory or even mutually exclusive, one can imagine the beginning of issues that may emerge based on such differences. Space therefore explains ethnicity and differences, of which some can be contradictory or mutually exclusive to constitute ground for possible conflicts.

It all starts with spaces and boundaries or borders. Spatial boundaries inhabited, occupied, and settled by communities are canvases of human activities. Activities and actions proceed through interactions. Such interactions allow the crystallization of a number of factors such as values and customs, as people collectively learn the behaviors that are welcome and those that are unacceptable. The same process justifies the establishment of norms. These processes occur and involve members of a community sharing the same space, whether they directly interact or are simply indirectly linked by a network of many interacting members. They all become socially and culturally glued together by the norms, values, and customs they produce. The collective of interacting community members who share the same norms, values, and customs in a given geographic space engenders the notion of *ethnicity*.

Ethnicity is therefore defined as a product of shared space, customs, language, belief systems (worldview or religion), aesthetics (intellectual and artistic senses: music, dance, literature, tastes, etc.), folklore (rituals, observed traditions, etc.), and consequently, diet and attire. It is the result of a process that produces a collective cultural identity.

Because there are a variety of space-bound communities wherein each has developed its own ethnic culture, we have a variety of ethnic communities throughout the world, for example, the Zulus in South Africa; the Cherokees in the United States; the Bavarians and Saxons in Germany; the Andalusians, Catalans, and Basques in Spain; the Bretons in France; the Massai in Kenya; and the Bashi in the Democratic Republic of Congo.

One of the distinct products of ethnic cultures is the aesthetics of their attires. The native Native American ethnic attire differs from that of the Bavarians of southern Germany or that of the Masai of Kenya.

The notion of ethnicity, however, has evolved from its primordial spatial context and sense to reflect the complexity of modern communities. Such complexity of modern communities can be explained through high mobility, moving in and out of original boundaries in which ethnic identity is first formed, and increased exchanges. It can be explained through increased interethnic relations, therefore expanding the basis of ethnic identification. It can be explained through reduced reliance on ethnic networks. It can be explained through the exigencies of modernity, which have forged more independent, self-determining human beings, emancipated from ethnic identification and embracing cosmopolitanism, etc.

Is Race a Constitutive Element of Ethnicity?

Historically people sharing the same phenotypical features (skin tone, color, hair, and others) have been associated with the same civilization, culture, or ethnicity. This is because historically, human communities are made up of individuals who share the same space, interact and develop kinships, have common gene pools, and share environmental influences such as climate, diet, public health, etc. The result is biological resemblance. This process links biology to culture, but the link is not apodictic or intrinsic. It can also produce a common civilization, culture, and ethnicity among various populations of distinctive biological backgrounds if people interact because they share what is called identity determining factors, which are land, customs, belief systems, languages, values, diet, attire, folklore, etc.

There is indeed a clear distinction between ethnicity and biology. While biology is natural, ethnicity is constructed. Biology is a natural phenomenon, and ethnicity is a sociological and cultural phenomenon. The distinction between biological identity and cultural identity is worth mentioning, since confusion at this level has led to identifying the ethnicity of a people or individuals with their biological phenotypes (how they look). How people look has been the basis for the nineteenth-century notion of race. Today's biology disputes derive from the notion of race based on the idea that there really is no biological basis for the categories we call races. The argument today is that there has been so much interbreeding among the human population that hereditary physical traits do not follow clear boundaries; "there is often greater variation within a racial group than there is systematic variation between two groups," as modern genetics argues (Eriksen 1993, p. 5).

The nineteenth-century elevation of race as an *explanans*, or the cause of sociological and cultural phenomena and behavior, has been detrimental to the notion of race itself. It has allowed race to be instrumentalized. Race was given a meaning, a centrality, and an importance it did not intrinsically have. Race became itself a social construct, allowing those who instrumentalized it to see in it whatever they chose, often serving the purposes and interests of those doing the choosing. This attitude of the nineteenth-century era of imperialism, which discredited the use of the notion of race, and thus transformed a biological concept into a social construct, can be reproduced today if and when not enough distinction is made between race and ethnicity. The consequence of amalgamating the notion of race and ethnicity has been to expect specific cultural attitudes or mindsets from people based on their "race." Amalgamated biology with culture has produced a false causal link, which assumed that "race" produces ethnicity/culture. Ethnicity, culture, and even civilizations are sociological (and historical) phenomena, responding to empirical imperatives and exigencies, but are not the result of biologically determined predispositions. The fact that people who are phenotypically different (with different skin tone, color, or other phenotypical features) may share the same ethnicity is proof. And so we have Black Hispanics in both

North and South America as a result of such historical processes, in this case the displacement of people of African descent in the Western hemisphere in the context of European expansionism. The nuance is of some significance to delink biology from culture, not to make cultural differences the product of race, as Eriksen (1993, p. 5) writes: "hereditary characteristics do not necessarily explain cultural variations." Cultural variations are the product of environmental stimuli and even of cultural value systems more than they are of race. Indeed, human beings are not predetermined. They are products of their environments.

The term *race* has remained nevertheless complex, and therefore "it has dubious descriptive value" (Eriksen 1993, p. 5). Efforts, however, have been made by most using the term race to be more nuanced in what it is and what it is not, what implications it allows, and what other implications it does not allow.

Race remains a relevant category in specific, appropriate cases. Some of such specific and appropriate cases can be found in the areas of sociology or cultural anthropology, which means areas in which biological factors are not used as an explanandum. For instance, the fact that a population of a specific origin congregates in a section of town, which is often the case in metropolitan urban areas in immigrant nations, and they happen to have the same physiological features is primarily a sociological and cultural phenomenon, in which race as a sociological variable may or may not play a role but in which race as a biological notion is not an *explanans*. That means, in this case, it may become knowledge worth having to find out why people of the same ethnic origin congregate together, which probably has practical, empirical causes and is probably not their biological makeup.

The enduring relevance of ethnicity has survived the prevailing argument of modernization analysis of both Max Weber's[1] material rationalism and Talcott Parsons's[2] functional structuralism. Indeed, the analysis of both Weber and Parsons focusing on the demands and imperatives of modern life saw in the ethnic dimension an obsolete feature of traditional societies, destined to be left behind as they transition into modernity. Ethnicity was particularism destined to make room for universalism (Stavenhagen 1998). The enduring notion of ethnicity is the product of a new identification with ethnic origins. Since 1945, through globalization, increased contact between societies and away from tribal communities has produced a need to reconnect with those fellow ethnic members found elsewhere (Eriksen 1993). It is in some ways a contradiction that modernity, which is supposed to lead us away from ethnicity, seems to lead us back to it. The answer to this question is provided by Friedman (1990, p. 311) when he writes, "Ethnic and cultural fragmentation and modernist homogenization are not two arguments, two opposing views of what is happening in the world today, but two constitutive trends of global reality."

The enduring relevance and role of ethnicity in modern nation-states is manifest in the cases of ethnic and nationalist conflicts, which we examine in the sections below. Such conflicts are part of cultural identity conflicts. Cultural identity conflicts are, therefore, the first global issue we discuss. It is the most immediate conflict, as it revolves around who people are.

Ethnic Conflicts

Before diving into such conflicts we propose revisiting the *notion of conflicts*, a familiar concept, as conflicts are inherent in societies. The notion of conflicts needs to be defined here to allow a proper understanding of the analysis. We suggest the definition by Johan Galtung (1998), who defines conflict as a situation arising when someone stands in someone else's way. The definition implies a "someone," or a "group X," having an interest (which can be anything from a car, money, or natural resources to political power) who cannot freely and easily pursue, reach, and achieve that interest because someone else or a group stands in its way—simply because they interfere with the pursuit of the object of interest or because they also are in pursuit of the same object of interest. Schematizing the definition, we have something like this: *Conflict: X (X') I*

Ethnic conflicts are those wherein a cultural element, in this case, ethnicity or one or more ethnic identity features, is interjected into the conflict. It is worthy to insist on the use of the verb *interject*. As some authors have noted, the very concept of ethnic conflicts can be deceiving when we take such a concept and assume it is simply about ethnic differences. Caution is needed because conflicts, as Galtung rightly noted, are generally about an object of interest and in only a few cases are solely about ethnic differences. Differentiating between the true natures of ethnic conflicts is what this chapter is about.

We distinguish two types of ethnic conflicts: those in which one or more cultural identity factors (or cultural identity determining features) and or biological identity factors of the actor or actors involved in a conflict are intrinsically the cause of conflicts. Such cultural identity factors are first the same as the ethnicity constitutive elements, namely religion, language, customs, and values, whereas biological identity determining factors are race and gender.

These cultural and biological identity determining features are intrinsic causes of conflicts such as the Muslims in Bosnia and Serbia, where their religion was the cause of persecution; apartheid in South Africa until the 1980s; Jim Crow laws in the US South in the 1950s and 1960s, which obviously were caused because of race; and conflicts involving gender discrimination around the world. We call these conflicts *identity* (cultural or biological) *intrinsic* conflicts. It is therefore conflicts caused by ethnic cultural features that are the *true* ethnic conflicts, specifically, when the difference itself is the problem. In such conflicts, there is X and (X') but not necessarily I. It is the classic case of conflicts.

There is another type of ethnic conflict. There are those wherein cultural or biological identity determining features of one of the involved parties in the conflict are *instrumentalized* for the purpose of gaining advantage, support, or sympathy. These are conflicts about a true object of interest (I) with two or more contending parties, X, X'. They may be competing over resources (I) for example, but if the contending parties X and X' happen to have distinct cultural and or biological identity determining features such as religion, race, or language, this distinction is used—instrumentalized—to depict the identity feature of the opposing party as the problem and thereby to galvanize the support of all those not sharing it or sharing the identity of the oppressor. Thus, if a predominantly Muslim group has a conflict with a predominantly Christian group over oil, as is the case in Sudan, to reach oil the Sudanese Muslims instrumentalize the difference of religion between the factions. The difference is then declared the true obstacle to exploiting oil. By so doing, the instrumentalization of the Christian Sudanese galvanizes the zeal of the Muslims, and vice versa. The phenomena is common because those suffering from political hardship, and therefore having grievances, often share common features, which explains their common predicament.

In modern societies and even more so in nations with advanced economies, such communality of features is often a communality of social class, profession, and interests. It justifies the existence of interest groups such as unions, corporations, the lobby, etc. Their communality of features is defined predominantly in economic terms, namely income. In many other nations those still predominantly traditional or semi-traditional or whose culture has barely modernized because of stalled industrialization (which is the prerequisite for successfully transitioning into modern culture), traditional structures still underline societal relationships. Here, traditional customs have not lost their relevance. They often remain the binding glue for social existence. The communality of interests, therefore, is not based on social class but rather on traditional affinity norms such as existing in geographic proximity, being interrelated, or sharing values, language, ideas, beliefs, interests, etc. This explains why communities that have common political grievances are at the same time bound by ethnic cultural features. Such ethnic features are those that are instrumentalized by their antagonistic counterparts.

When the intrumentalization of ethnicity happens we end up with a classical conflict situation, as defined by Johann Galtung, X (X') over I, which diverts focus away from the true nature of conflicts and renders it to be perceived as Muslim/Christian conflicts. It is this diversion that some authors have decried, calling ethnic conflicts a myth.

This scenario of instrumentalization of identity features in the case of conflicts has proven to be complex, as parties involved in conflicts do not always call identity determining factors at once distinct from those of their counterparts. Thus, we can have conflicts wherein one warring faction is Sudanese African and Muslim and the other Arab African and Muslim. In such a scenario, we have two warring factions sharing one identity feature, which is religion, namely Islam, but having distinct races, namely African Sudanese and Arab Sudanese, but each on opposing sides of the conflict about the exploitation of oil in Sudan. This was indeed the case in Darfur, an eastern province in Sudan. In general, these are classic conflicts as defined by Galtung, in which the identity of the warring factions is injected into classic conflicts, therefore making them *identity extrinsic conflicts*.

Recent history has provided a number of such cases from Cambodia (as a case of political identity conflicts, wherein people were killed for not adhering to Communism) to Bosnia and Rwanda, where the interest was access to political power by the Tutsis but opposed by the Hutus and therefore the ethnicity of one became instrumentalized. The notion of ethnicity in the case of Ruanda, it must be noted, is a bit tricky. The two main groups of people living in Rwanda are indeed Hutus and Tutsis. The former belong to a line of African people of the Bantus, and the later, are from the Nilotic, originally from the Nile region, or Hamitic people. One is essentially an agricultural people and the other essentially a pastoral people. These two groups spread throughout Africa and ended up producing ethnic communities wherever they went. The Bantus of Ruanda are those we call Hutus, and the Nilotic or Hamitic of Ruanda are those we call Tutsis. Each has distinctive physiological features.[3] Because both settled in the same land centuries ago, they ended up sharing the land, speaking a common language, and sharing the same customs and diet (although the Tutsis' attire remained distinctive from the Hutus'), ultimately marrying each other. By marrying from each other's groups, they increasingly blurred the historical distinctive features of each, which however remain visible by those that have not intermarried. The case of the Hutus and Tutsis is therefore tricky because they both share key constitutive elements of ethnicity and therefore should not be seen as different ethnic communities but rather as one; at the same time, they are generally referred to as two distinctive ethnicities. The reason is because of the distinctive physiological features that tell them apart, for the most part, and allow for that perception of two ethnicities. And it is based on their distinctive physiologic features, which underline their different historic origins, that the colonial power of

Belgium has used to further reinforce the sense of distinctiveness but also instrumentalized it for whatever political end and purpose it had in mind, often privileging the Tutsis over the Hutus. This as well contributed to resentments on behalf of the Hutus, who eventually, when the time came after independence, used their strength in numbers to impose their ethnic dominance over political life in postcolonial Ruanda. We have considered the Tutsis and Hutus as distinct ethnicities here mainly because political life in postcolonial Ruanda, and most particularly the quest for political power, has unraveled in the backdrop of such consciousness of distinctiveness and resentment of past rapport between these two groups.

In the case of Bosnia, the coexistence, resources, and power sharing were compromised by instrumentalizing the distinct ethnic identities of the parties in competition, namely the distinction between the Serbia Orthodox religion and the Muslim Bosnians.

In these conflicts, there is X and (X') and I, but I is rendered relative or overshadowed by the focus on the difference of identity of the warring factions.

Another type of intrinsic cultural conflict is the one entertained by *ethnopolitical groups*. These groups comprise members of a given ethnic community (often ethnic minorities, indigenous peoples, or underserved identity populations) with grievances they believe occur against their identity. The grievances are often about injustice, the need for self-determination, access to resources, power, recognition, etc. As they stand to address these grievances, they articulate their demands. They seek defending their interests against other ethnic groups or governments in countries in which they feel inadequately fully stakeholders.

Ethnic Conflicts and Civil Wars

Civil wars are the result of conflicts within a state, involving warring factions with specific grievances or diverging claims. These warring factions within a state may very well be the government itself and its military (the regime in power); rebellion groups (with or without arms) with grievances or political objectives of any kind (power, resources, freedom, economic hardship, etc.); the population at large, as the silent majority, often used as a pool from which the government forces can draw and mobilize to become militia, but also the uprising force uses to replenish their rank-and-file soldiers; ethno-political groups with grievances and/or claims; or ethno-nationalist groups also with grievances but emphasizing the claim of autonomy, secession, or separatism. The term civil is therefore an umbrella term for all kinds of intra-state conflicts, ideological, ethnic, nationalistic, and classic (wherein not cultural identity of warring factions plays a role but rather solely a political objective), between national entities.

Many conflicts that have broken out to produce internal wars have steadily increased since World War II. There are currently sixty countries involved in wars. Considering that the total number of nations officially recognized by the United Nations is 193, roughly one third of them are dealing with internal unrest (see Table 2.1). The number of all warring factions involved, militias, and guerrilla or separatist groups is 460. Across the globe, across cultural configurations, and across political actors and their grievances and claims, we have the following outlook of civil or intra-state wars considered to be *major civil wars*, as their casualties reach the thousands per year, as opposed to minor civil wars with fewer than a thousand casualties:

- *Major civil wars in Asia*: Afghanistan, Iraq, Yemen, North-West Pakistan, the Kashmir
- *Minor civil wars in Asia*: Kurdish separatists and Mujahedeen guerrillas in Iran; Kurds and Shiites in Iraq; Kurdish rebellion in Turkey; South Yemen insurgency; the Nagorno-Karabakh conflict; in India, the Hindu-Muslim skirmishes, Naga Rebellion, Mizo rebellion, Tripura rebellion, Assam rebellion, and Bodo rebellion; in Burma, Chechnya, Kashmir, Sri Lanka, the Philippines; the separatists on the Island of Bougainville in Papua New Guinea; Hmong in Laos; and in Indonesia, the west Papua rebellion, Aceh rebellion, Ambion ethnic violence, Sulawesi sectarian violence, Korea border battles, and Thailand
- *Major civil wars in Africa*: South Sudan, Central African Republic, Egypt, and Nigeria
- *Minor civil wars in Africa*: Algeria, Darfur, Libya, Casamance (Gambia and Senegal), Burundi, the Democratic Republic of Congo, the Ivory Coast, Liberia, Rwanda, North Sudan, Mali, Uganda and the Lord Liberation Army, the Cabinda separatists in Angola, the Chad and Central African Republic border conflict, Namibia, Nigeria in the Delta region, Niger and Tuareg rebellion, Ethiopia and the Oromo insurgency, and insurgencies in the Maghreb
- *Minor civil war in the Middle East*: Israeli-Palestinian conflict and Syria
- *Minor conflict in Eastern Europe*: the Ukraine
- *Major civil war in Latin America*: Mexico
- *Minor civil war in Latin America*: Peru, Colombia, and Paraguay

There are countries with serious internal communitarian tensions. Such tensions, although significant, have yet to reach a tipping point. These countries are Spain (Basques, Catalan), Belgium (the pressure of the Flemish commu-

Table 2.1. Number of armed rebellion groups in nations dealing with minor or major civil wars (some may be dormant but still exist)

Africa
- Algeria 3, Angola 2, Central African Republic 7, Chad 1, Ivory Coast 1, Egypt 6, Eritrea 4, Ethiopia 8, Kenya 2, Libya 4, Mali 11, Mauritania 2, Nigeria 5, Rwanda 1, Senegal 1, Somalia 10, Sudan 11, South Sudan 16, Uganda 3, West Sahara 1

Asia
- Afghanistan 8, Myanmar 27, China 1, India 33, Indonesia 4, Kazakhstan 1, Kyrgyzstan 1, Nepal 1, Pakistan 20, Philippines 7, Sri Lanka 2, Tajikistan 3, Thailand 4, Uzbekistan 1

Europe
- Northern Ireland 9, Spain 2, Russia 11

The Middle East
- Iran 5, Iraq 31, Israel 9 (including Palestinian groups) 42, Lebanon 6, Saudi Arabia 1, Syria 33, Turkey 4, Yemen 14

The Americas
- Chile 2, Colombia 3, Ecuador 1, Mexico 17, Peru 2

Source: Armed Conflict Database (https://acd.iiss.org/en).

nity against the Walloons), France (Corsica separatists), and Italy (the claim of the Liga Nord).

Many other major or minor civil wars have recently been resolved, have concluded, or are suspended. Many more will end, but others, old and dormant or new, may break out. Today, their number, their impact, and their humanitarian implications have forced the international community to pay attention. Like many wars, they produce extreme atrocities and casualties among unarmed populations produced purposefully, not as collateral of wars. They are not regulated and their conduct not subject to any international convention other than the crime against humanity clause. And here, even declaring that is itself an issue, as the numbers required to declare an occurrence of crime against humanity are not easily confirmable. When they are, the hesitation has been there from member nations, signatories of international laws to consequently intervene, as the debate on crimes in Darfur/Sudan demonstrated in 2007. Therefore, unlike classic wars, these civil wars have the particularity of targeting ad hominem anyone who is identified as "other." The result is often senseless, mass casualties; ethnic cleansing; massacre; rapes; mutilations; sodomy; kidnapping; forced labor; and dehumanization, as the cases of Rwanda, Bosnia, Cambodia, and the Eastern Democratic Republic of Congo have demonstrated, to name just a few. As a result, they all soon become major conflicts and wars, where easily thousands of people will die.

They have supplanted in many ways the interest that has often been reserved for international conflicts and wars. These international conflicts have diminished in their frequency and therefore in number and the hardship, destruction, and disruptions they cause. They indeed become a global issue. They affect more than the state within which they initially break out.

A number of reasons have been advanced to explain that increase. The cause of these many wars can be found in the nature of the conflicts producing them. But conflicts have multiple causes, dictated by a number of factors, as is often the case in the social sciences. Geography, resources, power, recognition, economic hardship, injustice, oppression, freedom, exclusion, etc., are just some of the causes that play a role, either alone or in combination with other factors, often producing ingredients that make the resolution of intra-state conflicts complicated. They do not simply end with a military victory or defeat. Often, military victory or defeat is not the best engine of producing the preferred outcome.

Structure of Civil Wars

Initially, intra-state conflicts have the following structure: a regime X (in power) with an interest I (secure power or and keep order, ensure security), being opposed by a resistance X' whose interest (access to resources, power sharing, or simply oppressed) is undermined by X and therefore must resist. X and X' stand in each other's way. If compromise is not an option, the conflict may remain dormant or break out and produce a civil war. The regime in power (X) often has the army and is normally better funded. The resistance movements (X') that arise because of grievances caused by X, the regime in power, are often led by ideological or ethno-political or ethno-nationalist groups or just a fed-up populace. The leaders of such groups, who may just be prominent and affluent members of the community such as clan leaders, charismatic peasant leaders, or just someone with an ambition, articulate a message aimed at galvanizing the support of their acquired constituency and appeal to potential sympathizers from whom ultimately they recruit militia members and financial support. This dynamic implies the possibility for additional support, or the lack thereof, both internal and external.

Regimes in power and group uprisings may or may not enjoy the population at large (the silent majority). Sometimes, this silent majority favors the regime. It may as well side with the uprising. Whether or not regimes in power enjoy popular support depends on a number of factors: the overall level of positive perception of the government's performance as guarantor of a more or less stable economic and peaceful status quo; the level of popular cultural identification with the government; overall government allegiance to a specific religion, ethnicity, or race that establishes a link to a popular base; the nature of the *casus belli*, etc. Conversely, support for the uprisings depends on the same variables.

Many regimes in peril, facing rebellion, have relied on such an internal population support with mixed results such as Ruanda, where the Hutu relied on their ethnic population making up the majority of the Rwandan population around 1994, and the Ivory Coast, where Laurent Gwagbo could not be saved despite the support of his ethnic-religious base in the southern part of the country in 2011. Other regimes use the assistance of surrogate forces to contain uprisings. Such is the case of the Islamic regime in Khartoum, Sudan, with the *Janjaweed* militia utilized to root out the SLA/M (Sudan Liberation Army/Movement) rebellion. Such support from the population at large is also crucial to uprising groups. They often do not have the same resources as the regimes in power. They rely on sources of financing often obscure or drawn from natural resources of regions they control. In Uganda, the rebellion of the Lord Liberation Army (LLA) has failed to galvanize the support of the population. Its unpopular cause and the economic stability of the regime of Yoweri Museveni explain that failure. There have been cases, such as in Angola between northern and southern provinces against the central province and in Sudan between the regime in Khartoum and the Christian South, where such an internal alliance factor was split down the middle. This increases the chances for a stalemate.

Extended Structure of Civil Wars

Civil wars rarely remain conflict in the territory where they break out. Whatever internal dynamics they incite, they do not remain bound by the territorial borders of the state. They attract external alliances. This explains the internationalization of civil wars.

These external alliances lend support of various kinds (weapons, personnel, financing, logistics, etc.) to warring internal factions, both regimes in peril and uprising groups, based on what are called *external alliance factors*. These external alliance factors are based on the level of sympathy (cultural affinity) and strategic political/economic interest from outside forces. The sympathy factor is contingent on the collective identity determining factors of warring factions. To the extent that an external entity (state or nonstate) identifies with a cultural identity of one of the parties to an internal conflict, there is potential to sympathize with it. When such a sympathy factor leads to favorable and active support, an alliance is created. Interest as a driving motivation for external alliance formation is self-explanatory, since geopolitical interests have historically been the grounds for countless alliance formations. The functional interpenetration of political power and economic resources often renders strategic political and economical interests contingent on one another. The sympathy and interest rationale explains the dynamics that internal conflicts create.

It is perhaps interest rather than the sympathy factor that constitutes the strongest motivational factor for external entities' involvement in internal conflicts. The reason for such interest-based realism is the quid pro quo nature implied in alliance formation, which necessitates a rational justification. Such external support may derive from foreign governments or nongovernmental entities such as multinational corporations. Note that rebel groups in one country may lend support to others in another. Such externally induced support may then produce the following combinations: a governmental external support to a regime or an external nongovernmental support to a regime. External support also occurs in favor of the rebellion when led by a *foreign government* and provided by a *non-governmental* entity.

The centrifugal structure of such a pattern that pushes civil wars to turn into regional conflicts begins with a state's regime X in conflict with its resisting group that we identify as X'. The resisting opposition X', or rebels, often has the support of another regime, in a different state, Y, based on a sympathy factor such as shared ethnicity, ideology, or religion but also based on a strategic interest, as Y stands to improve its own security or any other goal with X' power rather than X. However, in nondemocratic or authoritarian regimes, often any such state has its own internal opposition group. Therefore, often the state Y would have an opposition Y', which will now be assisted by X to weaken Y, who assists X' that is fighting X. This alliance formation then puts state X in an indirect and implicit conflict situation with state Y. We now have a skeleton or basic structure whose dynamic can be extrapolated and dissected as it is applied to similar or particular conflicts. With it, the internal dynamics dictated by the *internal alliance* factor can be scrutinized according to the dependent variables we have discussed (internal alliance with X or internal alliance with X'). With it, external dynamics dictated by the *external alliance* factor (*governmental external alliance or nongovernmental external alliance*) and its various possible combinations (governmental external alliance with X and governmental external alliance with X', the rebels, and/or nongovernmental external alliance with X or nongovernmental external alliance with X') can be examined.

Once again, African civil conflicts and wars adequately reflect this dynamic of external alliance formation with civil war warring factions or actors. Here, both governments facing rebels and rebels resisting governmental forces have always been able to count on external governmental or nongovernmental support or assistance from the regional neighborhood. The example of the war in Ruanda and the Democratic Republic of Congo shows this. The war involved all the neighbors, Angola, Zimbabwe, Uganda, Burundi, and South Africa, and continues to attract many others such as Tanzania or from far away. France, as governmental external support, is known to have done that

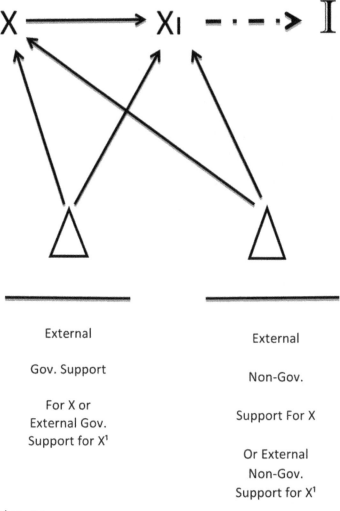

X ⟶ X₁ - · - · > I

External

Gov. Support

For X or
External Gov.
Support for X¹

External

Non-Gov.

Support For X

Or External
Non-Gov.
Support for X¹

Figure 2.1.

a number of times, recently in the case of the civil war in the Ivory Coast and Mali. Corporations as well as nongovernmental external support have been involved in these civil wars as the following examples show. Some multinational corporations without scruples have chosen to support some warring factions based on which party will guarantee access to coveted African natural resources. The most recent and publicized case of this phenomenon is the civil war in eastern Congo, the region of South and North Kivu, a region where the "wonder minerals of the moment" as Karl Wick (*Washington*

Post, March 19, 2001) put it, are to be found. Indeed, Kivu is the region where some of the richest tin, columbite, and tantalite, which is tantalum ore, are found. Columbite and tantalite, which together are called coltan, are incredibly important for new technology. They are used in the manufacture of advanced mobile phones, jet engines, air bags, night vision goggles, fiber optics, capacitors used in computer chips, smoke detectors, nuclear reactors, missile parts, and surgical and dental equipment.

Known cases of external involvement of corporations such as the Swiss-based Swipco, the South African–based De Beers, the Canadian-based Anvil, the US-based Mining Field International and Barrick Gold, the French-based Elf Aquitaine, British/Netherlands Shell, etc., have been documented by UN reports and studies by organizations in the international civil society and scholars such as M. Ross (2004) in *Economy of Armed Conflict.* Such companies have provided financial backing for armed conflict, aiding their economic allies in the acquisition of arms. In the Congo, the rebel movement to overthrow President Mobutu by Laurent Kabila had officially signed contracts with a number of companies such as De Beers even before he had won the war. Specialized services of organized, private armies of mercenaries based in South Africa and Namibia, and private military instruction firms in existence in countries such as the United States stand by to intervene in local conflicts. Some operational personnel of such organizations were recently caught in Zimbabwe heading to Equatorial Guinea with a purpose, based on their own testimony, of destabilizing the regime of Obiang Nguema.

These governmental and nongovernmental external supports are motivated by interest. Others are motivated by the sympathy factor, as shown by the support of Israel to the regime in Kigali Rwanda as a result of the genocide of 1994; the conflict in Ireland and the interest of Irish Americans in the United States; the Israeli-Palestinian conflict and the Jewish Diaspora and the Arab-Islamic world; the conflict between the North Muslim Sudan and the South Christian Sudan and the involvement of the US evangelicals; and the case of gender discrimination conflict in Islamic Pakistan in the case of the shooting of Malala Yousafzai and the outcry of all other young women and the rest of the world.

All things considered, external sympathy and external interest factors explain the dynamics of regionalization of civil wars. The dynamic is activated when formed alliances actually participate in the conflict by providing harboring space and political, logistical, military, and financial support to local allies. This dynamic has turned African foyers of local conflict into potential multiparty conflicts. When those conflicts spread, they seem to have a distinct pattern, which the following segment examines.

The Dynamics of Alliance Formation in Civil Wars

This need for state and nonstate entities to create alliances and be involved in the affairs of others has been theoretically explored in international relations literature. The need for states to protect themselves against threats justifies and explains the necessity for alliance formation. Small and weak states seek protection or opportunity by allying themselves with other partners. Kenneth Waltz (1979) has called this phenomenon "bandwagoning." They may choose to balance by joining forces with others (balancing) if they cannot arm themselves (arming) to deter the threat of open conflict. This theory addresses external threats involving states. Civil war context addresses both an internal threat between regimes in power and an armed opposition and potential external threats from antagonistic neighbors. This scenario necessitates a type of alignment that Steven David (1991) has called "omni-balancing." This type, according to David,[4] is the one we find in developing nations. He writes, "Third World countries' leaders' main aim is to ensure their political and physical survival, which is far more likely to be challenged by internal threats (with or without external backing) than from external threats."

But what is an alliance? We adhere to the definition given by Wolfgano Piccoli,[5] who sees an alliance as "a formal relationship of cooperation between two or more states involving mutual expectations of some degree of policy coordination on security issues under a range of conditions in the future." The definition proposed by Piccoli includes a variety of relevant configurations and motivations on which alliances are formed. It addresses, however, only state actors, not nonstate actors. We have pointed out that alliances may rise between nongovernmental forces (the case of two armed oppositions) or between governmental and nongovernmental forces (the case of a state supporting an opposition group).

Whereas the need for alliance formation is clear, the motivations of all potential allied nations are dictated by their different and specific security needs. They have different sensibilities and interests, different ideologies and ideals, and different cultures and identities. The complementary nature of any differences multiplies possibilities for alliances. As a result, alliances are always a result of a calculation expecting either an intangible dividend in the case of those based on idealism, morality, or cultural sympathy or tangible dividends in the case of those based on security and economic interests. Intangible dividends consist of the satisfaction resulting from the sense of a "we feeling" when the alliance has been driven by shared cultural, ideological, or religious norms. It may also consist of the prestige found in belonging to a powerful alliance. Tangible dividends are contingent on military and/or economic security that results from an alliance choice based on pragmatic interests. A government or nongovernment actor may seek alliance with another actor and expect a security dividend where it brought an economic benefit to the table or vice versa. The case of the United States and Saudi Arabia is such an example.

Despite their predetermined depth of involvement, alliances find a variety of expressions for common cause among allies. They begin with simple verbal and diplomatic support and may consist of logistics (military arsenal and technical material), financial aid, and the commitment of personnel and soldiers fighting alongside those of the supported allied. In the end, although threats justify military alliances in a world or region with an asymmetric power structure, the choice of allies is often driven not by the thought of which state offers more security (myopically defined in military terms by the realist view) but rather by which state identifies the most with another concerns and interests. Which state satisfies best one's interests (which may or may not be primarily of a tactical nature), and what dividend will be strategically gained from a given alliance? These questions are the questions that lead to alliance formation across conflict scenarios.

NATIONALITY

Cultural identity formation may exceed the ethnic realm. This has been the case, as through a rather messy process eventually nation-states were formed throughout the world. Our cultural identity has since increasingly been negotiated within the context of our nationality. It has been negotiated within the context of the national space. Nation-states are obviously spatially larger. Their larger nature implies incorporation of more than one ethnicity. Nation-states are, therefore, by nature, multi-ethnic, meaning they accommodate a variety of ethnic expressions and their amalgamation to form a new consciousness, which we refer to as national identity. This means that the same process that produces ethnicity is at work at the national scale to produce a nationality. Nation-states also produce national constitutive elements such as shared land, value systems, languages, aesthetics, folklore, diet, and attire as a result of both emerging interactions and exchanges but also because of binding mechanisms such as constitutions or laws as norm providers. Although there are other norm providers on the national level, the law prevails, as modern nations are essentially republics. The consequence of the notion of republicanism is discussed in chapter 5 on politics and religion. The law is the primary public space–ordering norm provider and in some ways a binding glue in so far as it is understood as the product of a social contract. It is this centrality of the law in the republic as a national space that explains the cohesion between multiple ethnicities of nation-states and justifies the extension of the national identity beyond not only ethnicity but also race, religion, and origin. Indeed, today, peoples of various ethnicity, religions, and origins are citizens of one and the same state. They become citizens based on the rule of law, which may rationally formulate and articulate determining criteria to citizenship. And when such criteria are based on and informed by the principles of justice, they open the door to people in their formal status as beings regardless of their particularities of origins, ethnicity, religion, etc.

Today, the context of globalization has extended the limit of national activity to a global scale, which means we can affect and be affected by world affairs today more than ever before, allowing an even greater functional permeability of national borders to foreign activity, and in the process to multiple cultural experiences. As a result the initial understanding of the nation-state as defined in the Westphalia Treaty has been transformed to truly be primarily a republican space and only secondarily about cultural ethnicity. It used to be that being French meant to have historically been part of traditional ethnic groups such as the Normans, Bretons, Burgundians, Basques, etc. Being German meant that one could trace his or her ethnic origin to the Bavarians, Franks, Saxons, etc., or being Spanish meant that one was of Galician, Basque, Catalan, or Andalusian descent. And so was the case with South Africa, where there are historical ethnicities such the Xhosa, Zulu, Ndebele, etc. Nationality derived from the notion of *jus sanguinis*, as the blood of any ancestry secures the rights to nationality, which means by birth. It derived as well from the notion of *jus soli*, which is based on the place of birth of a child, which means at birth, to determine their nationality.

Historically, multiple ethnic groups have integrated to establishing one national identity. Like ethnic identity, national identity emerges bottom up. The Italian, French, or German national identity is the product of that process. So we think of the French as being French, while insignificantly, alluding to their, let us say, Normand ethnicity.

Belonging to a nation is no longer a process grounded in the historicity of the ethnic presence to which one is originally part of. The same history as a factor has allowed for changes since the modern era that have displaced people or produced wars whose ends have forced an appropriation or expropriation of land that has contributed to a mixing of populations. Moreover, in the modern era, belonging to a nation has also become the result of a legal process of naturalization. There is a process through which one acquires a *de jure* citizenship or nationality. The result is that the descendants of the Bretons or Burgundians or Normans are French just as French as those who have acquired the French nationality but are descendants of Kabily in northern Africa or former French colonies of Senegal, Mali, Ivory Coast, etc. The identity of modern nation-states is today a growing pool of various cultural realities that are being woven together in a process that is ongoing today, and they are experiencing pains before producing new national identities of nations in which such cultural pools have increasingly diversified. In the United Kingdom, France, Belgium, and elsewhere, such new integration processes are indeed under way. The outcome of the process is yet to emerge. In many other nations around the world with a high influx and growing rootedness of new populations such a process is known and currently negotiated. It is the case from Dubai to Malaysia, from Portugal to South Africa.

In developing nations, generally, the process of integration has been under way since the introduction of the nation-state societal model, but it has somewhat stalled in many such nations because the driving engines of such an integration process, namely modernization, which in turn depends on industrialization and the efficiency of institutions to support it, have lack in many ways. The result is the still strong identification with ethnicity and the influence of ethnic ties.

In immigrant nations, such a national identity may not emerge bottom up but rather *top down* (Samuels 2012[6]; O'Neil 2010). Top-down national identity emergence is the case of immigrant nations where people having existing ties with an ethnic identity and a national identity of origin (already Italian, French, Irish, German, etc.) are immigrating into a new nation and having to immerse in the new ways of the new nations, only to find out that there was not one to be absorbed into or they voluntarily chose not to immerse themselves in the ones found. In the United States for instance, things were in flux as the new Americans figured out what to do as they cut client-patron ties with Great Britain and the old continent of Europe, declaring their independence in July 1776. They had to define what they were going to be about. To that effect, they met and designed a series of documents, the Federalist Papers and the Constitution and its Bill of Rights, in which they discussed the terms on which to ground their nation.

The terms have produced a certain idea of America, made of principles and ideals to which it was essential to subscribe to belong. Subscribing to those principles and ideals was primordial. It did not intend to induce a melting of identification of previous cultural identifications, as the term melting pot once suggested, but simply adhesion to the new. And even if it intended to produce melting, it has miserably failed, as Glazer and Moynihan (1970) or Wilson (2010)[7] have argued, pointing to the obvious formation in the United States of cultural identity communities such as Little Italy, Chinatown, Hispanic Harlem, etc., to illustrate the natural tendency to gravitate toward those like oneself for a number of reasons, as we explore in chapter 8 on globalization of space. As the people subscribed to the ideas and ideals of the new nation, they increasingly became Americans. The attempt of the Founding Fathers to establish America created a new culture. It is the one that today helps tell a US American apart from a French or an Argentinean simply after a relatively short observation. As immigration by people with far more distinctive backgrounds than the predominantly west Europeans grew larger, the idea of a culturally homogeneous America, closer to the Anglo-Saxon heritage, an intent documented through the pressure to force name changes on arrivals to Ellis Island, New York, from, for instance, Brusciani to Johnson, was unsustainable. Eastern Europeans, Asians, and Africans were arriving with their lingering accents and different physiologies and were not always ready to shed off features of their cultural identity of origin. Continuing pressure would have simply meant cultural intolerance.

In the 1980s, diversity was becoming the new sociological let-motive. The concept of cultural pluralism was resurfacing and the praise of the benefit associated with cultural diversity. It has continued gaining traction ever since. Today new Americans have become proud Americans who can proudly celebrate their ethnicity and/or nationality of origin without betraying their allegiance and commitment to the United States. They now call themselves Irish Americans, Italian Americans, Jewish Americans, African Americans, German Americans, Polish Americans, etc. The formula *Ex pluribus unum* was vindicated.

It is this spirit of the United States that has now been passed down through the two main mechanisms through which cultural identity perpetuates itself, namely *ascription* and *socialization*.

Ascription is a natural acquisition of biological heritage such as race, gender, and cultural heritage such as the language we speak and the religion we adhere to simply because our parents passed them down to us. *Socialization* is a process through which a biological human being becomes a social human being. These mechanisms explain our ties today to cultures of the past.

Ethno-Nationalism Conflicts

Nationalism conflicts are conflicts in which the ideology of nationalism is central. Nationalism underlies the notion of sovereignty and the uniqueness of a nation and its identity and therefore promotes loyalty and pride of the nation to its people. It is a notion that links identity to the concept of nation-state. Citizens of any given nation-state develop an identity tied to that nation-state. They can develop pride to belonging to that nation. They can all develop a sense of belonging to a nation. With that sense, comes a sense of pride. The sense of pride of one's belonging to a nation is the basis of *nationalism*. The result is that we have two types of nationalism. One is ethnic, based on ancestry, which we call *ethnic nationalism*, and the other is civic, based on allegiance, which we call *civic nationalism*. Civic nationalism is germane to patriotism in the sense that both express the attachment to the land, people, and culture one identifies with, and therefore naturally develops a willingness to serve or defend.

Such nationalism can be instrumentalized in various circumstances. It is often instrumentalized in cases of foreign attack, invasion, colonization, or imperialism, when the pride of a nation is wounded. The pride becomes the *cris de guerre* to galvanizing citizen's support when beleaguered and victimized by an opposing force and harnessing the energy and courage in a pursuit of reestablishing the integrity of their nation.

When such instrumentalization of national pride addresses civic nationalists it is simply seen as harnessing their sense of patriotism. It can as well address ethnic nationalists. This is the case in many of the *ethno-nationalism* conflicts around the world. There are conflicts around the world caused by ethnic factors or in which the ethnic factors are instrumentalized. In these conflicts, protagonists are ethno-political groups that often demand recognition, autonomy, independence, or secessions from any kind of tie with rival ethnic groups or governmental power they belong to. They seek separation. There are, indeed, a number of ethno-political groups around the world with ethnic-nationalistic demands for which they actively agitate. Among them are the Basques in Spain, the Corsicans in France, the Flemish in Belgium, the Muslims in East Indonesia, arguably the Liga North in Italy, etc.

There are a variety of expressions of ethno-nationalism conflicts. There are those between nations or a nation, or between a nation and and ethno-nationalist group, or between a nationalistic state and an ethnic community within that nation.

- *Nationalist conflicts between nations, which are not civil wars in which national pride is instrumentalized.* Examples: From the Chinese perspective, resisting the Mongols, the Manchurian and Japanese invasion was a nationalist quest; Hitler's quest to dominate Europe driven by the Aryan superiority claim and to Germany, the humiliating effects of the Versailles Treaty signed in 1919.
- *Nationalist conflicts between an ethno-nationalist group and a nation (government).* Examples: The Serbs under the Austro-Hungarian empire, the Basque separatists in Spain and France, Corsica in France; Tamil in Sri Lanka, Chechnya in Russia, Kashmir in India, Papua and Aceh in Indonesia, Darfur in Sudan, Kurdistan in Iraq, Iran, and Turkey, Palestine in Israel, etc.
- *Nationalist conflict between a nationalist state and an ethnic community within that nation.* Examples: Edward Benes in Czechoslovakia seeking ethnic cleansing; Ataturk conquest of Smyrna (today: Izmir) in 1922, Nazi

national socialism against the Jews; Turkish government in Istanbul in 1955 rolling panzers against Greek minority.
* *Nationalist conflicts between ethno-nationalist groups or communities (those will to dissociate from one another).* Example: In Cyprus between Turkish Muslims and Greek Orthodox.

Considering conflicts in which cultural identity factors are intrinsic or instrumentalized we can currently identity sixteen major dormant/active cultural conflicts. They are:

* Greece-Turkey: Muslims and Orthodox permanent tensions
* Chechnya: Muslims and Russian Orthodox rebels, on-and-off conflicts
* Armenia-Azerbaijan: Christian and Muslim tensions
* Serbia: Orthodox Serbs and Muslim Kosovar
* Afghanistan: Taliban Muslim against the rest
* Sudan: Northern Muslims/Arabs and Southern Christian/Africans
* Sudan-Darfur: North Muslims/Arabs and Darfur Christian/Africans
* Ivory Coast: North Muslim and South Christians
* North-East India: Hindus and Muslims
* East Timor: Christian and Muslim Indonesians
* Papua, New Guinea: Animists and Muslims
* Israeli-Palestinian conflict: Hebrew Jews and Arab Muslims
* Cypress: Turkish Cypriots in the North, Greek Orthodox in the South
* Turkey: Turks and Kurds
* Cashmere: Hindu and Muslims
* Rwanda: Tutsis and Hutus

NOTES

1. Max Weber, *The Protestant Ethic and the Spirit of Capitalism* (1905), 1930.
2. Talcott Parsons, *The Structure of Social Action,* 1937.
3. Hutus are generally robust and Tutsi generally slim. But intermarriages have blurred considerably these initial features
4. Steven David, "Explaining Third World Alignment in World Politics," *World Politics*, 1994, 43, pp. 233–56.
5. Wolfgano Piccoli, *Alliance Theory: The Case of Turkey and Israel.* Copenhagen Peace Research Institute, July-August 1999.
6. David Samuels, *Comparative Politics*, Boston: Pearson, 2012.
7. See Nathan Glazer and Daniel P. Moynihan, *Beyond the Melting Pot: The Negros, Puerto Ricans, Jews, Italians, and Irish of New York City*, second edition, Cambridge: MIT Press, 1970; or Sarah Wilson, *Melting Pot Modernism*, Ithaca, NY: Cornell University Press, 2010.

Chapter Three

Gender Issues as Space Issues

This chapter discusses gender issues as a global issue. It defines gender as an arrangement whose limitations and inadequacies explain the issues of gender. The chapter discusses as well that such limitations and inadequacies are mainly responsible for gender inequality. It discusses the role of space in producing such inequalities and the pushback against spatial gendered labor, role, and behavior, and how in advanced liberal democracies, more than in the rest of nation-states, the blurring of such space-gendered, roles, assignments, and behavior has been occurring, despite some areas of resistance. To continue pushing against such resistances, there have been institutional remedies applied in these nations such as quota systems and other mechanisms. The chapter finally looks at the ongoing success of the pushback against traditional gendered roles and at the set of new issues emerging in these nations, such as same-sex marriages, the recognition of third genders, etc.

We intend to demonstrate, primarily and specifically, that these issues are ultimately space issues. They are grounded in access, use, organization, protection, and control of various spaces in which the roles and assignments of men and women unfold, namely the private versus public sphere. They are about claiming spaces of exclusion for exercising roles and assignments by a specific gender. These roles are the products of a gendered arrangement primarily relying on biological grounds and which at face value make sense, such as, for instance, because women give birth they are expected to be caregivers and because men cannot give birth they are expected to be the protectors and breadwinners. The constrictive nature of the arrangement and its limitation of the spatial theater for female roles and assignments constitute the basis of gender issues. Gender issues, therefore, are primarily a contestation of a space ascribed for gendered roles and assignments. Such spatially

defined roles and assignments are eventually perpetuated through socialization, internalized and duplicated, and they sink into social consciousness to
become part of the social psyche of those identifying with given roles and
assignments.

We intend as well, secondarily and generally, to reaffirm the spatial charter
of gender issues in general, as such issues differ and vary in the way they are
dealt with, depending on different geographic spaces around the world. Different communities, cultural and civilizational spaces (East Asia, the Middle
East, Central Asia, Africa, the West, Latin America), have produced or are
governed by value systems that have produced their own gendered arrangements.

GENDER DEFINITION

Gender is generally understood as the social sex. This means that gender is
the expectations of society from each one of us based on our biological sex.
Generally we happen to be born male or female, and historically society has
built on that, organizing how the sexes relate to one another, ascribing roles
and assignments. This is what is referred to as gendered roles. Such an arrangement derives primarily from biological implications. Men do not get
pregnant but women do; men have more testosterone and women have more
estrogen; men are on average taller and stronger and have more muscular
mass and upper body strength.[1] These physiological facts seem to suggest that
men are better suited for physical, muscular, dangerous, perilous work and
women for nurturing, caregiving, and household activity and roles. The consequence has been a gender-based division of labor (GBDL), which reflects
primarily male and female biological attributes.

As a result, men are assigned roles that their physical attributes seem to
predispose them to do better. They can run faster, lift heavier weights, fight
more intensely, etc. They will become hunters, warriors, firefighters, builders,
high-contact sports players, and protectors of family and community when
dangers arise. They seem also predisposed, through biochemical makeup, to
have the skills and traits associated with tasks ascribed to them. These skills
and traits are assertiveness, competitiveness, aggressiveness, toughness, etc.
And they are socialized in a way that promotes and reproduces them. This
socialization reflecting social expectations produces male gendered roles and
behavior. As for women, the same process is at play.

Women, on average, are of a lesser physical stature through their body
mass than men and the one predisposed to give birth; they are ascribed
tasks reflecting those biological attributes. They are given less physically

demanding and less perilous labor and tasks associated with their natural attributes such as rearing children, caretaking, householding, nursing, and nurturing. The traits and skills associated with these tasks are sensitivity, compassion, cooperativeness, empathy, concealment, and secureness. Here, as well, women are socialized in a way that promotes and reproduces female-gendered roles and behavior.

Such considerations induce the gendered notion of masculinity and femininity. Masculinity and femininity are respective designations of a set of traits and induced behaviors reflecting the gendered roles. If being assertive and aggressive are traits that go well with being a male because they serve well the productive and protective role he plays, then assertiveness and aggressiveness are masculine. If being sensitive and compassionate are traits that go well with being a female because of the reproductive role she plays, then sensitivity and compassion are feminine. These traits of masculinity and femininity bring along subtraits, which are the enhancements or extrapolation of respective gendered behaviors. So, on one hand, for instance, *machismo* is a subtrait of masculinity that overemphasizes assertiveness or aggressiveness because it goes well with masculinity. On the other hand, wearing makeup or long hair for the female gender to underscore the attractiveness that goes well with the reproductive role of her gender is a subtrait of femininity.

The normalization of masculinity and femininity explains why in the end a father may react differently in the same situation whether involving his daughter or his son. There are many fathers who will hold tight their daughters when they cry over something and will tell their sons, in the same situation, not to cry and to suck it up. Such an attitude underscores the masculinity and femininity norms. Granted, many have been moving away from this mold. But it can still be observed abundantly around us. We buy pink for girls and blue for boys (in the West). The socialization process proceeds across gender lines, reflecting the gendered mold. This remains prevalent in non-Western cultures and less prevalent but still existing in the West, where men predominantly watch sports, during which car and tool commercials are shown, and women predominantly watch soap operas during which perfume and diaper commercials are shown.

Seen from this perspective gender is the result of a process of attribution of masculinity and femininity. It is a process of attributing cultural and social meaning to maleness and femaleness. This raises the question of how objective such an attributive process is. Is attribution a "natural attitude" (Garfunkel 1967 cited by Kessler 1978), or an "incorrigible proposition" (Mehan and Wood 1975 cited by Kessler 2000, p. 4), or a "corrigible proposition"? In other words, is gender an objective reality independent from us/society or is it a social construct? There is a reasonable case that can be made to substantiate answers that argue from each side of the question. There are physiological features that naturally allow the idea of leaving to the most muscular of two individuals the most muscular tasks. And if that individual is a male, the male will naturally be attributed that task. But there are cases where a female may do the task as well or may be stronger than a male. In such a case it will be the female who is attributed the task. But this process of attribution, whether the task is attributed to the male or female, remains a "natural attitude" and "incorrigible proposition." And if there are cases of tasks for which a specific sex generally performs better, that could lead to a general attribution of that task to that sex, and it would become a gendered task. An example would be a farmer in a village in Germany receiving a group of young visitors from the city, eager to participate in some field and agricultural work. That particular day, the farmer has the task of harvesting by picking strawberries. He simply says, "Please, guys, let women do this because from experience, guys tend to press and squeeze the berries harder and stain them. They lose their immaculate shine." Therefore, the farmer prefers, in his own words, "the finer female touch" to do the picking. He went on saying, "You, guys, I have something else for you to do." Is attributing to females the task of picking ripe strawberries, which in the eyes of the farmer has become a gendered task, a natural attitude, an incorrigible proposition, or unnatural and therefore corrigible? For such a task to be unnatural both males and females would have to have the same manual sensitivity and finger finesse, but if there is a difference in sensitivity and finesse of males and females, should that fact count? If it should, then in some cases, gendered tasks are a natural attitude and incorrigible propositions. Indeed, there are some deductions that can be made based on biology, which explains that in the army and on construction sites you find predominantly males performing. However, the fact that there are women in the army makes the deduction that males are more suited for the military or construction sites relatively, but not absolutely, true. And because of this nuance, one must side with the argument that refuses and refutes the absolutism of gendered tasks/roles. This means gendered tasks/roles should not be the applied norm, across the board. Furthermore, one must side with those who refute the absolutism of gendered attributions, taking gendered tasks as incorrigible propositions because such an absolutism may become an instrument of its own proof, as it also produces a male-dominant presence in any field, such as a battlefield or a construction site, by denying women the chance of entering such fields. Indeed, returning to the example of strawberry farming, there may be some females with the same agility as some males, and some males with the same lack of agility as some females, and this suffices to refute the absolutism of gendered tasks/roles. To further refute such an absolutism of gendered tasks, those lacking manual sensitivity and finger finesse to handle ripe strawberries could simply develop such skills and learn how to. Let us consider another example exploring the question of gender attribution and determine whether it was natural and incorrigible or whether it was unnatural and therefore corrigible. It is the example of a professor entering a classroom and realizing that all female students have long hair styles and all male students have short hair styles. The question here becomes whether that was accidental or whether it was natural, or rather the result of gendered appearance, to reflect the assertive maleness and attractive femaleness, which is what we called subtraits of masculinity and femininity, or whether the difference in hair was just to allow for better distinguishing between males and females? Based on biology, there is nothing natural about males and females wearing their hair short or long. That allows the deduction that a male wearing short hair and a female wearing long hair are rather a gendered and not natural attitude. This means wearing long hair for males and short hair for females is a corrigible proposition. It can change. We could even have it the other way around, and we would get used to it. However, although it is not natural for males to wear short hair and females long hair, what if, without any gender influence we were to find out that females naturally prefer long hair and males naturally short hair. Would that allow the suggestion that there was a "natural" disposition for males and females to look different? If so one would argue that despite the fact that males and females are not naturally gendered, there may be a distribution of natural preference that could reflect maleness and femaleness of both males and females. This possibility complicates further the total dismissal of the natural attitude that has initially driven the gender attribution process. A compromising attitude would have to lie in a certain fluidity in any gender arrangement that may emerge even after traditional gender attribution had been rebuked. That fluidity would consist in letting those comfortable with traditional gender attribution to be, just as those rejecting it to be, but also those tempering with either to be. And it is in favor of fluidity and against absolutism of gendered role attribution and therefore expectation that Plato, for instance, positions himself. In Book V of the *Republic*, Plato argues that gender itself does not tell us about talents or an individual, nor does physical appearance. He provides the example of a barber who himself may be bold or have long hair, which does not matter as long as he knows how to cut yours. Gender, Plato argues, does not tell us about the quality of the soul. And since Plato is primarily concerned with leadership qualities, he argues that they come from anywhere. In today's term soul should read as character. As a result, women can be leaders, or otherwise be utile for the state. The state should rather focus on how talents ought to be nurtured to constitute the pool of guardians from which leaders emerge. Caution therefore is required in any role attribution predetermined by gender.

The versatility of genders justifies that caution. The same caution, however, is not exercised by Aristotle, who in Book 8 of *The Nicomachean Ethics* seems to have made and agreed with that predetermination of gendered attribution based on the reasoning according to which in both males and females and infants there is a balancing between emotions and reason. In such a balancing, in men the scale tilts in favor of reason. In men, he argues, reason is in command, therefore justifying the role that requires the exercise of reason to be essentially the domain of men. In children, there is only emotion but no reason, whereas in women, the scale tilts in favor of emotion. Consequently, he sees no noteworthy public function for women. He is more in tune with the traditional attribution of gendered roles in Athens and elsewhere.

Such a process of gendered attribution, however, does not reflect the versatility of the genders. It is one that has allowed that muscular tasks become the preserve of the males and has become culturally and socially codified, anchored and duplicated through generations up to the point of identification of specific tasks with maleness. But aren't there tasks that are better suited to one or the other gender based on biochemical wiring, which means that there is an abundance of testosterone in one and estrogen in the other and that can affect attitude? Without overplaying its implications, such a reality has been observed. Or what to make of empirical data that find a concentrated number of females suited to one task and a number of males for another? Are these examples of a natural attitude about gender attribution, therefore making it an incorrigible proposition? The logical consequence would suggest some degree of empirical evidence to the notion of natural attitude, but the key is how much degree of importance one ascribes to such empirical evidence to answer the question of whether gendered attribution is a natural attitude. Indeed, there is evidence to the contrary, which means evidence demonstrating that gendered attribution is a corrigible proposition. Indeed, there is nothing naturally male about becoming an astronaut. There is nothing naturally female about cooking. These tasks may simply involve usage of brain. In so far as both males and females have brains with equal capacity, the attribution of the task of who should be an astronaut and who should be the cook should depend on who better uses his or her brain for either of these tasks, or the brain of which individual is better suited for each of the tasks. And because the outcome here is unpredictable, because it cannot be determined in advance by gender, indeed, there are today both male and female astronauts and male and female cooks. Only merit should then constitute the basis of attribution, not gendered expectations. There is nothing naturally male or female about these tasks; attributing them to one gender is a corrigible proposition. The growing consensus has been that gendered attribution is by and large a corrigible proposition. It is an asocial construct that can be deconstructed. But the process itself is complex. It is interactive, "involving the person making the attribution and the person she/he is making the attribution about" (Kessler 1987, p. 6). Furthermore, the attributor and the attributed can be simultaneously both. Here is where a game of cues comes to play. The interaction of gendered male and female proceeds through a game of cues about one attitude vis-à-vis gender attribution. It is about signaling whether one buys into gendered roles and assignments as a result of attribution. It is about sending such cues, receiving them, acknowledging receipt of them, accepting them, or rejecting them. An agreement must be reached for a smooth gendered interaction to proceed. Gender, in the end, is traditionally a designation of "psychological, social, and cultural aspects of maleness and femaleness" (Kessler 1978, p. 7).

The notion of gender and masculinity and femininity are the result of correlating nature with culture and the latter determining what to make of the former. To that Fausto-Sterling (2010, p. 8, cited in Goodman 2010)[2] writes: "Nature is opposed to culture, the body becomes the recipient of culture, and gender becomes the content of culture." There is a fluid interaction between nature and culture, in which society uses nature to establish the rapport of the sexes in culture. But as such usage of society is a construct and culture evolves, the construct is revisited primarily by the sex that disagrees more with such a construct. The debate is current. It evolves and progress is made to remedy some of the grievances articulated by feminism. The progress is relatively mobile or slow depending on cultures and societies. It is not fast paced because culture is slow to change, short of revolutions, and because change, even when it makes sense, may not be welcome simply because it is convenient to remain anchored in traditionally entrenched gender structures with whose logic we have been socialized.

Gender Categories

The empirical basis of gender categories is biological. It reflects the fact that most are born with either the male or female gender. Deviations from male and female distinction was either not acknowledged or simply suppressed. The consequence is that the history of gender has lived with a categorization that left out those in between. They are those born with both male and female anatomic features, called hermaphrodites; those whose features are ambiguous; the intersexed; and those who have the mind of one and the body of the other. In addition, we have transgender or cross-gender, which is "the condition of a biological normal person of being a member of the opposite sex" (Kessler 1978, p. 13).

The Complexity of a Simple Notion

The notion of gender seems derived from the basic premise and what seems to be a simple natural fact that human beings are generally born male and female. From this natural fact derives a proposition based on their biological difference, as they seem naturally to complement each other. They complement each other primarily for reproduction purposes and secondarily for production purposes. From this complementarity of purposes derives a social arrangement we call gender. Gender, as a social proposition, therefore seems to emanate from a fairly simple and natural basis. And its sociocultural and sexuality implications seem also that simple and that natural. What appears simple and natural to many is however not that simple and that natural to some. It is the complex nuances that this seemingly simple and natural notion that we should mention. There are indeed a variety of stations or stages that all play a role in the process through individual determination, identification, and belonging to a gender. Those stations or stages are the mind, which sends the information of adhesion to or rejection of a gender. It is the instance that reflects the biochemical balancing of the individual. When all is in balance we do not register or even assume the role of the mind in this process. We become aware only of such a role when we hear that such is not the case with someone. It is the station that determines our identification with one gender.

The second station in the process is the heart, which reveals the attraction to one given sex, whether opposite or same. It reveals in the process our sexuality. In other words, it is the station that reveals our sexual orientation. Indeed, a male may find out that his heart "beats" for a female. It is the indication of heterosexuality, just as a female may find out her heart "beats" for another female. That reveals attraction for the same sex and therefore for homosexuality.

Third, there is the biological sex we are born with, which may be male or female or ambiguous, and in some cases, the presence of both sexes and secondary gender features such as breasts. It is a biological organ with a function, like all other biological organs. It then becomes functional with the partner of one choosing. And finally, there is public expression. It is how one wants to reveal himself or herself to society and the world. Because of the role that each one of these stations plays and because of the link that ultimately exists between them, the process of gender identification, orientation, sexuality, and declaration can become complex to a portion, however small, of some people in society. Here is how. The mind signals the gender it feels one is but does not determine the attraction to others, which is determined by the heart. And both do not determine which biological sex they link to. But in turn, the biological sex itself does not determine with whom one will sleep. Once the determination about with whom one should sleep is done by the heart, then the biological sex goes to bed with whomever the heart has chosen. The complexity does not end there. It then becomes a matter of determination of homosexuality or heterosexuality. Indeed, if one has a female body but feels like a male and is attracted to a male, should that be considered homosexuality? Some feel the need to engage in surgical operations to reflect the gender they feel to be in their mind. Such a move clarifies the situation because it reveals the attraction based on a clear sex. There are as well cases when one has a female body and feels like a male but is still attracted to males. And the same scenario occurs in cases of a male body and the mind of a female and attracted to a female, or one with a male body and a female mind and still attracted to males, etc. To many, and as a matter of fact, to the overwhelming majority of human beings, such scenarios have never even been imagined. They have never occurred to most. This is the case because for most people, there is an alignment of mind, heart, sex and social identification with the social gender ascribed. This is because most people are naturally male or female. The reality, however, is that these questions have been the existential realities of some in any society around the world. Those to whom such questions are relevant have always existed, probably since the beginning of mankind. It is only now that we have started acknowledging and recognizing them.

The notion of identification with gender can, indeed, become complex. Such complexity used to be either ignored, unrecognized, or suppressed in premodern traditional societies. It was ignored because of inadequate or inexistent scientific knowledge, which often means ignorance and which in turn paved the way to superstition and elaboration of taboo pronouncements and societies grounding their social order in mythologies. In the same premodern societies, deviations from norms, articulation of any nuances that suggested abnormal behavior, led to suppression. In the modern era, an era that the German social scientist Max Weber saw primarily as characterized by emancipation from such superstitions and myths, at least in some modern societies, there has been an increasing acceptance and recognition of such nuances deviating from the traditional gender norms and sexuality. Modern societies are now facing the various societal challenges that such acceptance and recognition bring. Among such challenges, there is the question of accommodation of same-sex marriages (homosexuality); bisexuality; those not exclusively hetero or homo in nature; transsexuality, whose sexuality is considered to be a form of homosexuality, etc. There are as well challenges with respect to traditional norms of social morality, the adjustments or lack thereof of religious teaching on the matter, etc.

GENDER BENDING

Because the traditional gender categories have failed to account for the complexity of the simple notion of gender, there are other expressions of gender deviating from the traditional constructs. These new categories of gender deviating from the traditional categories have found no relevance for the subproducts and gendered attitudes we call masculinity and femininity. The result has been that these "new" expressions of gender have been bending the traditional categories and in the process, defying the notion of masculinity and femininity. They defy the traditional categories of gender both in their sexual and their cultural implications. These new expressions of gender are producing a number of gender-bending alternatives to remedy the reductionistic categories of the traditional gender, reductionistic because the traditional gender categories acknowledge just two and lead on one hand to a simplified sexualized expression, namely, heterosexuality, and on the other hand to a simplified cultural implication of heterosexuality, namely, a heterosexually conducted life. Gender bending describes the various expressions of rejection, refusal, deviation, alteration, reversal, or extension of the notion of gender and ultimately the division of roles and assignments based on it, but also of the sexuality associated with traditional gender.

There are those who have rejected, refused, deviated, altered, reversed, and extended the notion of gender. Such variation in attitudes vis-à-vis traditional gender have produced a variety of gender-bending expressions. Following are a few of such gender bending expressions:

• Reversing gender roles and assignments: Stay-at-home dads
• Rejecting gender cultural implications: Metro males

TAMPERING WITH GENDER CATEGORIES

There are a variety of expressions of gender identity around the traditional categories. Among them we have the Hijra (who may be transgenders, cross-dressers, or eunuchs) in South Asia. There are as well the sworn virgins in Albania and the western Balkans, who decide to escape fate and decide never to get married and organize their lives or are designated by their families in the case of the absence of any male, who may have died as a result of wars, accidents, or illness. For the family not to remain without a male presence, one female in the family is designated to play the male role.

There are a variety of many other social and cultural reasons compelling women to find ways of escaping the limitations and confinements of gendered roles. One of such many reasons has been reported[3] in Egypt, where an Egyptian mother, Sisa Abu Daooh, has dressed like a man for forty years, after the death of her husband, to provide for her family. Adopting the male gender attributes through disguise was the way out of her predicament. But she was in the predicament because of the rigidity with which gendered roles are attributed, so much so that being a woman, her gender did not compute with being the bread winner. She has had to transit from reproductive activities into productive activities.

The Bacha Posh (in Islamic cultures such as in Afghanistan and Pakistan) is a social cultural phenomenon through which the constraining implications of gender are tempered by women to overcome their limitations. A family of four with a father and a wife and three daughters may not have enough males to walk around with the women of the family in a culture where women are not allowed to walk around alone. One of the young daughters will simply transform her appearance to look like a boy and walk around with her sister or mother. The girl who performs such tasks will change her haircut, clothing, shoes, demeanor, and attitude to be believable.

The third gender category simply goes beyond the delineating distinctions between male and females in terms of gender attribution and gender expectation, defying them by identifying with a variety of features of both traditional genders. As they do, they mix or merge the biology and sexual and cultural implications of the traditional notion of gender, and consequently its derivative notions of masculinity and femininity.

Among them we have Muxes among the Zapotec people in South Mexico, who are young men identifying with the female gender or unable to identify with either, and therefore create a new category.

There are as well the Two-Spirits among the North American native population, which describes a phenomenon of going beyond the two genders and creatively imagining one that associates or merges masculinity with women and femininity with men.

The kathoeys of Thailand are transgender women or effeminate gay men. With a culture in which strict gender delineations are not strictly defined, self-identity determination is common in Thailand. The growing number of kathoeys and their active life in the entertainment industry in Thailand is part of the culture and less of an issue.

Fa'afafine in Samoa is a third gender of boys raised to be female or boys taking on traditional female roles.

A transvestite "is someone whose gender identity corresponds to her/his assignment, but who obtains erotic pleasure by dressing ("dress" includes hairstyles and accessories) as the other gender" (Kessler 1978, p. 14).

All these expressions of gender bending create a gray area that seems to grow larger as society loosens its grip on "enforcing" through cultural pressure the traditional gender understanding. This gray area can be primarily biological such as in the following cases: Some individuals while being male feel more like female or vice versa, or even feeling neither, or even feeling like both. This may primarily lie in the chemical wiring and balance of the body. It then has social and cultural implications, as those finding themselves in this gray area are human beings who live in a society that has yet to carve a role for their gray area in society. Their presence, visibility, and appearance in society must be asserted. The way they choose to express themselves may not fit the traditional gender role, as some will assume traditionally female roles while looking male, and others will wear female attire and appear female while being male. They choose intimate partners and create relationships that do not fit the traditional mold, etc. Many are creative and imaginative. They develop their lines of work, niche, or activity in business and entertainment, and assert in the process their presence and acceptance in society.

GENDER AND SPACE

As a social construct, gender is a cultural identity. Like any cultural identity, it emerges within a specific spatial context. This makes space, a molding agent of gender identity. Space is as well the canvas of gendered activity. Indeed, any given societal space attributes to gendered males and females their place in society. Society tells the genders where they belong. Such a place where they belong in society is their sphere of activity. Gender sphere of activity is about boundaries. The use of the term boundaries is crucial and central. It is used both literally and figuratively.

Literally, boundaries express the physical place where gendered activity occurs. Gendered activity occurs in specific spaces. Traditionally, for the male gender it is the public sphere, and the female gender is the private sphere. The public sphere encompasses spaces such as the battlefield or combat zone, the hunting ground, the stadium, the office of business, the neighborhood, the city, the entire world, etc. The public sphere is the theater of the male gender. The private sphere encompasses the kitchen, the household, the hospital. The private sphere is the theater for the female gender. The male gender exercises its activity in the *productive sphere*, whereas the female gender exercises its activity in the *reproductive sphere*. And it is this productive versus reproductive sphere construct that is repeatedly found historically in communities around the world. To use the Athenian Greeks in the time of Pericles, as reported by Thucydides in the *History of the Peloponnesian War*, in his Funeral Oration, in Book II, Pericles speaks about what an honor, in fact no higher honor there was, it was for the young Athenian soldiers to die for country in the battlefield, and to their mourning mother, simply exhorting them not to cry and to go back and make more soldiers for country, reemphasizing their role in procreation. Men are the defenders of the nation, making nationalism a gendered tool. It justifies the battlefield as a masculine space, and the traits and skills (assertiveness, aggressiveness, competitiveness, etc.) as essential for survival of country, and therefore vital to society. Pericles, a product of his time, like anywhere else, reflected the productive versus re-productive, which in turn reflects the private versus public sphere dichotomy.

The rigidity of this dichotomy has been contested by recent feminist re-search, Donansh (1989), Blunt (1999), Gowan (2003), arguing that the private sphere can be a space of public discourse, debate, and conversations about political matters or a space where support for public activity is organized, and that private activity or matters can be brought into the public sphere (Horton and Kraft 2014, p. 169). These authors, however, provide examples that do not go any further prior to the nineteenth century. Although there are indeed instances of such cases, of the private going public and the public taking place in the private, these cases are relatively recent. They reflect the changing times since the colonial and early twentieth century. Indeed time has been changing and the dichotomy itself. And its consequences, breeding gender inequality, have been questioned, as we address in the following segment. One of the ways it has further changed as time continues to pass is through the fact that even the private sphere itself has become a space of production as we can bring work at home and work in home offices, etc. The dichotomy and its consequence is changing around the world at different rates and paces. While it has been changing at different rates around the world, it has been crucial in affecting the fate of gender issues.

Figuratively, boundaries imply a gendered mindset that leads socialized individuals to "know their place" in society, not only "where they belong" but also what behavior they are expected to reflect. Knowing your place becomes an imperative urging both males and females to process, absorb, and come to terms with the attributions of their genders in order to be able, all themselves, to determine in any circumstance how to behave, even when no one tells them. It is a mental level of identification with one gender, making gendered individuals vehicles of gendered behavior. It is the level that allows one to see cues of gendered identification in the behavior of others. But such identi-fication with gender is mental. It must be consciously or subconsciously ac-cepted. It then is absorbed in the psyche. It explains why and how even when the activity of both male and female genders occurs in the same space, when they subscribe to gendered roles and assignments, subtly still know what their place is. Here, that place is not physical but mental. Knowing one's place in society and accepting, or not, to fit the mold of that "place" is therefore a mental process. Here, the mental space, the mind, becomes the canvas of that process of identification with or rejection of gendered behavior. That process can come to a conclusion that allows individuals, either male or female, to identify with or to reject their socially attributed gender and gendered roles and assignments. In the case of rejection, we do know that there are those who identify with the gender other than the one they are socially expected to belong, and they may behave accordingly. All this activity occurs in the mental space. This is as well the reason we argue that the mental space, like all spaces, is a canvas of activity. Even the mental space is a theater of human activity and therefore of issues. The activity here is to figuratively process the idea of one's place in society. And here as well there are issues that emerge, as there are those "taking issue" with the traditional gender definition.

HOW DOES SPACE EXPLAIN GENDER?

The causal link between space and gender can be established through the attribution of space of activity (roles and assignment) to males and females. Such an attribution process starts with the attribution of a productive nature for the male gender and of a reproductive nature for the female gender. These roles are exercised in different spaces, outdoors and indoors. These assigned roles require a certain number of specific skills (such as hunting, cooking, fighting, nursing, etc.). These skills require in turn special traits (such as aggressiveness, assertiveness, competitiveness, compassion, sensitivity, empathy, compassion, etc.). In the end of this attribution process there are roles, skills, traits aligned, corresponding to the genders. According to this scheme, being attractive becomes a trait associated with reproductive roles, just as an imposing stature and an assertive behavior suggest the ability to protect and provide for one's family as traits associated with productive roles. These traits are eventually reflected in the respective attitudes and behaviors of the genders. In the end, attribution produces types of behavior along the productive and reproductive roles. These attitudes and behavior are then codified to serve as norms. These norms underline the behavioral attitudinal distinctiveness and particularities of the genders, which are then validated by society. This distinctiveness and particularity become consequently the identifying markers of each gender. We are socialized to acquire skills needed to fine-tune the traits needed, to navigate and perpetuate gendered roles and assignments. The result is that we live lives whose gendered socialization is a vehicle of a message about our place in society, a message that serves to structure our behavior in society. This gendered socialization–induced structure comes with constraints. These constraints bound us. They are confining, limiting the ability to perform beyond the boundaries they set. Such constraints are, therefore, subject to a pushback on behalf, primarily, of those who argue they have been more affected, namely, the female gender.

HOW DOES SPACE EXPLAIN GENDER ISSUES?

Space explains gender issues because of the constraints that come with the traditional gender notion. Such constraints are first biological as the dichotomy of male and female gender has been contested, as we have argued. It has led to issues around gender identity beyond male and females, and it has led to gender bending, which entails various forms through which those discontents of the traditional gender notion find to express their specificity. The constraints of traditional gender roles have been as well about the spatial confinement in which they have placed the female gender in indoor and reproductive roles. The limiting spatial boundaries of the traditional gendered role attribution have been deemed to deprave the female gender of its ability to fully perform and to have produced gender inequality.

GENDER-BASED INEQUALITIES

There are various expressions of inequality. Here we focus on economic inequality or income inequality. Let us start by presenting the picture of inequality between the genders; then we can look at how we got there and possibly suggest a way out. Economic or income inequality is the key to examining overall gender disparity, and therefore it is where to start. It is because not only lack of income or inadequate income determines where you stand in the poverty scale, and therefore is the consequence of inequality, but also because there are deeper reasons why a specific group in society with a collective identity ends up suffering from lack of adequate income, and that, therefore, suggests that there may be structural reasons. When indeed existing, these structural reasons are the cause of poverty.

Throughout the world, across nations, regions, and continents, across wealthy and developing nations, and across cultures and civilizations, there is an independent variable, namely, that of gender inequality to the detriment of women. It is called the gender gap. This inequality although constant is not manifest with the same intensity everywhere. And so the gender gap is wider in some nations than it is in others. The UN data (Human Development Report since 1997 and 1998) show North European nations such as Sweden, Norway, and Iceland as nations with the most reduced gap between the genders.

The gap is wider in developing nations, where both traditional cultures more restrictive of women's status leads to exploitative and unremunerated labor and roles, and the precarious economic conditions exacerbate the gap.

The following UNDP (United Nations Development Program)[4] data illustrate the divide:

- Women make up 70 percent of the world's one billion poorest people.
- There are more women unemployed.
- Only 1 percent of the world's property is in female hands.
- Although two-thirds of the world's work is done by women, they earn just 10 percent of all income.
- Females comprise less than 5 percent of the heads of states.
- Sixty percent of all illiterates are females.
- Seventy-five percent of women have no access to bank loans because they have no job or only an insecure job.
- Women make up 50 percent of the world's population but own 1 percent of the world's wealth.

The figures suggest that women are "getting the short end of the stick" in what has been, and still is, the gender social contract, in accessing and sharing the resources and benefiting from the output of the world's national economies. They are generally the victims of violence, lack of professional recognition, unequal pay, etc. They are subject to restrictions of mobility and access to health care, education, etc. They remain generally socially dependent and vulnerable.

The subsequent question that the data beg is to have some degree of understanding of what accounts for the discrepancy in gender inequality. Because inequality affects women negatively, their collective identity becomes the primary suspect in analyzing the true causes of the disparity.

GENDERED SPACES AS CAUSE OF GENDER INEQUALITY

In light of gender inequality, the question then becomes whether the notion of gender itself accounts for the discrepancy in the data shown. This question compels us to focus on gender-based division of labor, which is the current arrangement, or the social contract between the genders. What we see from the start is that gender-based division of labor has allowed men to become active in the fields of production and left the field of reproduction to women (Peterson and Runyan 2011).

Gender-based division of labor is characterized by a spatial dichotomy through which inequalities are rendered possible, maintained, and reproduced. A closer look at this spatial dichotomy is warranted.

The spatial dichotomy ascribes and, therefore, confines the female gender to activity and duties in the private sphere (reproductive field) and the male gender to activities and duties in the public sphere (productive field). This is a typical dichotomy of the modern era. The consequence of it is that these sexes get to benefit from the fruits of their labor associated with their field of activity. The benefit, or fruit of their labor, however, is structurally unequal in a material sense.

The male gender fields are the battlefield, the hunting ground, the business world, etc.; the benefit or fruits are that those active in them get to earn money, bring home game from hunting and the spoils of wars, make decisions, etc. The female gender has been assigned and ascribed a sphere of reproductive duties, children rearing, householding, and nurturing, whose activity, as important as it is to society, does not entail money, game, or spoils.

In this dichotomy, the genders benefit, or not, from the fruits of their respective spheres of activity. The result has been that the male gender was/is the "breadwinner," the one to "bring home the bacon." The female gender had to depend on the male gender. The female was gendered into a dependent role. The spatial dichotomy empowers the male gender and renders dependent the female gender. This is the core of gender inequality.

Beyond the material empowerment that the spatial dichotomy produces in favor of the male gender, an even more enduring effect is the status it allows men to acquire. It produces societal dependency on their duty and activities, as they are responsible for protection of land and family, production in the community, decision making, healing, and extinguishing fires, both literary and figuratively. Their contribution is valued. Their duty and role procure them esteem, respect, and recognition. Their capabilities and abilities are appreciated. These abilities are physical strength, muscles, mobility, strategic thinking, etc. Their capabilities are aggressiveness, competitiveness, assertiveness, toughness, etc. These abilities and capabilities are cherished by society at large, as a matter of fact, so much so that they supplant any other abilities and capabilities of the female gender, namely, nurturing, compassion, affectedness, cooperativeness, peacefulness, etc. The result is that society is more accepting of the idea of a strong woman and less accepting of the idea of a weak man.

We socialize our children accordingly. They duplicate the gendered behavior but also abilities and capabilities. The consequence of a gendered socialization is that it perpetuates the resulting gender inequality of the spatial dichotomy of gender-based division of labor.

Examining women's participation in world politics and facing the unequal participation rate of women's active presence in world politics, Peterson and Runyan (2011, p. 87) identified the space factor as having the most obvious effect, writing, "Most obvious are the continued effects of the dichotomy of public-private that privileges men's productive and 'political' activities over women's reproductive and 'personal/familiar' activities." The argument we intend to make is the one generalizing the overall effect of this public-private dichotomy, which is spatial in essence to make the case of its being the epicenter of gender issues. The space dichotomy explains inequalities, as it is itself the product of control content of masculinity and femininity. Any change in the gendered inequalities must occur through the intrusion in all spaces by the "weaker" sexes, which in turn will not occur without pouring a new or different cultural content into the traditionally constructed gender-based division of labor. In other words, the structure underlying these inequalities must shift. The cultural content of gender-based division of labor therefore is what Peterson and Runyan call "structural absolutes of unequal participation." To this effect they write, "Clearly, stereotypes and structural constraints shape the gender of political activism, but the recurring differences in women's and men's participation must also be examined in relation to large-scale, interacting, and enduring social structures. Here we refer broadly to sets of power relations and/or social cultural institutions that determine the boundaries of individual behavior" (2011, p. 117).

GENDER DISCOURSE AND PUSHBACK

The prevailing discourse on gender is itself the reflection of an evolving mindset, normative values and ideas, and the zeitgeist of our time. The discourse around gender reflects issues raised by the arrangement on the coexistence between males and females in society. Such an arrangement has been questioned, as it failed to account for a number of questions raised by its limitations and inadequacies. The discourse around gender therefore is about denoting, describing, decrying, deconstructing, and denouncing all those limitations and inadequacies. The discourse summarizes all the issues arising around the notion of gender. Such issues range from gender recognition to gender roles, from gender inequality to gender discrimination, and the variety of ways through they manifest.

The discourse around gender, as far as it is critical, has articulated the issues around which a pushback against traditional gender understanding has been organized. Such a pushback has been organized by individual women in their private ways and local circumstances, women activists, feminists and various women's organizations, organizations with a focus on women's concerns, and most recently the lesbian, gay, bisexual, and transgender movement (LGBT). The critical pushback articulates the following grievances.

First, the confinement in specific spheres (space) of activity, division of labor that the traditional gender attribution has produced, and which we have addressed earlier, which as poststructuralist analysis contends, is too modern, based on the dichotomy (male versus female, masculine versus feminine), and therefore like many other modern notions, is reductionist, simplistic, and historic (Peterson and Runyan 2011). Second, the economic implication of gendered division of labor, as it explains gender inequality. Third, gendered attribution has been essentially based on biology and has not taken into account merit, leaving in the process, possibly untapped, the talent of many women. Fourth, the sexuality and cultural implications of gender categorization, which does not take into account the various gray areas, nuances, and identities of many people.

Critical gender discourse aims at revisiting and redefining the many assumptions upon which traditional gender attributions have been made, at bringing missing nuances and critical reasoning in the debate on nature versus nurture.

Such a critical gender discourse is about bringing about social change, namely gender equality. The change it seeks, like many other social changes, if not revolutionary, take root incrementally, sometimes making leaps forward or detours. There is as well resisting forces in favor of status order that any social change must reckon with. In the case of women in general, such a push for social change started in the nineteenth century with the suffragette movement, with demands for political participation in voting, which was a push against the activity of women in private space toward more visible and public space roles. Such movement has spilled into the twentieth century. This problematization of women's concerns since then has not stopped. Generations of women activists and organizations have kept articulating demands, leading for instance to the 1915 Women's International League for Peace and Freedom (WILPF), formed to argue against the belligerence around World War I. The need to come together and agitate, militate, promote, and push for causes of concern to women has gradually spread, geographically from Europe and North America, since the 1920s and is reflected in the North-South relations, and East and West (the Cold War), since the 1960s, as a linkage between women concerned with similar grievances (women's rights and gender equality) could be theoretically established. Different priorities have, however, hindered some kind of a fusion among women and feminist movements, as the status of women and their different developmental stages in advanced nations differed materially from those of the South, and as both liberalism and Marxism provide each, in their own way, different ground from which to argue in favor of women's equality. The result was a discourse that was essentially the same in its emancipative goal but different in its perspectives and therefore in the actions it induced. The ability to pull in one direction was undermined. Different priorities and sometimes division between women in advanced nations and those in the developing world have characterized the movement.

In the 1980s an international consciousness around issues of gender was becoming an integral concern of the UN. The result was a series of initiatives, starting with a world conference on women in Mexico, twice, in 1975. The UN had declared since January 1, 1976, a Decade for Women, promoting equal rights and opportunity for women around the world. In 1980, another conference was held in Copenhagen, Denmark, followed by another in Nairobi, Kenya, in 1985 and another in Beijing, China, in 1995, where the Beijing Declaration and Platform for action and the Convention on Elimination of All Forms of Discrimination against Women (CEDAW) were adopted.

The process of globalization, whose imperatives have dictated, accelerated, or provoked new phenomena, has here as well accelerated the urgency of women's issues, as some of the consequences of globalization on women have not ceased to become more visible, from victimizations in wars and conflicts, to their high unemployment rates, low income, high illiteracy rate, to producing inequalities. And, it is this turn toward a more unified world that women's issues will increasingly since the 1980s, be shaped en block, in fusion, and less and less undivided by regional considerations (Moghadam 2013).

There are today, individualized, local and regional, transnational, and global gender activists. They accentuate different dimensions in their quest for equality. Some therefore focus on the rights of all women (per se). Others focus on the equality of genders (relative to men); others again question the dichotomy of the notion of gender and its implications, among which we count feminists, whose perspective is of interest.

ABOUT FEMINISM

Feminism is a critical theory. Next to other critical theories such as poststructuralism, it deplores and critiques the intellectual culture of the modern era and structuralism, which it sees as confining, reducing the human experience to dualistic categories, objectivity criteria essentially materialist, and uncritical vis-à-vis itself. These critical theories consider the intellectual discourse of the era of modernity, if not responsible, as at least as bedrock for the shortcoming and the abuses of the era. Among such abuses, they count the dominant cultures against the weaker cultures in the era of imperialism and colonization, patriarchal domination and male machismo vis-à-vis women, the power hierarchy among nations, etc.

In the list of such negative manifestations of the modern culture, feminism sees the subordination of the feminine and the elevation of the masculine (androcentrism). Feminism as a movement and a school of thought undertakes to question androcentrism, to redefine gender as a social construct, and to suggest a different, or maybe many different new attitudes to consider. There are indeed many schools of thought within the feminism movement, each with its premise, approach, and proposed new attitude. These schools of thought within feminism have one thing in common, namely the quest for gender equality, which occurs through either questioning its gendered notions of masculinity and femininity and/or by attacking the inequality it genders through its gendered roles and behavior.

Following are the main current and succinct core arguments of feminists.

There is a liberal feminism, which sees the evident fact that some human beings are born male or female but does not see that distinction as relevant, consequential, or binding to the lives of both. As a result liberal feminism considers gendered roles as unacceptable and highly restrictive of women's potential and capacity. A woman can do all that a man can do, it argues. It advocates therefore a life of a woman disregarding the mold that society has created and its confinement. The woman, it argues, should aim and thrive to accomplish that which she sees enriching and fulfilling, even when traditionally and socially not expected of her such as smoking cigars, shaving her head bald, playing high contact sports such as boxing and wrestling, being in combat in the battlefield, etc. The liberal feminist perspective is as emancipating for women as it is challenging.

There is standpoint feminism, which acknowledges and recognizes the biological difference between men and women but argues that they should not constitute a basis for gender inequality. Men do not give birth, but women do. That is a fact. It does even have a social consequence and induces degrees of a different socialization between boys and girls, a standpoint that feminism concedes. It sees a mother as not the father and vice versa, but does not see in that acknowledgment a reason for a gender construct that unfolds to the detriment of the mother/woman. Men and women are different but not unequal.

There is postmodern feminism, which rejects both liberal and standpoint feminism by suggesting a different path. It is the path of deconstruction. Because gender is a social construct, and because the notion of masculinity and femininity is a social construct, they can be deconstructed. And because they entail the cause of gender gap they should be deconstructed. Gendered roles and behavior are not etched in stone. There is no natural imperative for girls to wear pink and for boys to wear blue. It is pure construct. We can undo or alter the entrenched and prevailing practice. And once we do we can assign a different expectation to boys and girls, and get the girls to wear blue and the boys to wear pink without any noteworthy consequence to society as a whole. With both the recognition that the power to enact such a change lies in society, and by extension, in women, and the recognition that such change, rejecting old cultural content and infusing new cultural content to the concept of gender, postmodern feminism focuses on empowering women and society at large to do just that. Postmodern feminism ultimately focuses on the empowerment factor. It exhorts women to take charge of the gender discourse and infuse to it their meaning. By so doing they will produce a postmodern culture that will overcome the reductionist, dualistic, and patriarchal structure of the modern culture.

THE RESULT OF THE PUSHBACK

There have been essentially two main results induced by the pushback on gender issues. They are essentially the blurring of the boundaries, reduced inequalities, implementation of institutional remedies, and the emerging of new issues, but primarily in advanced liberal states, mostly Western nations, wherein such pushback has been expressed with the most fervor. Let us look at each one of them.

BLURRING GENDER BOUNDARIES

The dichotomy of the gender-based division of labor, namely the private-public sphere construct, has increasingly been blurred. It has been blurred as more and more women have entered the public sphere. We now get to see women in sports, the military, offices, and politics, and we see women judges, long distance truck drivers, etc. They have entered the traditionally male-gendered space.

But the phenomenon is not observable everywhere in the West in the same intensity or degree. Sweden is more advanced in this regard than Portugal for instance. There are a number of factors accounting for the progress. Breaking away progressively from the gender-based division of labor of the Victorian era, the West has adopted the ideas and ideals of liberalism. They promote the idea of innate freedom and equality of rights. They do not presuppose gender, nor distinguish between genders. We are all created with the same prerogatives. These prerogatives are inextricably linked to the essence of being human beings. From there, the only forces still keeping women confined in any boundaries are simply those of tradition. The power of entrenched traditions compels people to faithfully hold on to their precepts, which renders change a rather uphill battle. Traditions are the pillars of society. Naturally there is a certain traditionalist or conservative reluctance to do away with them. If they have been around for years, why change them now? This seems to be the traditionalist or conservative attitude, supported by a certain anthropological view that sees human beings as creatures of habit. This traditionalism or conservatism worries more about the uncertainty of changes and therefore prefers the imperfections of the status quo. Whatever the imperfections of the status quo, we know that they are manageable because we live through them. No one, however, can say the same about the possible imperfections of changes, which carry the potential of unmanageability. The West has gone through another historical transformation sooner than any other civilization, namely, the advent of the industrialization and the rationalization of cultures, which forces society to respond and react to the changes caused by the use of machines and labor specialization. Such transformation necessitates adjustments, such as the need for education. Such transformation has ultimately produced a modern life that relies more and more on science and that could afford to leave tradition behind and its archaic customs, practices, rituals, superstitions, and irrationalities. It was therefore, historically, intellectually probable to see emerge from the West the social movements questioning fundamentally gender-based division of labor, leading to emancipation from its boundaries and producing increasingly blurring spaces between the genders.

REDUCED GENDER INEQUALITY

Women have increasingly been able to access education, the labor market, and income. They have become more empowered than never before. With such improvements they have been able to secure their welfare and economic independence. They now have the ability to take advantage of their needs and wishes and attain their goals and objectives in life. They can free themselves from many constraints. This improvement of the female gender's standing in Western societies can be evidenced through the UNDP's Gender Inequality Index. Based on this index, Western nations rank the highest. The different and new measurement set is called Gender Inequality Index (GII). The GII was introduced in 2010, the year of the twentieth anniversary of the Human Development Index (HDI) to measure and capture the degrees of gender inequality, using the following dimensions: *reproductive health*, which in turn uses two indicators—maternal mortality ratio and adolescent fertility rate. It uses as a second dimension the *empowerment of women*, which in turn uses two indicators—share of female parliamentarian seats and higher-level attainment. Lastly, it uses the dimension of *access to labor market*, which in turn uses one indicator, namely, women's participation in the workforce. In the end these dimensions and their indicators are calculated the same way the human development dimensions and indicators are to arrive at a ranking that looks like the following (starting with nations with the lowest gender inequality gap in the year 2013; see Table 3.1):

Table 3.1.

1. Netherland (0.045)	2. Sweden (0.055)
3. Denmark (0.057)	4. Switzerland (0.057)
5. Norway (0.065)	6. Finland (0.075)
7. Germany (0.075)	8. Slovenia (0.080)
9. France (0.083)	10. Iceland (0.089)

But has gender inequality disappeared in advanced modern nations as a result of the blurring of the spatial dichotomy in the public versus private sphere? In the United States for instance the labor market, although fairly wide open to both genders, still shows a certain demarcation suggesting a gender divide, as women gravitate toward less physically demanding labor. Women have preferences for specific fields, reflecting the gender-based division of labor, making, for example, 92 percent of registered nurses, 82 percent of elementary school teachers and social workers, 71 percent of psychologists, on the one hand, and on the other hand, 17 percent of women in Congress, 11.4 percent police officers, 9 percent construction workers, and 4.5 percent firefighters.

In the United States, data compiled by the Bureau of Labor Statistics (2011) suggest a repartition of labor by gender that suggests residues of the entrenched traditional gender-based division of labor, looking at the areas of occupations preferred by women, as shown in Figure 3.1 and Table 3.2.

In advanced modern nations, inequality among the genders has been reduced due to the removal of the spatial boundaries between gendered roles and labor. However, the chart above reveals a concentration of women in some professions and lines of work. It begs the question of a possibility of personal, independent, and voluntary choices by women to embrace the professions and lines of work reflected in the percentages.

Naturally, if indeed that is the case, the data suggest a reflection of a traditional gender-based division of labor, linking women to nurturing, low

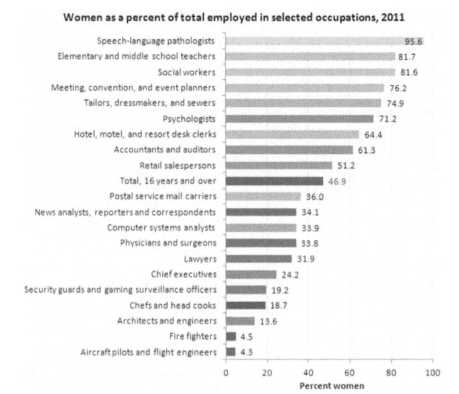

Women as a percent of total employed in selected occupations, 2011

Occupation	Percent women
Speech-language pathologists	95.6
Elementary and middle school teachers	81.7
Social workers	81.6
Meeting, convention, and event planners	76.2
Tailors, dressmakers, and sewers	74.9
Psychologists	71.2
Hotel, motel, and resort desk clerks	64.4
Accountants and auditors	61.3
Retail salespersons	51.2
Total, 16 years and over	46.9
Postal service mail carriers	36.0
News analysts, reporters and correspondents	34.1
Computer systems analysts	33.9
Physicians and surgeons	33.8
Lawyers	31.9
Chief executives	24.2
Security guards and gaming surveillance officers	19.2
Chefs and head cooks	18.7
Architects and engineers	13.6
Fire fighters	4.5
Aircraft pilots and flight engineers	4.3

Percent women

Figure 3.1. *Source:* US Bureau of Labor Statistics

physical impact, and spatially contained activities. If indeed the concentration in these professions and lines of work is voluntary, it lends credence to the traditional gender-based division of labor. The existing income inequality would then be the reflection of salaries found in these professions and lines of work. But if the concentration of women in these professions and lines of work is somehow induced by a number of factors other than voluntarily, then the persisting inequality will have its causes elsewhere, in those factors. We can identify among such factors the following: physical demands of some professions (the military, firefighters, etc.) and spatial and mathematics skills, as studies and tests[5] have suggested scoring gaps and differential achievement rates between boys and girls.

The other question is whether the low concentration of women in other professions and lines of works, those traditionally seen as male preserves, such as chief executives, architects, firefighters, lawyers, engineers, pilots, the military, construction, etc., is simply the reflection of their lack of interest or the reflection of roadblocks and discrimination. The roadblocks and

Table 3.2. Women as a percentage of total employed in selected occupations, 2011

Occupation	Percentage of women
Speech-language pathologists	95.6
Elementary and middle school teachers	81.7
Social workers	81.6
Meeting, convention, and event planners	76.2
Tailors, dressmakers, and sewers	74.9
Psychologists	71.2
Hotel, motel, and resort desk clerks	64.4
Accountants and auditors	61.3
Retail salespersons	51.2
Total, 16 years and over	46.9
Postal service mail carriers	36.0
News analysts, reporters, and correspondents	34.1
Computer systems analysts	33.9
Physicians and surgeons	33.8
Lawyers	31.9
Chief executives	24.2
Security guards and gaming surveillance officers	19.2
Chefs and head cooks	18.7
Architects and engineers	13.6
Firefighters	4.5
Aircraft pilots and flight engineers	4.3

Source: US Bureau of Labor Statistics

discrimination are subtle as a result of enduring traditionalist and conservative mindsets on gender, even among those living in these gender-progressive advanced nations.

If such roadblocks and discrimination are indeed at work, they constitute a cause, among others, of persisting gender income inequalities in the advanced modern economies. There is data indeed pointing to and documenting that such roadblocks and discrimination are at work. A case in point is the debate in the United States on equal pay legislation, by way of an executive order signed by President Obama in April 2014.

Questions have been raised about whether women are in certain professions and lines of work as a result of their choosing or whether they are constrained by certain factors such as maternity. Subsequent questions have been raised as well about whether they are less to be found in other professions and lines of work because of lack of interest or because of roadblocks and discrimination. The answer to these questions is that it is a little bit of all the suggestions entailed in these questions. Women have a lack of interest in certain professions and lines of work, with or without external constraints. And there are cases of roadblocks and discrimination against women in certain other professions and lines of works, traditionally seen as male preserves and denounced by women activists and organizations in cases of the glass ceiling in the corporate world, for instance, sexual harassment or unequal pay for the same amount of work for both genders. Indeed, according to the US Census Bureau, September 2013, women make 77 percent of what men earn for the same work. The general reasons that attempt to justify the discrepancy in earning by both genders states that women have a set of other concerns such as health issues (maternity and maternity leaves) and responsiveness to their children (motherhood) than men. The objection to such reasons has been they are themselves sexist to begin with. But a case that illustrates how all these factors (lack of interest, constraints, roadblocks, and discrimination) come into play to explain the low concentration of women in some professions and lines of work is the military, and most precisely the US military. There are currently in 2014, 15 percent of women in the US forces. This number remains low despite the opening of this particular space to women. The plausible and documented reason is that there are few women who think about a career in the military. And those who think about such a career must reckon with its physical and other demands. Contemplating these physical and other demands, it is fair to assume, based on the average physical attributes of males and females, that a lower number of males who want to become soldiers will be intimidated or discouraged to pursue such a career than females. And there are documented cases of roadblocks and discrimination in the military, from sexual harassment and assault to rape.[6]

Because such gender-based roadblocks and discrimination can permeate the various fields of human endeavor, leveling the playing field remains an uphill battle, which however is conceivably easier if and when the battle is not left to women alone to fight. In many advanced modern economies and increasingly many others, there have been institutional efforts to affirmatively induce gender equality in a number of domains of public life.

INSTITUTIONAL REMEDIES

There have been policy measures thoughtout and designed to remedy the residual effects of traditional gender-based division of labor in areas where such residues are most striking. Such areas are, for instance, public offices. The UNDP, as mentioned earlier, has public offices and more precisely a presence in the parliament by females as an indicator of gender equality. This indicator is used comparatively to assess empowerment as an index in measuring gender inequality or progress against inequality. To ensure increased women's parliamentarian presence, some nations have designed mechanisms, either voluntary or mandatory measures. The mandatory mechanism occurs through legislation that requires a certain number of women's presence in key functions. The number required amounts to a quota system, and the key functions where such female presence has been effectively and symbolically expected is the parliament. A legislated quota system still has to occur through the electoral process. Political parties are the gatekeepers, as they are the bodies through which elected members of parliament emanate. The mandatory or legislated quota system ultimately depends on political party quotas or must induce the requirement of a gender quota system within political parties. And beyond politics, the same quota system in the corporate world, or business in general, depends on the requirement of companies' gender quotas. The same goes for the labor market in general, and it can be extended to any other societal portal such as universities.

The requirement or implementation of gender quotas naturally has been a contested subject. There are those arguing in favor of a gender quota system and those arguing against it. Those arguing in favor have pointed to the fact that gender inequality is a problem that is not going to fix itself or naturally find a solution. The resistance against gender equality is a result of a centuries-long entrenched mindset and attitude vis-à-vis women, which would take longer to remedy without affirmative action. They argued therefore in favor of positive measures to either promote awareness of the issues and/or use legislation to induce the needed change in favor of gender equality. They argue further that women have been for centuries getting the short end of societal gendered arrangements and, therefore, a compensatory measure was called for. They argue in essence that a quota system designed to remedy gender inequality was in fact undermining its own premise of the quest for fairness by imposing it, since by so doing the imposition creates unfairness of its own. There are those among them who pose the question What difference does it make to have many women in politics (Dahlerup 2002)[7]?

Those against a quota system as a measure to address gender inequalities argue that such a measure undermines the principle of fairness, competitiveness, and competence. They argue that there were different ways it can be articulated. Nations responsive to the need for gender equality in public offices have been either creating legislation or promoting a minimum number of 30 to 40 percent of women presence. Some other countries simply focus on a gender-neutral promotion of public service involvement (the United States), and others seek parity, of fifty-fifty (France, Sweden).

Until recently the focus, with respect to women's presence and visibility in public offices has been on the Scandinavian nations of Sweden, Norway, Denmark, and Finland. The focus however is only conditionally warranted. Although these nations have been successful in showcasing a high rate of women's presence in parliament, this has been a spotlight earned and de-

Table 3.3.   Top Twenty Countries with Highest Women's Presence in Parliament (Lower/Single House of Representatives)

1. Rwanda: 63%	2. Andorra: 50.0%
3. Cuba: 48%	4. Sweden: 44.7%
5. Seychelles: 43.8%	6. Senegal: 42.7%
7. Finland: 42.3%	8. South Africa: 42.3
9. Iceland: 39.7%	10. Norway: 39.6%
11. Mozambique: 39.2%	12. Denmark: 39.1%
13. Netherlands: 38.7%	14. Ecuador: 38.7%
15. Costa Rica: 38.6%	16. Timor-Lesle: 38.5%
17. Belgium: 38%	18. Argentina: 37.4%
19. Mexico: 36.8%	20. Germany: 36.3%

Source: IPU 9, October 2013

served as a collective group vis-à-vis the rest of European nations. Individually, however, an international outlook reveals other nations more successful in producing a higher presence of women in parliaments under their own respective circumstances than the Scandinavians.

Following is the regional overview of the results of gender quotas effort, followed by individual countries' breakdown for women in parliaments (both houses combined when applicable):

* Nordic countries: 42.0%
* Americas: 24.9%
* Europe (excluding Nordic countries): 22.8%
* Sub-Saharan Africa: 21.7%
* Asia: 18.5%
* Arab states: 15.9%
* Pacific: 15.9%

NEW GENDER ISSUE: SAME-SEX MARRIAGE

The West has been progressive with respect to gender discourse, more than the rest. Such progressivism by nature "pushes the envelope." It forces new debate, as it questions entrenched traditional and existing gendered roles and behaviors. The push against entrenched traditional gendered roles and behavior is now being applied to the natural and cultural reality of marriage, natural because it is built on the biological male and female dichotomy known as heterosexuality (XX and XY), which aims at reproducing society, and cultural because heterosexuality is the basis for the gendered marriage model, which reproduces gendered roles and behavior as parents raise their children projecting their mom and dad roles and raising boys and girls reflecting cultural gendered norms. By so doing they reflect both the natural and cultural dimensions of social relationships. They produce gendered roles and behavior. Heterosexuality as the basis of marriage and therefore its productive purpose are questioned. This biological basis and its cultural implications are questioned by those who feel left out because of their homosexuality (XX and XX or XY and XY) and its nonreproductive nature.

Those questioning the traditional natural and cultural reality of heterosexuality as the basis for marriage seek the extension of its basis to include same-sex relationships, even though they are naturally nonreproductive. The extension would then admit the following configuration (XX and XY, XX and XX, and XY and XY).

But the push against the gendered notion of marriage does not question the existence of marriage. It questions its biological (natural) premise of it, which because it is built on the biological difference between male and female (heterosexuality, or XX and XY) and its reproductive purpose, naturally precludes the possibility of same-sex unions (XX and XX or XY and XY) and therefore their claim to legitimate marital status.

The push against gendered roles has always acted on two fronts: the biological and the cultural. These two fronts are intricately linked. Those in support of the gay and lesbian movement, which is the force behind the push to be recognized in the mainstream, are now pushing the envelope to be recognized and now question the basis of their exclusion from legitimizing the union. This claim that questions the entrenched biological basis for male-female unions also questions the entrenched basis of the roles between the genders when the couple is of the same sex. Here is also where the biological meets the cultural.

These new changes in the gender discourse in the West are pushed by those left behind in the biological gender dichotomy of male and female and the roles that it ascribes to them. There are, in addition to gays and lesbians, transgender, intersex, etc.

The push against gendered roles and behavior raises a set of new issues that society must grapple with. Among such issues, society must address the social normalization of same-sex marriage and the legitimization of same-sex marriage. Should such questions be answered, all other related issues such as adoption, etc., must fall in line.

These issues create tension and possibly conflicts in society, as there are always those who refuse to embrace change, as change always brings degrees of the unknown, surprises, and an uneasy transitional phase and forces us to adjust. All that implies effort we may not be willing to make and leads to a new status quo we may not be willing to embrace either because we do not welcome the nature of change and its implications or because we are satisfied with the current status quo. The tensions around change are therefore dictated by the fact that what may be a new unacceptable status quo induced by changes to some may be welcome to others.

New issues around gender create new dilemmas and challenges to the norms and value system of individuals, society, the legal system, and the culture. These dilemmas and challenges explain the debate that ensues as change occurs.

The debate around same-sex marriage seems to be the ultimate gender debate, ultimate because other gender-related debates such as access to all professions including the military and the corporate world, or equality of pay, etc., although not over and not definitively settled, have already taken place. They were about extension of space of activity (role); they were about income (economics); they were about equal rights (justice). The debate around same-sex marriage is about social and cultural recognition.

The push for social and cultural recognition of same-sex unions seems to be ultimate because it breaks through a new territory, a territory that encompasses simultaneously, roles, rights, income, and recognition. It questions the historicity of the institution of marriage and its grounding in biology, its grounding in religion, morality, and legality. It challenges the notion of sexuality in marriage, as it encompasses both reproduction and pleasure, but here naturally precludes reproduction, and therefore unacceptable to many who see reproduction as the primary natural and organic reason for marriage. It questions the status of the institution of marriage as a harbor of reproduction and the pillar of society, civilization, and mankind itself.

Society must deal with it. Societies are social systems. As such, like any system, they must adjust to change. The current change occurring is the shift toward more acceptance of a pluralism of gender roles and behaviors. The debate that the change implies is currently under way in many Western nations but also in others.

The debate so far has produced the following picture (see Table 3.4):

Table 3.4.   Nations that allow same-sex marriage

Scotland (2014)	New Zealand (2013)
England/Wales (2013)	Uruguay (2013)
France (2013)	Brazil (2013)
Denmark (2012)	Portugal (2010)
Argentina (2010)	Iceland (2010)
Norway (2009)	Sweden (2009)
South Africa (2006)	Spain (2005)
Canada (2005)	Belgium (2003)
Countries with partial legislation	
Mexico (2009)	United States (2003)

Source: Pew Research, Religion and Public Life Project, February 2014

Regardless of how the debate unravels, change is a manifestation of a shift induced by specific forces. If, therefore, there is a shift in gender-based roles and behavior around the notion of same-sex marriage, then there must be forces driving the shift. What are the forces behind such a shift? Are these forces conjectural or structural? If they are conjectural, the outcome of the debate will simply be that of today and will not have a lasting status quo effect. However, if what is driving the movement for same-sex marriage is structural, then it will become part of the social fabric, the new status. The history of gender social movement in the West builds on previous gained battles. It is known to focus on specific gender issues such as women in the military, women in politics, etc., and has not relented until the issues have considerable success. The gender movement today is focusing on same-sex marriage, seen by proponents as an issue of rights, civil rights. It shows signs of relentlessness. It is a structural feature of the gender push in the West. The current movement on same sex-marriage is structural. If that is the case, then same-sex marriage will become a feature of the new status, a feature of the social fabric in the West.

The world of politics must deal with it. It presents a conundrum, as legislation reflects culture, customs, morality, and reason, but here all these factors seem to rather complicate the matter. Indeed different cultures, customs, and morality, even when having the same reason, render legislating on this matter challenging.

The conundrum lies in the fact that new issues are generally too complex because of the complexity of the world we live in today. They are, therefore, challenging. But society must deal with them. Society must find a way to diffuse the tensions within and between proponents and opponents of the issues. It is part of what systems do. They integrate new elements of change while not causing disruption in the functional dynamism of the system.

NOTES

1. A US military survey states that the average female recruit is 4.8 inches shorter and 31.7 pounds lighter and has 37.4 fewer pounds of muscle and 5.7 more pounds of fat than the average male. She has only 55 percent of the upper-body strength and 72 percent of the lower-body strength.

2. Cited in Jacqueline Goodman, ed., *Global Perspective on Gender and Work: Reading and Interpretations*, Lanham, MD: Rowman & Littlefield, 2010.

3. *The Huffington Post*, Egyptian Woman Dresses Like a Man For More Than 40 Years To Provide For Family, 03/23/2015.

4. http://www.undp.org/content/undp/en/home/ourwork/povertyreduction/focus_areas/focus_gender_and_poverty.html.

5. "The Development of Gender Achievement Gaps in Mathematics and Reading During Elementary and Middle School: Examining Direct Cognitive Assessments and Teacher Ratings." *American Educational Research Journal*, April 2011, 48, pp. 268–302. First published on June 7, 2010.

6. Sexual assault complaints reported in 2012–2013 were 3,700. Fifty-six percent of reporters were between sixteen and twenty-four years of age, and 79 percent were females, according to the Department of Defense/*Washington Post.*

7. Drude Dahlerup, "Quotas—A Jump to Equality?" The Need for International Comparison of the Use of Electoral Quotas to Obtain Equal Political Citizenship for Women, IDEA (Institute for Democracy and Electoral Assistance, September 2002.

Chapter Four

Structured Spaces as the Cause of Global Issues

This chapter examines the concept of structure, a rather familiar one, which, however, can be understood in specific ways that induce a number of implications and consequences to individuals, communities, and the entire globe. We will therefore start by defining the concept of structured spaces, describing their attributes as spaces to serve as a canvas of activity (action and behavior), mental and physical. We will establish the reason why such spaces exist. We will establish the role they play in the establishment of our cultural identity. We will explore their claims, demands, and expectations, which may be both harmless and harmful. Last, we will explain how in the process, demands and expectations of structured spaces interfere with agency and the ability to exercise free will and that when such demands and expectations are harmful in their consequences, the demands and expectations of structured spaces indeed may become causes of global issues.

STRUCTURE DEFINITION

Like a system, structure is a concept generally describing a variety of contexts in which there are recognizable patterns that by design serve a purpose. As such, there are recognizable patterns in a variety of contexts such as society, molecular composition, architectural buildings, etc. There are therefore structures in many processes, situations, organizations, designs, etc. The result is that the concept of structure can be used and explored in a variety of fields of academic inquiry.

Our definition is purposefully not the one you will read from a sociology manual on the subject of structure. It is purposefully so because from a sociologist's view, structures are defined with an emphasis on society. We intend here to use the concept beyond its sociological limits. This is the reason why the concept is understood broadly.

We define structure as an organized space. This definition expands the use of the concept of structure. It includes and expands the sociological understanding to encompass other forms and dimensions of structures, from anthropological to economic, from cultural to physical, etc. The definition sees structures primarily as spaces. And we established in the first chapter that spaces can be both material and tangible (found in the geographic space such as a classroom, a stadium, downtown) and abstract and intangible (such as the mental space, the cyber space). All these spaces can be organized in the purpose of ordering life. And when they are organized they become structures, as they allow for patterned processes to occur. Defining structures as organized spaces and knowing that some spaces are abstract results in the existence of intangible and abstract structures. This allows us to extend the understanding of the concept and consider the following as structures also: political parties, the constitution, religions, cultures, and civilizations. These structures go "beyond sociological comprehension" (Hays 1994, p. 60).

These different levels of structures are, however, acknowledged by sociologists, even though it is unfamiliar territory for sociology. These structures exceed the sociological realm. It is not limited to those we know as social structures such as families, government, the constitution, defined more rigidly, whose rules and norms, when not followed, bring direct and specified consequences. There are necessarily no direct punishments from not heeding cultural, religious, or civilizational customs, norms, and value systems. Yet like sociological structures, these structures are norm providers. They provide guidance for social action and behavior. They order social life. Like social structures, they are "resilient patterns that order social life" (Hays, quoting Sewell (1994, p. 2). They are fluid, loose, and flexible, as they are carried out by those in space and time that abide by their canon. They earn their structure status more by their social life–ordering content rather than their frontiers.

STRUCTURED SPACES AND CULTURAL IDENTITY

We are socialized to use structures, to function in them, to adjust to them, to thrive in them, and to fit their molds. The process is designed to make us suitable to society, to become contributing members of society, to find utility in society, but also to help society fulfill its mission, that of preserving, protecting, and sustaining community members, and at the same time while doing all those things to the individuals, it does them for its own sake. The process makes structured spaces the instruments of what Michel Foucault has referred to as "governmentality."[1] They are venues through which and in which our cultural identity is molded, exercised, defined, and therefore limited. They are spaces in which our roles, assignments, and attributions are validated. They are canvases on which human activity proceeds in patterned processes.

PURPOSE OF STRUCTURES

We exist within structures as organized spaces, from family homes to churches, from classrooms to offices, from parks to stadiums, from restaurants to airplanes, etc. We belong as well to a variety of other structures such as a particular religion, political party, union, kinship, culture.

These structures emerge as a result of an organic process, for instance, kinship, family, cultures. Others are designed by people such as sports teams, political parties, governments, the constitution, the law, etc. They respectively serve a specific purpose. The purpose is to service or serve a particular existing and recurrent need in society. Hospitals exist because people regularly get sick. A bakery around the corner exists because many people regularly eat bread for breakfast. The National Football League exists to produce champions. Schools and colleges exist to convey knowledge, academic skills, and education. The military exists to repel threats to national security. Religions exist to align believers with the will of their maker or with the precepts of their worldviews. Families exist to raise future generations.

Beyond their respective purposes, all structures contribute to their higher purpose, which is to order life. As they order life, structures serve as anchors. They provide a benchmark. They become to guide, around which social behavior is normalized. They are norm providers. They remove the burden from individuals, from having to figure out on a daily basis what to do and how to go about it. This is indeed viewed by some of the most prominent conservative thinkers such as the likes of Edmund Burke[2] or Arnold Ghelen[3] as the key benefit of entrenched structures in society. Structures provide support for the productive need of society. They provide support for the reproductive need of society. They provide support for an organized coexistence in society.

COMPLEMENTARITY OF STRUCTURES

There are a variety of structures. Individuals become associated with structures. When we become hospitalized we become associated with hospitals.

We acquire a temporary membership with hospitals. We can as well voluntarily become a member of existing structures out there. Some athletes sign with specific clubs. Some people become members of specific political parties. We may have a US citizenship, which makes us members of the United States, which is a nation and as such a structure. So we may find ourselves belonging to a variety of structures because human beings live within and are part of a variety of structures, at once. This leads to the fact that the existence of and belonging to structures can be complementary.

One may be a US citizen, a male, a Muslim, and a Democrat. Another can be a Republican, a female, a Buddhist, and a General Motors worker. Yet another can be an atheist, a feminist, and a mother.

THE CLAIM OF STRUCTURES

The notion of claim of structures is closely linked to the notion of purpose. They are two sides of the same coin. The reason is because claims are the promise of structure's fulfillment of its purpose. If religion, for instance, exists to save souls, which is its purpose, the claim of religion then becomes the promise to ensure salvation. If family exists to raise children, the claim of parenthood becomes the ability to provide the environment conducive to fulfillment of that promise. Specific claims of structures derive from their very purpose. The existence of structures implies their ability to deliver on their promise (claim). Structures, therefore, must secure the ability enabling them to fulfill the claim of their purpose. A school that lacks resources cannot claim to fulfill the purpose for which it has been created.

In cases where structures lack the ability to deliver on their promise, they must start by claiming (demanding) the conditions be met in which they can fulfill the claim of their purpose. Using the example of cultures, which we identify here as a structure, Seyla Benhabib (2002) noted that many are not even recognized. As such they lack the necessary basis and ground upon which to start the effort of serving the purpose for which they exist. Therefore, their claim is to seek recognition before anything else. In such a category, we find a few cultures such the Kurds in Turkey, the Palestinians, and the Armenians and their claim to Nagorno-Karabakh in the South Caucasus region to name just a few. It is a case in which a cultural structure must claim (demand) first the conditions in which to fulfill the purpose for which it exists before claiming to fulfill the promise of a culture, namely to serve as a value and norm provider to a group of people.

DEMANDS AND EXPECTATIONS OF STRUCTURES

The existence and functioning of structures is characterized by guidelines designed to help them service and serve the need for which they have been created (purpose) and therefore to fulfill their promise (claim). To better provide care and heal patients, hospitals establish a series of rules to regulate the coming and going, the communication, the treatment mechanism, etc., for all those involved in the process and its procedures. These process and procedure rules and regulations are not optional. They are expected to be followed. They constitute demands that the hospital addresses to all. All structures are in their very essence about a specific purpose, which induces the need for a functional organization and order. All structures therefore demand a specific behavior.

COMPLEMENTARITY OF THE
DEMANDS AND EXPECTATIONS OF STRUCTURES

A variety of structures we belong to all have their demands and consequently their expectations on us, their members, or subscribers. Often the demands and expectations of structures are complementary. Using the examples above, we find that one may be a US citizen, a male, a Muslim, and a Democrat without any complication, problem, or conflict arising as a result. Another can be a Republican, a female, a Buddhist, and a General Motors worker because belonging to these structures does not raise any conflict. And finally, one can be an atheist, a feminist, and a mother and find that all these structures contribute to her identity as an individual. The reason is because whatever expectations these structures respectively formulate toward their members can be fulfilled by one unique member without this member finding himself or herself in some kind of contradiction. The expectations for US citizenship are complementary with the expectations to belonging to a political party or being of any gender or being of any religion. Belonging to any specific religion does not impede on being a US citizen or belonging to any given gender.

There are however cases and a combination of structures to which we belong that can cause and raise a number of issues, as we explore in the following segment.

INCOMPATIBILITY OF THE
DEMANDS AND EXPECTATIONS OF STRUCTURES

The demands and expectations of structures are primarily tailored to fit their respective purpose and claim. Just as taken together the multiplicity of demands and expectations can be compatible and therefore complementary, they can as well be incompatible and therefore mutually exclusive. The demands and expectations of one structure may collide with the demands and expectations of another. A concrete example is the abortion debate in the United States. Being a member of the Democratic Party and a Catholic is belonging to two structures with specific demands that oppose each other. Their demands are mutually exclusive. The Democratic Party advocates a prochoice policy, and the Catholic Church is the proponent of the prolife position. People belonging to or having membership in both these structures poses a problem. People who are Democrats should vote for the prochoice candidate or at least are expected to reflect the views of their party. On the other hand their belonging to or membership in the Catholic Church projects the opposite expectation on them. People must reconcile these two expectations. Belonging to different structures with opposing or incompatible expectations poses a problem. There is in this case a conflict that needs to be sorted out. There is as well a variety of possible solutions. People can quit one structure to fully embrace the expectations of the other. Or they can choose to ignore the expectations of one. By so doing they risk being in disagreement with the structure whose expectation they choose to ignore. The structure whose expectation was ignored can choose to retaliate. Indeed, structures have mechanisms in place to repudiate those who disobey their demands. The Catholic Church, for instance, historically is known to have practiced excommunication as one such repudiation or retaliation. There are today cases where the Catholic Church refuses communion. It is a form of punishing a structure's demand-deviation behavior. There are many more cases of incompatibility. They all dictate such responses. Take for instance a real case of a Sikh student[4] who happens to be an American citizen and wants to serve his country in the US Army. As a man of the Sikh faith he is expected to wear a beard and long hair under his turban. The US Army, however, has grooming rules, requiring a shave and short hair. The faith to which the student belongs and the US Army are two structures whose demands/expectations collide. The student had a choice to make. In this particular case he chose to sue the US Army to seek accommodation. The Jehovah Witness Church has similar colliding expectations with government with respect to allegiance and the draft. These two structures collide, as their respective demands and expectations are in many instances on a collision course.

Yes, it is indeed a struggle, an uphill battle to be both a feminist and a Muslim in areas where Islam is understood in fundamentalist ways that defy the claims of liberal feminism. Such dilemmas can become even more complex. Take the following example: One can be a US citizen who happens to be Muslim and in the US Army. He may be called on to fight in Afghanistan or

Iraq, where he will probably have to gun down fellow Muslims. There is, in this scenario, a number of built-in conflicts that need to be sorted out by the individual. Here we are dealing with religion, government, and the military. They are structures. They each have expectations that collide. For the Muslim it may be not to kill a fellow Muslim. For the citizen it may be to follow the law. For the soldier it may be to obey orders.

Each one looking at the scenario will have his or her own approach to dealing with the possible conflicts. These approaches may vary. There are those who suggest responding to the expectations of the highest structure. If such is the approach one will have to heed the expectation of religion. For this member of the US army, that would mean to refuse the order to kill his fellow Muslims. He would fail to follow the expectations of the government and the army. For someone else the approach might be to do what she signed up for, namely, to go to war when needed, and anything else is unacceptable. To another, the duty as a citizen primes everything else, as the soldier in question has taken the oath of protecting the country.

There was a case in Fort Hood, Texas, on November 9, 2009, in a killing at the military base, whereby US Army Major Nidal Malik Hasan doing the killing reflects belonging to a variety of structures whose demands for him eventually conflicted. For the soldier involved, we know what the outcome of a necessary negotiation of such a conflict ended up being. He went with his religion.

There are other cases of complex dilemmas in which multiple demands and expectations of various structures collide for an individual member. For instance, Palestinian Arabs who practice Judaism have to live through the Israeli-Palestinian conflict. The complexity of the world of increasingly convoluted structures complicates matters more and more, creating what Flint (2011, p. 249), analyzing the geopolitical world, contends is the "messiness of geopolitics."

THE HARMFULNESS OF THE
DEMANDS AND EXPECTATIONS OF STRUCTURES

For the most part, the demands that structures place on their adherents, followers, or members are designed primarily to service and serve the purpose that justifies their existence. As a result, these demands are motivated and driven by noble intents. They may have a restrictive nature, as they produce rules and regulations, and these are naturally restrictive and or constraining. Rules and regulations, which have the same essence as laws, are either prescriptive or proscriptive. And although restrictive and constraining, they do not aim at harming adherents, members, or followers. They often read as follows:

- Religions demand believers not to sin. Governments demand citizens to follow the law. Athletes must follow the rules of the game. In a marriage, married partners must remain faithful. Members of ethnic communities must heed their customs.
- Members (adherents, believers, and followers) are expected to honor them. These demands are harmless. And following them does not cause or pose any major problem. However, not all the demands of structures are harmless. Some demands are consequential. Indeed, a number of structures demand their members to commit harmful acts, to engage in atrocious and malicious behavior.
- And so we fight in the name of structures, as in the case of soldiers in various armies around the world, in the name of the military, the government, or the state; al-Qaeda and terrorism in the name of Islam; the Knights and the crusaders in the name of Christianity, etc.
- We kill in the name of structures, as in the case of the military and wars of any kind. We kill in the name of ethnicity and its customs, as in the case of honor killing, ethnic cleansing, and genocide. We kill in the name of Islamic Jihad. Some urban gangs in Mexico, the United States, Brazil, etc., demand rituals and initiation rites and later their members to kill. Structured social classes such as the Samurai, in case of dishonor of the Bushido code,[5] demand their members to take their own lives by performing harakiri, or seppuku.
- We die in the name of structures, as in religions to earn the status of martyrs and as soldiers in wars.
- We hate in the name of structures, as in the cases of the Ku Klux Klan, the Westboro Baptist Church, the Nazis against the Jews, the Hutus against the Tutsis and vice versa, etc.

These demands translate into expectations, and when heeded, they produce harmful consequences. These consequences are a true cause of global issues.

THE DEMANDS AND EXPECTATIONS OF STRUCTURES AS A GLOBAL ISSUE

A case can be made, considering the number of conflicts, atrocities, and destructions caused by harmful consequences of the demands of structures, that indeed structures are some of the causes of issues we face as a global community. Some of the most pressing issues around the globe are linked to the expectations and demands of structures. Many global issues can be linked to the demands of religions, governmental policies, ideologies, organizations' charters, etc. They directly or indirectly drive, motivate, or explain the existence of issues. One can in all plausibility conclude that without some specific demands and expectations of structures, some issues would not have any reason to arise.

Among such structure-linked issues are ethnic conflicts and wars. Ethnicity as a structure and its demands and expectations can cause, motivate, or drive conflicts and wars. We have mentioned a number of such conflicts in chapter 2. Honor killing is another one of these issues today. In Warren, Michigan, a man killed his stepdaughter in April 2011. Still in Michigan, the parents of a teenager daughter of immigrants from Palestine killed their daughter because she dishonored the Palestinian custom, causing harm not because of their own desire to stop short the life of their daughter but because of the demand of the custom of the ethnic structure to which they belong. Additional cases have been brought to courts in Arizona, Texas, and Virginia, to name just a few.

We count as well religious conflicts. If the Muslim rebels in Chechnya have no other reason to fight than simply because they seek separation from Orthodox Russia, the conflict is linked to structures. If in East Timor, the only reason Muslims in the northwest seek secession is because they are Muslims who do not want to associate with Christian East Timorians, then this is a structure-linked issue. In India, the tension between Hindus and Muslims is an issue. The conflict in Ireland is motivated and driven by the memberships of the involved parties in the Catholic and the Protestant churches.

Terrorism is a global issue, as well as a structure-linked issue, in so far as it is motivated and driven by the argument of Islamic Jihad. Jihad is a demand and an expectation of a religious structure of Islam.

The very notion of the clash of civilizations, considering the fact that civilizations are organized spaces and therefore are structures, is itself a structure-linked clash. It is a structure-linked global issue. Indeed, when civilizations clash vast regions and a huge number of adherent members who are scattered everywhere on the globe are affected. Although not all adherents are automatically affected, and many may distance themselves from such clashes, many others may sympathize with their respective civilizations and either actively or passively assist or support it.

This perspective then begs the question that has been raised by others before this book, namely, could it be that structures hinder some of the basic natural, organic fusion in favor of peace and harmony to produce barriers that complicate human encounters?

John Lennon wrote a song in 1971 whose lyrics simply exhorted the world to think of a community of human beings not subjected to the constraints of structured spaces, arguing it would be a better world. He called his song "Imagine."

Before John Lennon, in a different time frame, a different context, and a different level of inquiry, Jean Jacques Rousseau, the French-Swiss enlightenment philosopher, posited a reflection in his *Social Contract*, claiming and arguing (paraphrasing his argument) that civilizations have removed human beings from their natural selves, which he saw as essentially good and uncontaminated, only to make them subject to structures that interfere with their natural good instincts. Civilized people must now defend property. They have interests they must defend. They have artificially created needs that have to be met and serviced, and such imperatives produce confrontation, competition, worries, greed, conflicts, wars, and casualties, all of which are unnecessary if society had not created the conditions that induced them. These structures (here, interpreting Rousseau's thought) explain why George W. Bush or Barack Obama would not befriend Osama Bin Laden. The only reason this possibility was deemed impossible was the fact that these personalities belonged to different civilizational and religious structures (the West and Christianity and Islamic civilization and religion), with their respective demands and expectations that ultimately erected barriers between these protagonists.

The assumption is that without these civilizational barriers, there is no reason why Bin Laden and George W. Bush or Barack Obama would not have been able to meet for a few glasses of beer or a meal in a restaurant of their choosing, or at least not seek to kill each other, as they eventually came to do.

STRUCTURE AND AGENCY

Structures are inert without people within them. People animate structures. They function as agents within structures. These agents allow for the structural processes and procedures to occur. They act. They make decisions and choices within and on behalf of structure. Agency is the ability of these agents to act, make choices, and decide.

As a result structures do not function without agency. Universities and colleges do not function without students. Churches do not exist without believers, nor do armies win wars without soldiers. But colleges and universities also need administrators and faculty. Churches need priests and pastors, and the military needs commanders.

Agency within structures, therefore, is made of personnel and clients. Both personnel and clients act within the limits of the demands and expectations of structures. Actions, decisions, and choices are not made randomly. Walking into a supermarket, we socially, as second nature, know what behavior is allowed of us as customers and what behavior we should expect of other shoppers and clerks and cashiers. Clerks and cashiers in the supermarket also know what their roles are. We do not walk into a supermarket and start playing ball. This is because a supermarket is a structured space that is organized and regulated.

In such organized space that we call structures, interactions are regulated. These interactions occur between personnel and clients. Both personnel and clients are subject to the demands (regulations) of the structures and therefore are expected to heed them. So soldiers do not behave as they please. Students do not get to do what they want in class. Driving downtown, we do not get to take any turn we want in the middle of traffic, etc.

Agents within structures agree to this restrictive nature of space organization, as they voluntarily adhere to their role as personnel on one hand and as client on the other. Walking into a bank to open up a savings account makes a person a customer/client of the bank and at the same time a voluntary adherent to the restrictions that come with the functional organization of that bank. The same thing is true of becoming an NFL player or umpire, etc. Adhering to a church implies the same consequence.

In the end, it seems that we voluntarily agree to become subjects of all these structures we happen to belong to as we go about minding our business in life. And considering that there are so many such structures out there to which we voluntarily adhere, routinely, on a daily basis, and every time we do we relinquish implicitly or explicitly some of our own ability to act, decide, and choose as we please, one has to wonder whether structures around us limit our ability to practice free will. If such is the case, how really free are we in society?

STRUCTURES' DOMINATION OF AGENCY

Agents create structures. Although they do, agents are the ones that ultimately have to follow the rules, regulations, laws, and commandments and must meet the eligibility criteria and other standards established by structures. Yes, these standards are established by agents, and the latter can always change the former. But it does not happen as naturally as it theoretically seems. Here is an example: One agent cannot simply change the mechanism of denying or granting mortgages simply because he or she wants to. Even in such a case, there is a structured mechanism under which any change becomes possible. This example shows how eventually entrenched structural mechanisms dictate the actions of agents, even though agents are the ones without whom structures do not function and whose interests structures are designed to service.

Under this circumstance, does that mean that agency is powerless or at least has limited influence over structures? Who then has primacy over the other? The question has been at the basis of a debate carried out in the social sciences for a while. It has yet to be settled. Let us here briefly present the prevailing schools of thought.

In the debate on primacy between structure and agency, functionalists, Marxists, and structuralists argue that structures considerably limit the ability of agency. Although agents can still act, decide, and make decisions, these actions are restricted by the entrenched structures in which they proceed. Callinicos (2004, p. 1), quoting Marx, writes: "'Agency or men in general, operate within circumstances they encounter, limiting their actions, in range of alternatives open to agent.'" This is a deterministic argument, also known as structural determinism. Others have argued that agency has ascendency over structures due to the fact that individuals still have the ability and capability of influencing their fate and history, even in the midst of existent structures. In this category, Max Weber,[6] for instance, sees in the debate on primacy between agency and structure that "'the latter is the unintended consequence of the former'" (quoted in Callinicos 2004, p. 4). They are called voluntarists, among them, the interactionism school of thought. To bridge the gap between these two sides of the argument about primacy between structure and primacy, there have been nuances suggested by, for instance, Perry Anderson[7] (1980), who proposed three different levels at which agency acts: the private (private goals), the public (military conflicts, political struggles, civil rights), and the collective or self-determination level (pursuit of global social transformation). He submitted that the ability of the agency to influence structure and history depended on the level at which the action occurs. Based on this assertion, it is easiest to influence things on the private level and less so on the public level. On the collective level, it is much more difficult.

There have been attempts to reconcile the fronts between structuralists and voluntarists. These attempts to bridge the gap argue that the distinction between agency and structure is too strict, too dichotomic and reductionist. These attempts suggest instead an emphasis on the interactions between structure and agency. Among the proponents of this perspective are Bourdieu, Anthony Giddens, and Sharon Hays. Giddens (1984) has suggested a theory of structures to underline the interaction, and Sharon Hays used the term interconnection between structure and agency to suggest a rather unnecessary quest for establishing the supremacy of one over the other. To underline her argument, Hays (1994, p. 7) writes, "People make structures, structures at the same time as structures make people." She argues that structures are both the "enabler and container of agency."

She acknowledges the ability for individual choice by the agent who is the creative force of social life but as well, a component of social life and ultimately the subject of the structured social life.

Structures are undoubtedly the overarching constructs in society. And even though they become overwhelming, we need them to order life, as we fear more how miserable life would be without them. Relinquishing a bit of the ability to exercising our free will becomes the trade-off. Hence, the entire endeavor of human organization becomes a tension of managing social life between order and freedom (Alexander 1987).

STRUCTURES AS BOUNDARIES OF FREE WILL

Because we exist within structures that tell us what to do and because there are so many such structures around us, one must ask, How free are we really, or how much freedom do we have? The question might be surprising to many. After all, they live in free and democratic countries. This is the case in liberal states based on the principles of individual freedom and equality of rights. Individuals in such liberal states may have never felt limited in their choices, and if they have, it is in minimal ways that do not constitute cause for alarm about their freedom. Furthermore, they see the reason, and they explicitly or implicitly agree with the reasonable limits that society puts on human freedom. Average people therefore do not think of themselves as *not* being free. It is living according to the rule of law. Although free will is not exercised at will even in liberal states, it is constrained only out the necessity of safeguarding the public common good.

Those living in nonliberal states and countries where the rule of law is not the norm or the laws are not produced through a democratic legislative process or in societies wherein the principles at work are based on premodern customs or ideologies endure more constraining limits to the exercise of their free will than those living in liberal states. Indeed, traditional customs or ideologies may be guided by aims other than individual freedom or equality of rights. Consequently, the exercise of free will may be more constrained in such cases.

In both cases, minimal and considerable constraint to the exercising of free will, individuals have to put up with limitations. Such limitations are caused and induced by the necessity to create order to ensure the peaceful coexistence among society members. Douglass (1975) contended that it is a fundamental preoccupation of society to have to deal with the tension between *freedom* and *order*. Reasonable individuals recognize the necessity of complying. Societal peaceful coexistence in fact seems to be the highest good, high enough to allow the scaling back of our freedom. Indeed, without peace and security nothing else will thrive, and life itself is in danger. Our freedom is therefore a matter of perception. As a matter of fact, freedom, to the dismay of liberalists, may not be and is not the highest social good. We are more than happy to relinquish our freedom for the promise of other higher social goods. In fact, we do that more regularly than we care to admit. We give up a portion of our freedom every time we agree to be in a steady relationship with someone else. We lock ourselves down in relationships when we elope and when we get married. This implies that love is a much higher social good than freedom. We agree to spend at least eight hours of our time working for some firm or employer because money is more valuable than the eight hours spent somewhere else.

These limitations are socially induced by our membership or belonging in various societal structures, such as marriage, employment, or churches, as they are expressions of demands and expectations of these structures. The consequence of accepting the limitations exerted by structures is that we internalize their demand and expectations. We agree to the power, authority, and supervision of us by them, so much so that once accepting and internalizing these demands and expectations, the power and authority of structures silently and constantly continue to order our lives even when there is no boss around, no parent around, or no police around because we know what is permissible and what is not. We become kin to complying with structures if we are not defiantly deviant or criminally inclined. Our socialization processes prepare and reinforce compliance with structural membership. This led Marcuse (1964) in the *One-Dimensional Man* to state that there was a police inside our head. This means that even our mental space is infiltrated by structural demands and expectations by being aware of them and their implications to us.

A wicked thought then becomes internally reprimanded by the internal policeman before we even get to think it through because it is not in compliance with structural demands and expectations. This structural policeman inside our heads is not the same as our conscience. Our conscience is about right and wrong, but what structures deem right or wrong may not be the same as what our conscience deems right or wrong. Often, we find ourselves disagreeing with the demands or expectations of structures, finding them unjust, unfair, or even morally questionable and therefore not right. But there are norms and standards to uphold, sometimes structural demands and expectations and even conflicts within our sense of morality. For instance, it does not make moral sense to demand and expect a higher interest rate from a low-income earner and reduce it for a higher-income earner. The logic of the economic structure of the bank demanding and expecting low interest rates for the high earner is based on the risk factor. This factor is not necessarily moral. Some would even call it cold-blooded. Morals are here not the guiding norms for the bank, and therefore conscience is not the basis for structural demands and expectations. Rather it is based on functionality and therefore material rationality, as Max Weber has described in his seminal book, *The Protestant Ethic and the Spirit of Capitalism*. One is natural and precedes human action; the other is unnatural, a human's construct.

Under these circumstances, although we get to exercise our free will, the policeman is either internal, within us, or external through all kinds of institutional personnel or the mechanism of surveillance, checking whether our actions and behaviors are in compliance with whatever structures they are designed to be performed in. We are limited in the exercise of our free will.

We still get to exercise free will because we still have decisions to make and choices to take. Choosing which college to go to is an expression of exercising free will; however, we are limited here as well in a number of ways. There may be many colleges out there, but they are not unlimited, which means our ability to make decisions is limited with the unlimitedness of colleges to choose from. A number of many other restrictions apply here.

Society, however, does not validate the valiant cases of rebellion against the restrictions imposed on us by structures. There are punitive consequences of defying the demands of structures. Prisons and jails exist to dissuade such acts of deviance from structural norms and standards. There are people in jails, whose only fault consists of not having acted within the limits of what was permissible by some structure. They do not get to argue that they were only exercising their free will.

THE QUESTION OF INDIVIDUAL FREEDOM: A BRIEF PHILOSOPHICAL PERSPECTIVE

We have established the constraints that structures exercise on human agency. We have established as well that human agency is both limited and enabled by structures. In any case there is no doubt a limiting effect of structures. This now leads to the question of which one, human agency or structure, has the upper hand in determining the course of history.

Answers to these questions vary. Scholars have suggested a variety of arguments. Anderson (1980) argued that the ability of human agency to influence reality depends on the level at which an action occurs. We are still in charge at the private level of human agency despite the existence of structures. Hays

(1994), Giddens (1984), and others believe that there are constraints through society (structures) that limit us but also enable us to do more. As we interact with structures and through structural processes that necessitate individual input, human agency gets to make its mark.

Karl Marx in *Historical Materialism* (1926) and in response to Friedrich Hegel emphasized the limit within which human agency acts and therefore is less enabled than enabled by structures to determine man's fate. Hegel, in the context of human agency and history, in his work *Philosophy of History* (1837) argued that history already has a meaning and the task of human agency, more through the mind than through action, was to find out was it was. In the previous phrase, the expression "more through the mind than through action" seems as well to summarize the difference of approaches when it comes to the philosophy of history for these two theorists. Hegel, being the idealist that he is, starts with abstract reasoning to make sense of the world he sees. On the other hand, Karl Marx, reading what Hegel writes about history, does not recognize it. Hegel's abstract description of the world makes reality unrecognizable and smaller. That is revolting to Marx, who sees the world primarily as it is and wonders, how come? Marx therefore starts with the reality, origins, and implications. That reality and its implications are that human beings are conscious of their material conditions. Their history starts there, as opposed to animals that did not have that reflexive capacity. History begins and is reproduced by the consciousness of the material conditions of human beings. His view of history is materialistic. He argues that history can only through that perspective be really understood and not the other way around as Hegel suggested. Thus, we have two of the frontal face-offs in the world of theoretical reasoning. Underlining this theoretical face-off, Marx simply concludes by stating that history was not determined by consciousness but rather consciousness determined history.

Althusser, a structuralist, sees history occurring without any noteworthy influence of human agency. He sees history "as process without a subject or goals" (Callinicos 2004, p. 2). For Althusser, changes occur as a result of accumulated structural contradictions in which human agency has a say. Human agency is powerless, a puppet, in the powerful waves of the sea of history. Contradicting Althusser, a few examples out of the history book can be used. Mikhael Gorbachev, the secretary general of the Communist Party and head of the Soviet Union in the 1980s and early 1990s, initiated the policy of reform called glastnost (openness) and perestroika (restructuring). He almost single-handedly succeeded in bringing about change that ultimately led to the collapse of the Soviet Union and heralded the shift away from Communism. This is not an example of human agency's insignificance in the course of history. But structuralists such as Althusser may argue that the demise of the Soviet Union was structurally programmed by forces of history and that Gorbachev was just an instrument utilized by history.

On the other side of the structuralist argument, there are those who argue that history is "a process through which human beings constantly make and remake their lives." Thompson, (Callinicos 2004, p. 2) who argues from this perspective, situates human beings at the center of changing the course of history, which makes his approach a humanist one. Humans have only to struggle with "the objective conditions of their actions." Human agency is here in charge, at the private level, the public level, and the collective level. Karl Popper (1957) argued in *The Poverty of Historicism*[8] that history is a canvas that has neither sense nor purpose in and by itself until we, humans, give it that sense or purpose.

Max Weber (1978) in *Economy and Society* argued as well for the supremacy of agency over structure, stating that "'the latter simply was the unintended consequence of the former'" (Callinicos 2004, p. 4). For arguing from the centrality of agency, they are in that regard, humanists.

For Thompson and Popper, in the example of the demise of the Communist Soviet Union, they would see in Gorbachev the vindication of the centrality of human agency in determining the pace and the path of history.

But we do have here once again in the debate, a dichotomy, a dualism of perspectives, which some other theorists seem to deplore as fruitless. Anderson, whom we have mentioned, is one of them.

The suggestion by Anderson seems indeed to provide a way out of the dichotomy, as it proposes a more flexible and nuanced approach to the question of whether human agency does indeed have control. He argues that agency sometimes has more and sometimes less control of the course of events and history. Individuals have control and can influence through their actions their own immediate private field of action more than any other. The questions whether to attend college, to marry, etc., are much more easily handled than questions about the fate of the Republican party in the United States being impacted by a single individual human action, even though it remains within the limits of the possible.

MEASURING THE IMPACT OF
HUMAN AGENCY IN INFLUENCING HISTORY

When human agency influences the course of history, at a collective level, it is indeed often complicated to pinpoint, to unequivocally state, the influencing impact of human agency. European expansion leading to colonization was a historical phenomenon that took place three hundred years ago.

Globalization is one such historical level change currently occurring. There are always many factors at play, many protagonists with their contributions, sometimes contradictory ones, practical circumstances that facilitate or impede the advent of historical change, etc. In so far as social phenomena ultimately contribute to producing history, these examples of colonization then and globalization today illustrate an old problem of social science, that of multicausality and multifactoriality. Such phenomena are often induced through the concurrently acting forces (multifactoriality), which complicate the establishment of a causal link (causality) to a qualitatively and quantitatively identifiable clean source.

DIFFERENT VENUES THROUGH
WHICH HISTORICAL CHANGES OCCUR

It remains, however, a fact that history does indeed continually change. Historical changes occur mostly at the third level of Anderson's scale of private, public, and collective agency actions. But at any level, human agency is the driving force behind any change, although actions influence the pace and path of historical change with variable impact.

What are those driving forces? Because we are in a social and historical world, forces that drive processes in this world are all triggered by human agency. Human thoughts and action initiate directly or indirectly historical changes, indirectly through scientific and technological inventions and innovations, whose tools and products have the ability to alter entrenched patterns of relationships between agents (in society) and between agents and structures (change in functional process), forcing structures to adjust. They may change structures' purpose or claim, even demands an expectations. Sometimes they induce even the demise of structures, leading to the disappearance of some and the birth of others. Examples of dying structures and emerging structures are a social phenomenon in and by themselves. In the world of economics, companies die if they do not keep up. Kodak in Rochester, New York,[9] is one such example. The automobile industry in the United States, more precisely that in Detroit, Michigan—Chrysler, Ford, and General Motors—found itself on the verge of disappearance in late 2008 had it not been for a five billion dollar government bailout they received to avoid bankruptcy. There are many more examples in other areas of society where we have structures that need to adapt. So just as the demise of Kodak is a historical fact, an eventual death of the automobile industry would have been an even bigger one. The impact of technology, however, can have a big historical impact, as the advent of the Internet shows. It has induced a change in behavioral patterns in society, led to a number of adjustments in structural demands and expectations, and induced a new historical epoch, the digital technology era. Scientific and technological inventions and innovations are a driving force. In the social and historical world the changes they indirectly effect are initiated by human agency, but human agency does not determine their impact, and which ever that impact, human agency has himself to adjust. Human agency initiates but does not determine the impact and must submit or adjust to what impact the scientific and technological invention or innovation has to society and history.

Another category of indirectly induced changes by human agency is that of cultural shifts of ideas, ideals, values, and norms. Culture is dynamic because factors that underlie it are themselves dynamic. Ideas are dynamic because new ones emerge. Values are dynamic because they can change and morph and new ones can be adopted and old ones shed off. So do ideals. As a result norms shift to reflect the changes of ideals and values, and the shift is manifest in the behavior. The sum of this process is what we call culture. When culture changes, and however it changes, society, agents, and structures adjust. This adjustment is indirect, as we do not individually and voluntarily decide to do so and we do because we are social animals.

But there are changes that occur as a result of driving forces that are directly triggered, initiated, and induced by human agency. Such is the case of social movements, social militancy, advocacy and interest groups, lobbies, etc. They are in the business of inducing change, sometimes of resisting change or even of dismantling change, as the later chapter on social movements will show. It is in this case because of direct human agency involvement in changing society and history that revolutions occur.

These changes, at any level they occur, may occur in increments (little shifts that accumulatively occur and over time change previously established patterns in individual life, structural processes, or collectively). Changes may occur transformatively when they profoundly alter patterns of relationships and processes within a structure by freeing both agency and structure from what holds them back. Changes may occur in an evolutionary manner, simply because structures are functionally dynamic. The dynamism of structures implies the necessity to evolve. Evolution is a "progressive modification of the structure in response to input from the environment," Lazlo wrote (1972, p. 39). Events within the environment (society and life in general) simply and naturally produce changes that we, people and structures, must adjust to. Adapting to these changes produces the evolutionary effect of driving forces of change. Changes, however, may also occur through revolutions. Revolutionary changes are drastically and suddenly induced changes in a crisis form as a consequence of imbalanced and unaddressed structural functionality. Revolutionary changes are induced by structural agents on the losing side of the imbalance, whenever a critical mass has been reached. They may not all be successful, but they do break out when the time is right. It is no accident that historical revolutions have often been initiated, at least carried out, by the peasants, the poor, the disenfranchised, and the oppressed, for example, the American Revolution; the French Revolution; independence movements in Africa, Asia, and Latin America; during European colonialism; the revolution in Romania, which overthrew Ceaușescu; the Bolshevik revolution, etc. It is as well no accident that if revolutions break out because structural imbalances have not been addressed, it is because there are those agents within structures that benefit from the status quo and therefore are reluctant to address the need for change, may be just because change itself is to some a risky endeavor, as conservatism would argue. Historical change may finally occur as a result of a dialectical process, as described primarily by Friedrich Hegel and much more practically by Karl Marx. The process ensues when concurrent realities (thesis and antithesis) in society produce a compromising third alternative (synthesis). The third alternative ends up generating its own opposition or contradiction, and the process draws its dynamism from there. The dynamism of history, as explained by Hegel, is justified by the fact that human realities or constructs are often imperfect, incomplete, and imbalanced. They end up producing a countering alternative. As the first reality or construct concomitantly exists with its opposition, they inspire a compromise, as in the following example that Hegel himself uses in *Philosophy of Right* (2005), namely, that there should be an abstract universal law (a thesis) that is contradicted by our having personal conscience to follow (antithesis), not universal law. Both these propositions have to find a compromise, which becomes the need for an ethics of society (synthesis). History, according to Hegel, follows this dialectic process. The main reaction to Hegel was Karl Marx's, who agreed with the dialectic mechanism but rejected Hegel's ideational or rational perspective, as everything starts with our conscience to order our existence. This suggests the opposite, namely, that it is our material existence that dictates our conscience and therefore that history is generated from the bottom up. From the material and sociological reality of an individual starts the conceptualization of human history.

To conclude this segment, we should reiterate that different social forces produce different kinds of changes, affecting both human agency and structures. These forces of change occur with different paces and intensities. They may occur concurrently, successively, or suddenly, which helps determine whether they will impact structures incrementally, evolutionarily, revolutionarily, transformatively, or dialectically.

NOTES

1. Davidson 2004.
2. Burke 1986.
3. Gehlen 1988.
4. A case reported by the *Huffington Post*: http://www.huffingtonpost.com/iknoor-singh/sikh-army-rotc_b_6147686.html.
5. Articulating the virtues of the Samurai, among them poutiness, courage, honor, loyalty, self-control, honesty, etc.
6. Max Weber, *Economy and Society*, New York: Routledge, 1989.
7. Quoted in Callinicos (2004, p. 1).
8. Some translations use the term "misery." Both poverty and misery are acceptable translations of the German term *das elend.*
9. The company failed to adapt and adjust to the use and consequences of the digital technology in film and photography, which precipitated its competitive inviability and financial fall.

Chapter Five

Religion and Politics

Competing for the Public Space

Some of the issues we observe around the globe surprisingly have something to do with the tension between religions and politics, surprisingly, because we modern societies have evolved to reach the twenty-first century, and behind us there is a junction in history where such a conflict between matters and prerogatives of the church and those of the states have been debated and settled. In that sense issues around politics and religions today sound anachronic. It seems to have reemerged as an issue. But it is not the only issue modern societies have seen reemerge. The issue around ethnicity is, in that regard, another one. Indeed, about religion and politics, we observe issues arising around the appropriateness of the display of religious signs and symbols in the public space. In France, for instance, the wearing of Islamic attire—burqas, niqabs, hijabs, chadors, khimars, al-amiras, or shaylas, which cover the body from head to toe, including the face, or cover only the head, leaving the face open—in public spaces such as schools and other security-sensitive places has prompted the intervention of the state and reignited the debate about *laïcité*.[1] In the United States, there is, for instance, the case of the law on abortion, which is contested by some on religious ground. In Iran, secular principles of governments are rejected in favor of Islamic precepts. There are new forms of terrorism. The Islamic State,[2] for instance, seeks to reintroduce the Caliphate, and by so doing negates the idea of the republic or the liberal state, which is secular, to embrace the notion that public space is as well the space that ought to be governed by the precepts of the Quran and other Islamic holy books such as the Sunnah and the Hadith. Among the issues arising about the coexistence of religion and its precepts and politics and its principles of the liberal state is the notion of the freedom of the press, which allows caricatured images as a matter of political norm in liberal states,

97

and essentially in the West on one hand, and the inadmissibility of carica-
turing or depicting through images the prophet of Islam, Muhammad, as a
norm of the religion of Islam. This issue led to the killing of journalists of
the French newspaper *Charlie Hebdo* in Paris, France, in January 2015, and
in Copenhagen, Denmark, in February 2015. This is not only a case of collision between two principles and their claims to governing the public space;
it is as well a case illustrating the kind of issues borne out of the crossing of
religions' and civilizations' paths into each other's spaces of origin. Such a
crossing of religions' and civilizations' paths brings about issues of value
systems, which we discuss in chapter 6.

The interest of this chapter, therefore, lies in exploring the inherent potential tension between both politics and religion. There is a congenital, natural
in-built tension between the world of politics and the world of religion or
worldviews. This tension is grounded in four fundamental realities intrinsic
to both: their respective essence; their sense of purpose, and their legitimacy,
influence, and prestige; and finally in the functioning principles of each. With
respect to their essence, both religion and politics are intangible structured
spaces, as defined in chapter 4. With respect to their sense of purpose, both
religion and politics are norm providers. They have the purpose of ordering the lives of their constituents. Politics has laws and the constitution to
do just that, and religion or worldviews have their teachings, precepts, and
commandments. Their constituents are respectively citizens and believers.
But the believers are citizens. The result is that both politics and religions or
worldviews have the same constituents.

This opens up the possibility of a tension. Such a tension does not necessarily have to induce conflicts or break out into an all-out open strife, as it
has been the case in many places, at many occasions in history, because such
an inherent tension can be negotiated. The tension is therefore an inherent
possibility. This tension leads us to the third fundamental cause of tension
between politics and religion, namely, their sphere of influence and prestige.
This tension potentially and inherently exists because believers and citizens
are a collective and come in aggregate numbers. And what they collectively
do occurs in the public space, that is, in society. And how they do whatever
they collectively do in the public space is informed by their shared values,
which are themselves informed by the teaching, precepts of their belief systems, which we called in chapter 4 demands and expectations, to be followed
by the constituents. And so polygamy is a norm in Islamic public cultural
spaces while monogamy is the norm in Christian public cultural spaces. They
are both linked to these respective religions or worldviews. This explains
why religions, as norm providers induce cultures and even civilizations, as
we discuss in chapter 5.

But next to religions or worldviews, politics as well inherently has a vocation or ordering activity in the public space. Indeed, the purpose of politics is ordering public space activity for the commonweal. It does so by guiding its actions through principles other than those found in the teaching and precepts of religions and worldviews. In the end, we have two norm providers, religion and politics interested in providing norms for their constituents, believers, and citizens, who happen to be the same. This is the context on which the potential between religion and politics is grounded.

Before going any further, we need not to define politics, but we need to allude to the nuance or difference between religions and worldviews, as these two terms will be mentioned next to each other. Although similar in some ways, they are dissimilar in their essential purposes. We define religions as structures governed by a teaching and its message that speaks of a god, an afterlife, and conditions to access both that god and that afterlife, also known as salvation. Religions do entail that metaphysical component of a spiritual world, accessible only through the path they propose. Any of the belief systems, large or small, that meet these criteria are religions. Worldviews on the other hand are also known as moral philosophies simply because they make no claim about the afterlife. Although some worldviews recognize and premise the existence of God,[3] some do not,[4] and some are indifferent,[5] they are all essentially about this world and life here on earth, and their purpose lies in proposing guidance to make sense of them and to find an anchor in order to make the existence of an individual or a culture meaningful. Although many worldviews from the West have practically had to live in the shadows of Christianity and in the Middle East to Asia, in the shadows of other monotheistic religions such as Islam, Buddhism, and Hinduism, in East Asia, worldviews such as Confucianism, Shintoism, and Daoism have been successful in playing the role of providers of meaning to human existence. In their claims to provide meaning to individuals, religions and worldviews lay claim to ordering the pubic space of activity for the collective number of followers, differently. This explains why some religions and worldviews are more or less present in the public sphere than others. This also explains why the inherent potential conflict between politics and religions or worldviews is more pronounced in some cultural spaces around the world and less pronounced in others.

The tension between religion/worldview and politics revolves around legitimacy, influence, and prestige. If both religion and politics have the vocation of ordering the lives of citizens and believers, whose order (demand) should be expected (expectation) to have ascendency or precedence? In other words there is a question on the primacy between religion and politics. The issue is not new. Sophocles in his play, *Antigone*, written in 442 BCE, has already thematized it. The New Testament of the Christian Bible reports an encounter between Jesus and the Pharisees in which obedience to the demands and expectations of religion and politics has clearly been given a guideline in the answer provided by Jesus. The Pharisees asked Jesus whether it was right to pay imperial taxes to Caesar.[6] Jesus answered (paraphrasing) that they should give to Caesar what belongs to him and to God what is His. Just as the question then already illustrated the tension of supremacy between church and state, the answer that Jesus gave was indeed a first attempt to separate the prerogative of either.

Just like in the time of Sophocles in Greece and the time of Jesus in Judea, communities and societies since have had to negotiate and manage the inherent tensions between politics and religion. Such tension can be dormant, silent, and explicit, and can sometimes even blow up in the face of society. And because such tension can blow up in the face of society, and because it can blow up in many societies, it is a potential global issue. And because it actually *does* blow up in the face of many societies around the world it is indeed a global issue. We have, as a matter of fact, defined as global issues those that are recurrent and structural (because all societies have both a political order and religious allegiances) and can be observed or witnessed anywhere in the globe. Tensions between politics and religion are one such an issue.

And finally one last fundamental cause of natural tension between religion and politics lies in the functioning principles of each. Whereas religion and worldviews function based on the ordinance explicitly stated in their holy books, teachings, and precepts, politics, timidly since the time of Cleistenes of the Athens (508–494 BCE), experiencing with popular participation of citizens in matters of governance of the city, we know as democracy, and later the Romans since Cicero, in the first century CE, introducing the notion of the *republic*, to delineate matters of public interest from those of the private, modern political societies have evolved, though a lot of pain and historical detours increasingly since the Enlightenment movement to function based on the principles of liberalism. It is this basis that justifies the description of modern democratic states as the liberal state. Indeed, functioning principles of the liberal state are the presumption of innate freedom for all individuals on one hand and the equality of their rights on the other. Today, among the 193 nations registered with the UN, we can count fewer and fewer, as years go by, nations that do not subscribe to the liberal state model. With their different functioning principles, based on rational principles of positive law for the liberal state, and based on religious principles for religion, the principles of politics have succeeded in most modern nations in claiming influencing primacy of the public space.

But how has the inherent potential tension between religion and politics been articulated in the various forms of political societies until and including the liberal state? We can break these societies into categories to scrutinize their attitudes vis-à-vis religion or worldviews found within.

If we begin with tribal, ethnic, and communitarian societies of the premodern era, tension between religion and politics is nonexistent simply because in these societies social order was established and maintained through customary laws, which were themselves products of premodern cosmogonies and worldviews. Such cosmogonies and worldviews were inspired by their belief systems. This made belief systems at the basis of the social order. In these traditional premodern societies often there was no distinctiveness between politics and belief systems. There were often no political superstructures, institutionally and functionally detached from society. Their political organizations had not developed a reason d'état, a set of imperatives proper to the organization of society and away from their belief systems. Their laws were organically codified into customary practices designed to ascribe to society its higher meaning and purpose and to keep members in compliance with that meaning. Societal order (politics itself) was legitimized by religious practices. Hence, there was no possible tension to speak of, as political order was itself part of the belief system of the community. This has been the reality of many tribal societies in a number of non-Western cultures, from Africa to Pre-Columbian America, from Asia to Australia, before changes occurred as a result of Western colonization. Yes, there were cases of existing political organizations with statehood and statecraft, central governments and courts, such as in kingdoms and empires in these cultures. But even their powers were explained, justified, and cemented in a narrative that invoked higher power and legitimized them. They secured in that manner their authority and subordination. The phenomenon is not limited to these non-western cultures mentioned above. It has been practiced under the mantle of divine right elsewhere in Europe, Great Britain, and France, where Jean Bodin (1576)[7] argued in favor of institutional monarchy and the legitimacy of the king, which did not derive from the people but rather from God. The idea of divine right was to suggest cohesion between politics and religion but also the need for such cohesion is in itself recognition of the potential tension, which needed to be nipped in the bud, in case believers had religiously grounded objections to political power. And it will be in Europe where the tension between politics and Europe will break out.

In Asia, where we have both a long history of established religions (Hinduism and Buddhism) and worldviews (Confucianism, Taoism, Shintoism) and centrally run statecraft, the tension between politics and religion developed in the following manner. Hinduism has been essentially preoccupied with

spiritual matters of righteousness and removed itself and encouraged the removal of the followers from earthly concern and its material preoccupation.
In *Sociology of Religion*, Max Weber (1922) speaks of an ascetic *Hinduism*
rejecting of the world and its discomfort, which they seek to escape but not to
change. By so doing Hinduism has removed itself from earthly preoccupation
and from the public space, which politics, uncontested, occupies. As for *Buddhism*, again Max Weber argued, it is accepting of the existing order, building
on it and promising a different fate through eternal cycles of reincarnation. It
surrenders to the discomfort of early order but does not question or confront
it. Here again, Buddhism, like Hinduism does not have vocation to interfere
with social order, and therefore its action must develop a different theater
outside the public sphere or space, which is left to the political.

Elsewhere in Asia, the worldviews of *Taoism* and *Shintoism* in their quest
to finding the way to inner peace, to finding harmony with nature, are inherently introverted, not seeking the public theater or aggregating the body of
followers for a collective goal. *Confucianism* is a bit different in the sense that
as a worldview it was essentially secular, essentially political, as it encourages a virtuous life both in society and politics. Confucianism is essentially
political, as it promotes civic life, civil service engagement, commitment
and dedication to family, society, and the nation, to seek peace and harmony
as measures of virtuous life. But as Confucianism engages politics, it is an
ethical and moral approach and therefore practical. It does not articulate nor
propose idealistic normative goals that may or may not conflict with political
claim to public order. It did so by harmonizing the objectives of an individual
good moral life with those of a good citizenship. Confucianism allowed a path
of fusion to the follower and citizen between the objectives of the state and
those of society. Confucianism itself harmonized its teaching with the state's
reason d'être. By not articulating idealistic goals and by just harmonizing its
own with those of the state, Confucianism did not position itself as a potential competitor to the state as a public norm provider. Thereby Confucianism
conceded the claim to public space. This essential feature of Confucianism
was well received and appreciated by various Chinese dynasties.

And so, in China, a nation with a long history of statecraft and citizenry,
the tension between politics and religion and/or worldview was dealt with
through various dynasties[8] coopting, adopting, and declaring either Buddhism
or Confucianism and even legalism as the official dynastic guiding philosophy. Buddhism and Confucianism in Asia did not propose goals, promote
behavior, or demand allegiance competing with the prerogative of the central
state. Nor did they claim to influencing public life independently from or
even in competition with the state. Chinese dynasties did not have to worry
about the claim of the religion or worldviews around them. Buddhism was an

ally to guiding both decision makers and citizens, and Confucianism offered itself as a support for statecraft. A third support for statecraft was known as legalism. When Chinese dynasties did not coopt, adopt, or declare either Buddhism or Confucianism to state philosophy, legal scholars were those relied upon to ordering the lives of citizens. This third support for statecraft was closer to the rule of law and constitutionalism now in practice in the West, even though not sharing the same customary sources of laws. It was legalism.

In the West the tension between religion and politics has existed as well. Christianity, since the Roman Emperor Constantine's conversion in 310 AD, has had a good run. Over the history of the West, Catholicism, and since the 1500s, Protestantism have been the binding glue of Western civilization and the foundation of its culture and in many ways, next to liberalism, which came later, its main driving force. Christianity drove processes in the West not just in religious but also in political matters up until a few historical events started to bend history into a different direction. Indeed, different European local and regional feudal lords, all the way to the Holy Roman Empire (tenth to sixteenth centuries), monarchs and emperors have had to deal with the claim of the Catholic Church to ordering public life, a true amalgamation of secular and sacred authority. The pope saw himself above the king and the emperor, and his authority was stressed by his prerogative to crown emperors[9] and to appoint bishops and other church officials with no consideration of political authority within the confinements of the Holy Roman Empire. There was an ambiguous two-way street between political and religious authority claimed by the Church, which provoked a quarrel of investiture (appointment). The raging quarrel of investiture begged for clarification, and in 1122 AD, the Concordat of Worms produced a first arrangement to ordering the tension.[10] The Church was in no way weakened. The Catholic Church had remained a towering power throughout the Middle Ages and claimed authority over the public space above politics. The intertwinement of the power of the Church and the state can be demonstrated both anecdotally and structurally by the existence and role of the infamous Borgia family in the fifteenth and sixteenth centuries.

The Catholic Church abused its authority, prompting a monk's dissent. Martin Luther, the monk in question, published his *Ninety-Five Theses* in 1517, denunciating and repudiating practices such as indulgency, among others, and generally a Church that has forsaken its mission and purpose. The Reformation movement was to become the consequence of his action. The Reformation movement was at the beginning of what was to become a long process of secularization. Indeed, Martin Luther argued in favor of a principle of two kingdoms, a church and a secular one in an effort to turn the Church's focus back to matters of salvation. The principle was another attempt to produce an institutional arrangement in regulating the tensions between church and state.

On the political side, the prerogatives and essence of the modern state had been increasingly suggested and argued by the precursor of the Enlightenment movement, the likes of Baruch Spinoza and John Locke. In his *Two Treatises of Government* John Locke (1689) underlined the rational man's natural quest for freedom of choice, which implies free choice of commerce (in pursuit of his or her happiness) but also other choices such as religion. They ought not to be tempered with. Not even government or the state was to be able to interfere with it. Hence, the government was to be of rational men who understood that their freedom was at stake if the state was to be generated by any other source or means but them. As rational and conscious, they stood to choose what government and what laws, but also what religion they practiced. As a result religious practice was to fall under the prerogative of the individual conscience. God was a matter of concern to the individual, not to the state, and therefore a matter of concern to the individual, not the citizen. And since choice is pluralistic in its own nature, it implies a possibility of a variety of religions. The state or government will deal with them by allowing each individual his or her own exercise of freedom of choice and by protecting that choice. From this perspective, politics becomes the towering entity above religious practices.

In the meantime, the Reformation movement had culminated with a war of religion that ended in 1648. The result of the stalemate produced by the outcome of the war was the Treaty of Westphalia, with a number of principles. Among those stipulations two addressed a new *modus vivendi* on church and religion and tolerance. The principle of *cuius region, eius religio* stipulated that different rulers could pick the religion of their jurisdiction. The other about tolerance stipulated that if the religion picked was not that of some inhabitants, they could still practice freely their own. These principles were another milestone in regulating the cohabitation of two norm providers with claim to ordering public life of their shared constituents, citizens, and believers.

Many other incremental milestones were produced by a number of political theory works, irrespective of their focus, all contributing to the clarification of the prerogative of politics and political power, from Machiavelli to Locke, from Montesquieu to Burke, from Hobbes to Rousseau, from Adam Smith to Marx. Modern Europe was on its way to finding an arrangement on the coexistence between politics and religion, between church and state. It was separating the prerogative and competence of these entities in what we now call separation of church and state. It was reinforced by the novel ideals of the Enlightenment movement and the era of modernity and formalized in the spirit of the French and US constitutions.

In other words, the process of removing God from the center (theocentrism) of human affairs to replace Him with human reason (anthropocentrism) was under way. Faith in human reason's ability to fulfill its new function was strengthened by the successes in scientific discoveries that induced a scientific revolution, which practically accompanied the process of secularization since the offset of the Renaissance, the late 1500s to the eighteenth century. All this to the delight of the philosopher Friedrich Nietzsche, who argued[11] in favor of an emancipated human mind and body from fear of any kind, and who saw in religion the repressor from whom the human mind had to be emancipated. We are full into the Enlightenment era. The notion of the Republic was taking root, cemented in the intellectual mind of Europeans by philosophers such as Jean Jacques Rousseau,[12] who argued in favor of a society of citizens, all conscious of the common interest and justice, and the rational rule of law mechanism to achieve a common existence. Rousseau wrote in 1762 (1968, p. 59), "I therefore give the name of the 'Republic' to all states governed by laws." The republic was becoming the political ideal frame of reference, containing the influence of the church, and in which secularism will be molded. The novelty of the republic and what it stands for is an arrangement that is not uncontested. Nowhere will the resistance to what it stands for be more displayed than in France, a nation with a long history of statehood and deeply anchored in Catholicism. Napoleon Bonaparte attempted to appease the Catholic Church in the Concordat signed in 1801, which while limiting the influence of the Church in the public sphere, still allowed Catholicism to remain informally the state religion. A portion of the French population was in tune with the novelty of the republic. They were called "Republicans." Others had not yet given up on monarchy, dethroned since the Revolution of 1789, and they argued in favor of a closer church-state relation. They were called "Royalists." In the tension between both parties, the momentum was on the side of the Republicans. The tension boiled over into a crisis during the Third Republic and sealed the defeat of the Royalists in 1877. With the defeat of the Royalists and their support for a greater church role, France was on its way to ordering public life without the influence of the Church. It established a national education system in 1882. In the early twentieth century, in 1905, the secularization process of France was sealed by the signing of a law that codified the separation of church and state in the principle of *laïcité*.

In the newly formed nation-state of the United States of America, where the new federalist republic was being formed, it has as well to ponder the rapport of the state and its nature and power with that of religion. This ponder justifies the formulation on December 15, 1791, of the First Amendment to the Constitution, refraining the state from overpowering hands to make laws regarding religions, and the rights of the people and religions to be exercised freely in the republic. In a new republic wherein politics was not competing with church for supremacy of the public sphere, as was the case in Europe, the spirit of the amendment, although not explicit about church and state separation, induced just that in practice. Here, again, there are attempts and voices arguing in favor of more blurred lines between these two entities.

Indeed, in the West, religion has since made room for politics in ordering the public sphere. The removal of religion from the public sphere is explained in modern political context by the need of the state, its purpose, to ensure stability and justice (O'Neal 2013). And this can be achieved only through recourse to public reason to regulate public discourse. From public discourse, which relies on public reason, states' actions and laws derive their legitimacy. In this process, arguments shared by all reasonable citizens constitute the basis of state action. Public reason itself is guided by the principle of good citizenry grounded in the recognition of shared mutual freedom and equality of rights. As a result reasonable citizens are "those will to show respect for their fellow citizens as free and equal persons" (O'Neal 2013, p. 2). These are principles of liberalism. The state's purpose, therefore, becomes to ensure stability and justice on the basis of those principles. This, however, cannot be achieved on the ground of nonpublic reason, which is any reason that citizens may have for themselves based on their own beliefs, convictions, ideologies, and of course religion. Religion is a nonpublic reason, which consequentially cannot constitute ground for public discourse nor ground for states legitimizing action such as laws.

Those agreeing with this process are liberals or liberalists, in favor of constraining religion in the public sphere. Among them is John Rawls.[13] To them religion is more comprehensive, while the state is more essentialist. Religion demands absorption, immersion in all its tenets; its expectations are comprehensive and possessive. In other words, religious order or rule, meaning theocracy, can only be authoritarian if not totalitarian. If and when in charge of ordering public life, any religion would be the only source of law. And citizens/believers would live their lives to reflect the theology of the religion in question.

It is this very comprehensive and possessive nature of religions that constitutes a handicap for a public quest for coexistence with other norm providers, first, because it leaves room for no other source of behavior-legitimizing norms, and second, because not all citizens are of one and the same religion. The freedom and equality of rights of some citizens would be undermined should the demands and expectations of just one religion prevail, which is a possibility, given the number of states around the world in which there is a predominance of specific religions or worldviews and knowing that some of them do lay a claim of control over the public sphere. It is the comprehensiveness and possessiveness of demands and expectations to adherents that render problematic that claim of religions to order the public sphere. As a result, the claim of religions to ordering public life undermines the essence of the republic and that of liberal societies. Both the republic and, even more so, liberalism, begat pluralism. Pluralism subsumes religion without undermining its existence and purpose. Moreover, it guarantees such existence and purpose. Religion, however, cannot subsume liberalism without undermining it. The claim of religion to ordering the public sphere is not accommodating but a source of conflict in the republic or liberal society. And in case there is more than one religion competing for ordering the public space, the potential for such a conflict for undermining the viability and stability of the republic and liberal society is even greater. Let us imagine for a minute what would become of India with its multiple religions should they all seek influence or control in ordering the public space. Such potential for undermining the viability and stability of the republic is as well given, as religious currents compete for influence in ordering the public space. It was historically the case in the mid-1400s AD Europe within Christianity, between the claim of the Catholic Church and the forming Protestant church. It is as well the case within Islam when Kemalism, reformism, and fundamentalism are nothing but different answers to the question of how much competence should Islam have in ordering the public Islamic life.

In the light of all the potential conflicts among and between religions in their quest for authority to order public space, and their potential for undermining the viability of public life, the liberal state appears to be the solution. It subsumes without undermining religions and their believers-citizens while providing space for nonbelievers-citizens to live in the state without constraints from any given religion. The liberal state, argues the liberalist, is the guarantor of public stability and justice. Consequently, this adhesion to a liberal state solution implies the removal of religion from ordering the public space and life.

The removal of religion from the public sphere or space does not sit well with all believers-citizens. They are revisionists who can be found in different places, driven by their individual beliefs or aggregated interest groups. To gain an insight into the revisionist perspective, let us use the argument of Nicholas Walterstorff (2012),[14] who arguing for more religion in the public space, pleads for an integralist approach simply because the separation or distinction between a religion experienced privately and expressed publically is untenable because the private believer is at the same time the public citizen. As such he or she is both a private and a public actor. His or her private beliefs inform his or her public choice or behavior. Coming from the citizen such a revisionist perspective is arguably logical. It does not dent in any way the liberal-state argument, as far as such a revisionist citizen can still link his or her belief to his or her public choice, such as voting, without undermining the principles of the republic. As long as individual choices do not undermine the principles of the liberal state, even private beliefs can, and do, inform public choices. This revisionist approach does not question the validity of the liberal-state claim, namely, to be the guarantor of legitimate individual choices for all, which in turn implies respect for each.

This is exactly what Jurgens Habermas (2013) suggested. He argued that there is room in the public sphere. The public discourse can resort to, or use, or rely on, or be based on religious arguments. That does not harm anybody or any liberal state principle. Religious argument can even find its way into public reason and constitute a basis for legitimizing states' actions, but provided such discourse and argument has passed a test, that of public suitability, which means respecting the notion of justice for all, whose discourse and argument are universalized and formalized to address all citizens regardless of their particular identity and features. And when identity particulars are addressed, they must be addressed in formal and universalistic terms, which serve as an insurance against discriminate and selective validation of public discourse to becoming public reason. Only then, can any discourse and argument be used to guide or influence life. If not, the discourse and argument remain in the domain of the private sphere, where nonpublic reason prevails. Only when a discourse and argument have passed the test can they become institutional material. Only then can they find their way into the administrative regulatory or normative legal texts.

This process and transition implies a legislative process. Such a process is in essence a filtering process through which lawmakers examine any discourse and argument based on its universal and formal application to all its citizens. Habermas, therefore, sees institutions as thresholds. He sees in institutions a hurdle that nonpublic reason must clear to become material for legislation. Through such a transition process even religious material can succeed in entering the sphere of public reason. It a process that allows the content of a religious text, demand, or expectation to become part of legislation provided it has been screened and scrutinized and has   passed any public reason that discourse must undergo. There are indeed texts, demands, and expectations of specific religions that coincide or harmonize or are compatible with the principles of the liberal state. The transition process as a hurdle will keep out only the content whose demands and expectations diverge from the liberal-state principles.

As a result, Habermas considers this legislative process as a passage that "religious materials advanced by citizens from outside the threshold must undergo, to become secular" (O'Neal 2013, p. 5).

The religious must pass a republican test, as one would say in France, or a liberal state test, as one would say in the Anglo-Saxon world, to become secular, to cleanse it from the danger of imposing one religious norm on the rest of the citizenry, often citizens of the minority religion. Despite the separation of church and state in liberal states, many have found a way to acknowledge the influencing role of religion in public life. They have created a special status, that of "state religion" or "national religion."[15]

In the Islamic world the rapport between politics and religion is decisively contentious. Politics in the Islamic culture has to deal with a religion that lays claim to all aspects of the life of the Muslim. Islam is ubiquitous. It lays claim to the intimate, private, family (umma), and communitarian life as well as the public life of the Muslim. There is no aspect of Muslim life exempted from communion with Allah. The argument is that the forces keeping the Muslim from expected purity are everywhere. And they must be met everywhere with a personal or even collective jihad. Not to go astray, the Muslim has the Quran, the Sunnah, the Hadith, and the Sharia to guide him. And when in doubt, the ulamas, mullahs, and muftis, the legal scholars of Islam, enlighten the Muslim on which behavior to adopt. Islam naturally supersedes the provisions of politics, its prerogative and its laws. There is no institutional arrangement to fundamentally address the role of politics. There is no formal formula of separation of church and state.

The prophet Muhammad himself did not separate matters of religion from those of the state. He was both a spiritual and a political leader. The institution of the Caliphate, until it was abolished in 1924, did not. Political matters are man-made and as such ought to take a backseat to Allah's intent for the Muslim, wherever he or she is. Not even politics ought to stand in the way of that vision.

Different states in the Islamic world have had to deal with tensions between Islam and politics differently. We have those states that have officially declared the supremacy of the Islamic law in Iran and most recently, the Brunei in Southeast Asia. We have those that have Islamic monarchies, both absolute and constitutional, and officially must demonstrate their allegiance to Islam in the exercise of their political power, as is the case in the United Arab Emirates—Saudi Arabia, Kuwait, Bahrain, Oman, Qatar, and Jordan—and recently Brunei in Southeast Asia, whose court has now elevated the Sharia to be the law of the land. There are those that have attempted a political balancing act of modernizing while remaining committed to Islam, the moderate, reformist states such as Morocco and Tunisia. We have those that have decided in favor of the state over Islam as the national norm provider, the likes of Turkey, the Kemalists. We have authoritarian rulers who, while being Muslim, want to protect their state from a supremacist Islam. Such was the case in Egypt under Nasser, Sadat, and Mubarak, and in Iraq under Saddam Hussein. In Islamic democracies such as Pakistan, Algeria, and Egypt since the end of Mubarak, holding democratic elections has become a worrisome occurrence for those fearing the rise to power of Islamist parties. States with a majority Islamic population call themselves officially Islamic, recognizing the influence of Islam as a state religion. Among those that have not is Turkey.

RELIGION AND POLITICS: A RECURRENT GLOBAL ISSUE

If we discuss religion and the public space today in the context of global issues, it is because there has been in a number of nations, not the least significant ones in world affairs, a resurgence of claims by religions or claims by religious groups for a heavier, larger weight or larger share in influencing the public discourse. These claims from religious groups seek to infuse the demands and expectations of their respective beliefs into policy measures. They seek a society whose legislation reflects those beliefs. After all, it is their state and they are its citizens. And since the state should mirror the culture of its people, it is their belief that the state's laws should mirror theirs. Although there is some legitimacy to this argument, it fails to acknowledge that the culture of a people is only one of the many sources of liberal-states' laws. And it is because other sources of inspiration of liberal states' laws, such as reason, simply reject the validity claims of some religious discourses and arguments, many in some religions have been frustrated. Their growing frustration is exacerbated, possibly by a number of many other factors such as the pace of today's cultural value and norm shift, and the socioeconomic impact of new digital technology. Indeed such resurgence in favor of religion has been linked to the unsettling malaise of shifts, which generally induces the need, for some, to hold on to the familiar. The phenomenon has been observed time and time again throughout history. We seem to witness the rise of conservatism in politics after revolutions.[16] Other examples are US conservatism rising partially as a result of the cultural shift of the 1960s, the birth of fundamentalist Islam as a reaction against the intrusion of modernist culture from the West in the Islamic sphere,[17] etc. These drivers of cultural shifts in many ways drive the need for reassurance. This need is satisfied by religions, which are perennial, whose teaching is immutable and whose directions are clarity defined.

All these changes are responsible for the complexity of current global issues, from the stem cell research debate to abortion, from same-sex marriage to same-sex adoption, from legalization of marijuana to the increase in trivializing pornography, etc. They all challenge the historical, traditional, ethical, religious, and societal status quo. The modern liberal state must deal with them and find essentialist solutions, which means those solutions that are based on the foundational basis of societal coexistence, which allows individuals to pursue their happiness in freedom and equality of rights. It is what public reason dictates. Anything beyond may very well fall under the category of nonpublic. Solutions that the liberal state may come up with to address these challenging issues are reflective of its reason d'être, namely, to secure peace and stability. Religions struggle more with challenging issues of our time, as they compel churches to revisit their teachings, which happen to be rigid and less flexible. Hence, there is here once again the possibility of a tension between state solutions and church stances with respect to challenging issues.

But a distinction must be made here as well among religions, such as Islam, Catholicism, and Protestantism, to name just a few, and the attitudes of their followers. Whereas these religions often show categorical, unapologetic rigidity in their stances, their followers display an array of different sensibilities. This difference of sensibilities allows the following classifications: liberal, reformist, and integrist. Liberal believers in any religious tradition are advocates of a more private exercise of their faith. They concur with the constraining of religion's role in the public discourse and sphere. Reformists seek a common ground where both the state and their faith meet to allow them to be both good citizens and good believers and each to fulfill their respective purpose, even if that means more or less church here and more or less state there. Integrists, also known as fundamentalists, are those found in any religion who resist the changes of the time and the shifts they induce in societal behavior, mores, and lifestyle and the challenges they pose to the status quo, but who also diverge from or disapprove of the solutions, often pragmatic, that the liberal state proposes to dealing with such challenges. And it is through integrists that the resurgence of religion today has been infused into the public discourse and the public sphere of politics, pushing back against some of the liberal state solutions to fundamental questions dictated by the changing times.

How do integrist believers and integrist religious currents enter the public sphere? Integrist religious currents can directly challenge the nation-state, liberal or not. Through their teachings, they can encourage their followers, who happen to be constituent citizens, to influence the political discourse through anything from debate to the electoral process, from interest groups to lobbying, and from activism to terrorism.

And it is this process of seeking to influence the public discourse and opinion that Habermas referred to as transition, a filter that allows religious nonpublic discourse to find acceptance in the public sphere and to become part of the public discourse. If and when it succeeds, the religious stance stands a chance of becoming material that informs the institutional mechanism and its decision-making process. And so we may have as a result, theoretically, an integrist stance serve as the basis for legislation or informing the political decision-making process. But to deserve such consideration, any religious stance must stand the test of modern state liberalism. Any argument in the public discourse must be guided by public reason, which produces principles acceptable by all reasonable citizens. A result of the exercise of public reason is the establishment of the premise of freedom for all and equality of rights for all. Such criteria are acceptable to all reasonable citizens. The premise is a way to immunize the polity in a liberal state from the danger of nonpublic opinions and beliefs that are based on nonpublic reason, that of individuals or churches, and that may not find adherence from all reasonable citizens; therefore, they should be disqualified as material for public discourse. Integrist discourse runs the danger of not standing the test; therefore, there is a need for a transition to ensure the republicanization of its nonpublic discourse status. This is necessary, as religious integrist stances have a particular origin but have a universal expectation in their application. Such universal application of their stance includes nonadherents. It therefore needs their consent and approval. Without such approval the freedom and equality of rights of nonintegrist citizens in a liberal state are not ensured. This is unacceptable to the liberal state. These are conditions that integrism fails to meet and provide guarantees for to nonintegrists. It is therefore the nature of religious integrism issues and conflicts that we find around the world. In some states the issue and conflict are dormant, such as in Turkey, where the military sees, since Kemal Atatürk, its duty as preserving Kemalism, or the choice made by Turkey to modernize, to the dismay of potential Islamist tendencies. These tendencies can be displayed at almost every election in Turkey. The Islamist political party in Algeria, the Islamic Salvation Front (known in French as Front Islamique du Salut), has once already been brutally kept away from political power in 1991. In Iran, reformist and liberal Muslims, and let alone secular Iranians, are simply on the losing side of liberal state citizenship due to the integrist Islam of the Supreme Leaders and their grip on power since Khomeini and the Iranian revolution in 1979. In some other states the issue and conflict are open, such as in Egypt, where the military, almost like in Turkey, must serve as a buffer zone between the integrist forces of the Muslim Brothers and other Islamist organizations and the state that wants to modernize. In other countries, such as in Afghanistan, where although they have found their demise since 2012 as a result of the war led by George W. Bush, the integrist Talibans continue to undermine the establishment of a viable state. There, the issue and conflict between religious integrism and the aspiring modern state led by Karzai are both dormant and open as strikes, bombs, and attacks surface and recede at will.

In the United States, the religious right movement has been reflecting the pattern of religious nonpublic discourse attempts to enter the public discourse and the political sphere. Like in any other integrist attempt to enter the public and political sphere, guarantee for a liberal state is an essential promise and premise of protection of citizens; freedom and equality of rights must be ensured. The danger here and elsewhere, where there is a majority religion, not even legislation is a sufficient guarantee for liberal state essentialism of individual freedom of choice and equality of rights, as integrist positions may gain the upper hand in the legislative process.

The only sufficient guarantee for a liberal state to ensure the respect of its principles is the willingness of the polity not to give up on them. This is, we concede, a conjectural guarantee since not even the willingness not to give up on principles of the liberal state is perennial. And it leads to the realization that nothing in life is guaranteed, not even the perennial triumph of the ideas and ideals of liberalism. Both religious integrism and liberalist principles are ideological structures that remain inert and with no impact without the action and effort of their adherent members. The success of religious integrism and liberalism therefore will depend on the effort each makes in the defense of their cause or on the ability of one to win the debate of the public discourse in the public sphere.

NOTES

1. The concept of *laïcité* in France is about the areligious character of the republic, which on one hand does not promote religion and on the other does not interfere with the practice of faith. This concept is mentioned later in this chapter.

2. The Islamic State, ISIL, ISIS, the al-Nusra Front, and Daesh are names used by these groups with the aim of establishing an Islamic state through violent means.

3. There are, in the Western tradition, many worldviews recognizing and premising God's existence, among them deism, pantheism, humanism, and naturalism, and in Asia, Taoism, Shintoism, and Confucianism.

4. Among them are atheism, nihilism, and existentialism.

5. Among them are apatheism, deism, and agnosticism.

6. Matthew 22:15–22.

7. Jean Bodin articulated his theory of absolutism in his *Six Books of the Commonwealth.*

8. Chinese Buddhist dynasties: Sui and Tang. Chinese Confucian dynasties: Han, Sung, and Qing. Chinese Legalist dynasty: Qin.

9. Later, Napoleon I's self-coronation was a symbolic refusal to acknowledge the authority of the pope over him and in a way a refusal to recognize the ascendency of the Church over his authority.

10. The compromise was that the pope would invest Episcopal nominees with spiritual office and the ruler will bestow them temporal power.

11. Friedrich Nietzsche, *Thus Spoke Zaratzustra.*

12. Jean Jacques Rousseau, *Social Contract*, Book II.

13. John Rawls, *Theory of Justice.*

14. Nicholas Walterstorff, *The Mighty and the Almighty*, 2012.

15. A few such nations are for instance

16. Edmund Burke, *Reflections on the Revolution in France*, 1986.

17. Abd al-Wahhab and the need to preserve the purity of Islam.

Chapter Six

Civilizations and Space

WHY AN INTEREST IN CIVILIZATIONS?

The interest in civilizations here is justified by the fact that despite all the changes in world history, politics, and commerce and despite the sophistication of today's modern society and its people, we have not created any new structural beliefs and value systems that we hold to be referential, we call civilizations. We have, for the most part, succeeded in adjusting or adapting a few aspects of our old structural beliefs and value systems to suit the changing times. We have not come up with revolutionary ways of approaching humanity and existence. This may simply be a reflection of the anthropological essence of the human being. The familiar does not seem to go away despite the new and exciting changes of the moment. Whatever change comes, it has the potential to impact life around us. We worry about how the change will affect us, society, our material interests, and political order, but we do not worry about how change will affect our civilization or civilizations in generations to come. Changes that occur seem to be integrated, absorbed, and digested by a greater construct that are civilizations.

Next to religions, civilizations appear to be the independent variables in the midst of changing times we call history. They seem to subsume even change itself. And when they fail to subsume change, which is what happens to some of them when they run out of energy, they disintegrate. They often simply accommodate change and pursue their long run in history. We have come to reckon with the enduring forces that civilizations are. Even the smallest of civilizations remain relevant despite the assaults of might and conquest, despite the wealth generated by commerce. The US military, for instance, can win the war in Afghanistan or Iraq but cannot win the war against Islam. China is becoming wealthier, but no one expects the Chinese to leave behind

Confucian teachings as they ascend. The Kurdish culture endures despite the repressiveness of politics around the Kurdish people, just as Judaic civilization did through years of dispersion of Jewish people, etc. Civilizations endure because of their values. Once permeated into the culture of and consciousness of their adherents, uprooting them becomes a gargantuan task. It is the measure of such a task that has often been taken lightly when dominant powers and civilizations set out to subjugate smaller ones. Political, military, and even economic victories over smaller civilizations aren't enough to destroy them. And when military might has been used to spread civilizations, the result has been at best very diminished. This was exactly what the European expansion experienced, as it expected non-Western civilizations to lay down or fade away as they colonized their territories. They did succeed in taking over and transforming these colonized territories, but not in uprooting them from their cultural anchorage. These non-Western cultures have opened up to the benefits of modernity, and even the values of liberalism brought about by the West, but they did not substantively transform the civilizations of Islam, Confucian, Buddhist, Orthodox, Hindu, and Africana.

Today's civilizations remain strong in their plurality, and we are learning that neither might nor wealth had eroded their relevance and role as noted. To that effect Katzenstein (2010, p. 2) wrote: "By their mere existence, civilizations undercut both the realist confidence in the superiority of the military and the liberal presumption that universalistic secular liberal norms are inherently superior to all others."

To conclude, Katzenstein argues that "civilizations deserve more attention than they have received." It is that attention that we are giving here. Just like sociologists generally avoid the cultural and the civilizational, so too do political scientists avoid them because they exceed the frontiers of society for the sociologist and the frontiers of the state for the political scientist. The relevance of civilizations, as it was stated by Samuel Huntington in the post-ideological world since the collapse of the Soviet Union, has been reiterated in the globalization era as it becomes apparent that there is no civilization-periphery dichotomy. Every civilizational center has a prestige to uphold in a context wherein resisting, competing, and winning is no longer about politics but about economics. And this economic competition ensuring the attractiveness and propagating the merits of one culture and civilization occurs through economic success. It is this dynamic of multiple modernities that Eisenstadt (2000) described.

THE SPACE DIMENSION

We live in a world made of regions. Different regions constitute geographic spaces. These spaces have produced their own civilizations. The relevance of space and civilizations here lies in the fact that civilizations are structures that embrace value systems and norms. They are norm providers. These value systems and the norms they produce differ as each civilization develops its own cosmogony. In fact each major civilization is a product or has seen emerge the manifestations of specific cosmogonies or worldviews and/or religions. Looking at the categorization of world civilizations suggested by O'Neil (2010)[1] we find the following: Confucian civilization in China, the Christian (Catholicism and Protestantism) and liberalism in the West, Islamic civilization primarily in the Middle East and North Africa, the Slavic-Orthodox civilization in Russia, Hindu civilization in India, and the vitalist civilization in precolonial Africa and pre-Columbian Americas (see Figure 6.1).

Civilizations inspire political cultures. And these cultures are geographically localizable. They constitute the centers of world geopolitics. Using this perspective Samuel Huntington (1995) suggested a categorization for a world geopolitical map, which he saw as a coming together of religions and/or worldviews with political cultures. He proposed a map made of the West, Russia, East Asia, Africa, Latin America, and the Middle East.

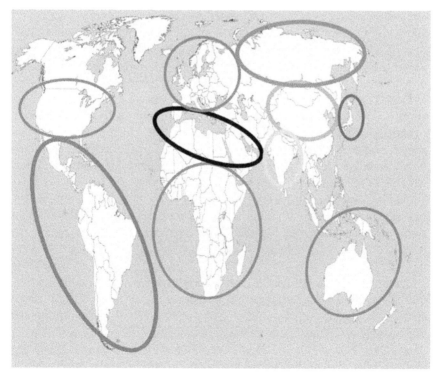

Figure 6.1.

Granted, both O'Neil's and Huntington's categories are based on a certain idea of importance in size and number of space and peoples to be seen and included in these categories. So these categories overlook small but old and historically entrenched civilizations such as the Judaic or the Nippon.

Earlier in the text, we defined worldviews as a canon of guiding principles to approach life and choices of adherents. And we see on the other hand religions as worldviews that furthermore entail a metaphysical component, as they suggest the existence of a supreme being, the creator, which addresses the afterlife and eternal damnation and the condition of salvation here on earth. Both worldviews and religions have the potential to and in fact inspire civilizations. Where they did not inspire a civilization, as is the case in the West, Christianity even if it is not the basis, has at least over the years become a binding glue as a value system and norm provider, next to the worldview of liberalism.

We understand civilization the same way William MacNeil (1990, p. 8) does, namely, as "a shared literary canon, and expectations to orient human behavior." A second definition by Randall Collins (Kaztenstein 2010, p. 18) sees "civilization as zones of prestige organized around one or several cultural centers." Both definitions complement each other and suit the underlying argument of this book. The first emphasizes the expectation dimension of civilizations, which we have established as an essential feature of structures, and we have identified both religions and civilizations as intangible structures. The second emphasizes the dimension of space as the point of departure before they engage in the civilizational dynamics of either conquest (offense) or resistance (defense).

Indeed, civilizations initially claim specific spaces. In these spaces reign specific core beliefs, value systems, and norms. As such, civilizations are overarching structures with specific demands and expectations. Their core beliefs, value systems, and norms are reflected in the multiple structures below their overarching shadow, which are the various institutions of administrative or social life.

Although civilizations' core beliefs may vary, their value systems and norms may be the same. In all civilizations we generally find an exhortation to cherish and support life, to protect one's own and others' lives. As a result, in all civilizations we generally find the demand and expectation "you shall not kill."

Although the core beliefs of civilizations may vary, such variations produce different value systems and norms that may be different but still can be compatible. The value and norm of going respectively to church on Sunday or a mosque on Friday is different, but not incompatible.

However, because civilizational core beliefs vary, such variation may also produce value systems and norms that are both different and incompatible, as an example, polygamy versus monogamy. Polygamy is a value and a norm in the Islamic civilization, whereas monogamy is a value and norm in the West.

And because civilizations' core beliefs vary, they can produce value systems and norms that are not only incompatible but also mutually exclusive. For example, we have Sharia law or secular law. The process of secularization in the West produced the prevalence of the rule of law to order public life as opposed to many Islamic nations, wherein Sharia law is preferred. The incompatibility here lies in the fact that their intrinsic inspiration difference renders them mutually exclusive and dictates that a necessary choice be made as to which one shall order public life, as both cannot at the same time. Such intrinsic difference of inspiration is manifest for instance in the notion of equality of rights to all, for all genders, etc., which may be the inspiration to one but not to the other.

ENCOUNTERS BETWEEN CIVILIZATIONS

There are many civilizations around the globe, as identified earlier. They may exist apart from each other. That, however, was the case in the distant past. In the meantime, civilizations, which tend to expand their space of validity, have eventually encroached into each other's initial spaces. See the image below, suggesting the dynamics of spread.

The consequence is that the value system they carry or bring finds expression in these recipient spaces, and their value system must find validity there as well. And so we find adherents of Hindu, Confucian, or Islamic civilizations in the United States, just as there are Westerners in China, which adheres to a different civilization. In the end, this underlines the fact that civilizations can coexist with each other. Indeed, various civilizations around the globe coexist. They encounter each other through transcivilizational engagements and intercivilizational encounters. Civilizations complete each other. The notion of positive law inherited from the West has been adopted by many non-Western civilizational nations. Civilizations borrow from each other. The West did benefit from paper, the compass, and gun powder from the Chinese civilization. Islamic scholarship benefited from the Greek philosophical and intellectual culture, etc. Such positive cross-fertilization and engagements occur through dialogue and debate in areas of differences and incompatibility of value systems and norms (Katzenstein 2010, p. 1). There are, however, the cases of differences, incompatibility, and even mutual exclusiveness of value systems between civilizations. This is the context in which encounters between civilizations may produce contentions and clashes. This is as well the context in which value systems compete against each other.

It is the context that explains the notion of competing civilizations. Civilizations compete over value systems.

COMPETING FOR THE VALIDITY OF VALUE SYSTEMS

The notion of competition here is to be understood in its various complex and subtle expressions. Competition need not primarily imply confrontation, antagonistic context, or presumed enmity or even disagreement. Indeed, competition can occur in a cooperative context, such as in trade. Competition can be friendly, which means it is not just enemies who compete. It also means that the outcome of competitive exercise need not produce enmity. One can lose a competitive outcome to someone else and remain of good spirit and a good sport, as pugilists do after a fight, sometimes after a bloody fight. And sometimes there needs to even be a disagreement to prompt a competition, as it is in the case of two basketball teams or soccer teams about to start a game. In such a context of competition, the terms or rules under which the competition unravels are articulated and known. It is the context in which there is a need for a referee or umpire. And in some other contexts, competition may not even be declared and still occur implicitly. It can as well be occurring when only one protagonist is engaged in it without the awareness or knowledge of the other. And finally in the midst of peers, with comparable attributes, one can be the most competitive and start benefiting from it without actively seeking such benefit.

There is a little bit of all those different contextual scenarios happening when it comes to competing civilizational value systems. In competition in the contexts described, foes indeed occur between civilizations. Although today's various civilizations cooperate economically, they compete as well for the "prestige of their cultural centers." They compete for the attractiveness of their value systems and norms. They compete because their value systems and norms in specific ways are contested. There are therefore civilizations that are interested in attracting others to adhering to their value system and norms and in propagating their value system and norms toward others' civilizational spaces. After all, we would rather have others live like us than us live like them. The conditions of such a contest are given in the event when and where civilizations have value systems and norms that are different and incompatible and in the event when and where civilizations have value systems and norms that are different, incompatible, and mutually exclusive.

The contest can unravel from a distance. It is the case, when a given civilization is known to occupy a specific space on the globe but still manages to attract followers and adherents from different, faraway spaces. An example would be the case of Buddhism and Christianity. Both Buddhism and Christianity are religions, structures that have inspired civilizations. Their respective teachings (demands and expectations) explain the difference in these respective civilizations. In their respective teachings lie the origin of the contest and the reason why based on the case they make, may spread to gain ascendance, influence in each other's spaces. There are numbers of people from the West adhering and integrating Buddhism or other Asian religions or worldviews. There is a growing number of Buddhist temples in California wherein most members are Californians. They have found the religion and by extension the civilization and value system it inspired attractive enough to adhere. Depending on their degrees of adhesion, some start organizing their lives according to the ordinances and precepts, which we call demands and expectations of these new faiths, and the value systems they inspire and propose. Some others accommodate aspects of their lives to suit both the old and the new.

The contest can unravel directly. Historically, it has been a quasi-natural tendency for civilizations to expand, a process that produces the encounter of two or more civilizations in one space. Some civilizations have been more expansive than others, among them primarily the Islamic and Western civilizations. Islam, the religion, spread since the seventh century from the Arabian Peninsula and brought along the Islamic civilization to reach practically all regions of the globe. The West since the dawn of the modern era, around the 1500s, expanded through European trade and colonization, triggering a new paradigm that was to unleash an all-out civilizational encounter, from Africa to Australia and from Asia to the Americas. Along with its quest for trade and territories, the West exported its civilization. The West has succeeded, in some areas more and in others less, at imposing key features of its civilization. Among such features we count the beginning of liberal trade, even though protectionist at first; the nation-state model; and Christianity. The success of Europe since the Industrial Revolution has nothing but cemented European claims to global hegemony. Europeans attempted to impose the idea of a dominating and single civilization. This dominance has been criticized under the concept of cultural imperialism, not as primarily understood by Antonio Gramsci (1975) or later by Michel Foucault,[2] but broadly as an instrumentalization of the agents and institutions of non-Western nations to adjust their societies to fit the Western mold. Because of that, we cannot overemphasize how instrumental colonization was in the spread of Western civilizations and ways, but also ultimately how instrumental colonization was in laying the foundation, for better or for worse, of the global culture we are developing today.

Today, direct encounters have been increasingly the result of interconnectedness and the movement of people, which has thus inflated big cities to create cosmopolitan spaces. The process has allowed a coexistence of peoples of various and different civilizational backgrounds in shared spaces. We now have spaces in the United States where the values of Hindu civilization are now negotiated within a Western context, in Paris, France, or London, United Kingdom, or Sydney, Australia, where the values of the West encounter those of the Muslim populations. More specifically, there are cases in France where some marital rights of Muslims have been deemed against the human rights of the wife. This for instance constitutes a concrete case of contested value systems.

The effects of such coexistence can be measured through the number of conversions into or out of religions that inspire civilizations. The consequence can be measured by the adhesion to value systems that such religion-inspired civilizations produce. There is a growing number of Muslims in the West as a result of new conversions, who are themselves the consequences of direct encounters of civilizations. The immigration process continues to increase the prospects of the continuation of such a phenomenon.

The contest between civilizations unravels, therefore, primarily at the individual level. There is a civilization fault line at the individual level consisting of the need to position oneself when faced with the influences of another culture or civilization. Such a position is a fault line insofar as one can fight a clash of civilizations at the very subjective level, having to either fend off such influences or even cave when overwhelming. In that case, one simply integrates the value system of another civilization. One can also voluntarily integrate the value system of another civilization simply because of its attractiveness. One can as well successfully resist. There are as well cases of selective positioning when one picks and chooses which value system to live by. But by and large, such a selective approach often goes for superficial features and visible expressions of civilizations. When it comes to core values, often an adhesion to one system of values becomes necessary. Likely, such a positioning between civilizations at a personal level is just that, a matter of personal choice, which often occurs without fanfare. As a result, there are constantly individuals adhering into one civilizational value system or leaving another. It does not constitute a cause for alarm. Civilizations can handle such transfers in and out, because they are superscale structures. This development suggests that the notion of fault lines, as described by Huntington (1995), as a territorial demarcation line between the end of one civilizational space and the beginning of another, has become less a matter of geographic bordering regions between civilizations and more within civilizations.

The contest between civilizations can develop as well at the aggregated level. This is the case when there is a conscious and concerted effort by an institutional group, or just a group, to articulate the aspirations of a civilization and to carry, defend, or promote them against or above the aspirations of other civilizations. Often such carrying out, defense, and promotion of civilizational aspirations occur through political means. It is the level that helps explain the notion of the clash of civilizations, as proposed by Samuel Huntington. At this level, any contest between civilizations is as well political, as civilizations have no armies of their own. If any, they use those of the political power whose culture they inspire. It is a phenomenon at the basis of nationalism. Russia found itself involved in World War I, a political war, on the side of the Serbs not only because they share with the latter a common civilizational heritage but also because the Serbs fought under the mantle of nationalism, whose underlying culture and civilization they share in many ways with Russia. At this aggregated level of contest between civilizations there is a geographic fault line. In such civilizations the political power and military might behind them can geographically position their resistance if they are not willing to cave or voluntarily adhere to the rival civilizational quest. We have been witnessing the rise of nonstate actors, creating groups or organizations in the name of the defense of their civilization, as in the case of al-Qaeda, or the "Islamic State" insurgency demonstrates.

As part of new developments, there is as well another aggregated level not based on civilizations' value systems but on humanitarian concerns or just simply on the humanity of mankind living on planet earth, a goal that by definition transcends civilizations. There are indeed new forms of alliances that bring together as members individuals, groups, or nations of different civilizational spaces to service specific needs of mankind. People and groups organize across civilizations to service issues around women, gender, human rights, labor, the environment, health, etc. Such needs vary, and so do the diverse forms of new alliances we find at that level. For instance, we have the case of nations organizing beyond civilizations' fault lines, as is the case of the European Union, which includes Serbia and Bosnia and awaits the membership of Turkey and Albania, traditionally not part of the Western civilizational heritage. The context of globalization has continued to facilitate the emergence of cross-civilizational space arrangements and alliances. This development runs counter or parallel to ethno-centrism, nationalism, and civilization-driven value systems, as it allows the focus on issues relevant to humanity regardless of culture or civilization of origin. Such a development continues to blur the notion of fault lines.

The contest between civilizational value systems therefore are more and more to be observed not at the fault line territories between civilizations but within a civilizational space, cosmopolitan cities, which host chunks of residents or just citizens who have adhered to values of a different civilization. The laws of the republic often suffice to manage public life, and therefore the cultural tensions and conflicts that occasionally arise within cosmopolitan spaces are to be seen as proof of internal fault lines.

CIVILIZATIONS AS CAUSES OF GLOBAL ISSUES

Competition between civilizational value systems has the potential of producing tension and conflicts. We argue that if civilizations are the cause of issues, it is primarily because of their value systems. We make this distinction because there are issues in which civilizations' value systems are the cause and others in which civilizations' value systems are simply instrumentalized but they are not the cause. For each case, following is an example. If the United States fights a war in Iraq because it wants to introduce democracy into the Middle East, in so far as some would contend that it is not historically an Islamic value, such a war and its underlying conflict qualify as a civilization conflict. It is then a conflict or war driven by an element of the value system of one and resisted on the ground of the value system of the other. And the argument will apply if and when the West should seek to export gender equality or any other typically Western norm in a civilization where the norm is gender hierarchy. If the United States fights a war in the Middle East because it needs access to oil and argues that it is because of the need for democracy, here, a civilization value, namely, democracy, is instrumentalized. The same reasoning is valid in case of a fundamental Muslim fighting the infidels simply because they are infidels (this would be a civilization conflict), whereas as if the fundamentalists sought political power in the name of Islam and its civilization, both the name of Islam and its civilization would then be instrumentalized. The use of civilizations in conflicts is often not about them but about the initiators of conflicts. It is often not about value systems of civilizations but about the interests of those claiming to belong to a specific value system. But can a value system of a civilization coincide with the interest of the belligerent? Yes, such is the case. For instance the spread of the value of liberal economics coincides with benefiting, let us say, US businesses. But even then, the coincidence does not necessarily employ the use of force. Civilizational value systems are generally carriers of positive ideals. It is the attractiveness of their positivity that should justify their spread, not the use of force. The use of force is, however, the product of material interest of political power. It is therefore politics that justifies force through its civilizational value system.

Indeed, the aspirations of civilizations (their demands and expectations) can be carried out or safeguarded by political power and through political interests of those adhering to that civilization. And it is this amalgam that has brought civilizations into the midst of today's global issues. It is possible because of the merging of civilizations' aspirations and political interests through political cultures. Political cultures synthesize material interests (politics) and their ideational interests (civilizations), which become manifest through foreign policy. But it is as well the amalgam that complicates the exercise of foreign policy, namely, when the value system of a civilization does not coincide with the political interests. Indeed, just as value systems coincide with material political interests, they can however differ. Such is the case for instance, when national security needs (political interest) interfere with upholding basic human rights (value system), as it appears in the debate whether to torture detainees for information.[3] Although this example is drawn from the perspective of the West, it remains valid for any other entity, any nation, to align its political interest with the value that it claims to subscribe to.

Even in the scenario of mixing civilizational aspirations and political interest, clash has not always been the means of negotiating the outcome. Many non-Western civilizations under siege by European expansionism have managed to resist in ways other than through confrontation. Asian civilizations have proven that incompatibility or exclusivity of value systems and norms with the West could be dealt with in other, more subtle means. Passive resistance has been another one of such means through which to resist, even in the case where one civilization had the upper hand, using the political and military might of the people belonging to it. European colonization of non-Western territories introduced the value systems and norms of the colonizing forces, which were celebrated on the surface but never deep enough to replace the traditional value systems and norms.

The West in East Asian has not succeeded in altering the core entrenchment of long established worldviews (Buddhism, Confucianism, Taoism, and Shintoism) as well as the ethos of peoples whose cultures have preceded the European culture. The resistance was simply daunting. What is true for China with its millennial civilization is as well true for Japan. When Catholic missionaries (Franciscans and Jesuits) made progress in their attempt to convert the Japanese people, reaching considerable numbers, up to one third of the Japanese people, in the 1500s, the Shogunate of Hideyoshi, in power since 1536, organized a stop to the process, ordering the expulsion of Spaniards and Portuguese traders with their missionaries and a renunciation of the Christian faith by as many as 37,000 Japanese.[4] The exception to the expulsion was the Dutch traders, the only Europeans who did not bring missionaries along. China revealed itself to be too much work for any attempt to Westernize it. Korea, indeed then, was too much under the tutelage of successively both China and Japan to have made much in this context. When the West came back in the aftermath of the Industrial Revolution, in the eighteenth and nineteenth centuries, the tables had turned. Europeans came in full force. They were not just Portuguese, Spaniards, and Dutch. The Dutch and Great Britain joined in and later the United States. To engage Asia in trade and to access pieces of territories for trading posts, they simply took what they needed. Sometimes this has to occur through wars, at the end of which China and Japan were on the losing side. The result was the many treaties in which portions of their territories went to Europeans. These treaties, known as *extra-territoriality*, were the causes of humiliation felt by both China and Japan, and most arguably, inspiring Asian nationalism. This nationalism was politically induced, as all nationalism movements do, an instrumentalization of cultural and civilizational pride. So the few clashes and wars and the unrest recorded in East Asia (the Opium War [1840]; the Sino-French War [1883–1885]; the Taiping Rebellion [1850–1864], a civil war against the foreign Manchu Dynasty of the Qing; the Sino-Japanese War [1894–1895], fought in the early phase of Japanese imperialism against its neighbors; and the Boxer Rebellion [1900]) were primarily political. These wars were about the integrity of their territories and their claims to their land, and their respective cultures were the fuel used to drive their resistance. East Asian civilizations have been around in many instances longer than Western civilizations. The West has simply succeeded to force trade on East Asia and eventually got the region to engage with modernity, Japan first, and others have followed suit since: South Korea, the so-called Tigers (Taiwan, Malaysia, and Singapore), and now China. The rest are as well doing just that: the Philippines, Indonesia, and Vietnam, to name just a few.

About the West in Latin America, the continent was initially massively colonized by European settlers primarily from Spain, Portugal, and Italy. These settlers, like those in North America, eventually cut their political affiliation to their mother countries. The continent was therefore essentially Western, but as Huntington (1995) argued, it has been developing a civilizational space, drifting away from the traditional West. It is in the process of asserting its value system and norms that do not copy or emulate the ones found in North America or Europe. They have a communal life of family and community with a different emphasis than in the West. Their gender relations, although evolving like elsewhere, still recognize and acknowledge the distinct male-female roles in the family, community, and society. Their language is proficiently resilient, challenging more and more the supremacy of English in the Western hemisphere. Their aesthetics differ from those of the West with respect to music, sense of beauty, literature, diet, sports, and folklore, and more importantly the ethos and consciousness of it all that led them to clearly identify with a "Hispanic world," not an Anglo-Saxon one.

The continent has recovered from the difficult decades of the 1970s and 1980s, and has been progressively modernizing, beginning with Brazil. Yet this process of drifting away from the West has been taking place. With the relative diminishing clout of the United States and the growing significance of an economic partnership with China, a sense of distance has been felt like never before. If Latin America used to be the backyard of the United States, the latter has been preoccupied with other urgent matters (the war, the economic downturn, internal political divide, etc.), while the former has grown tired of feeling neglected and sought other ways to feel relevant.

In Africa, although the process of modernization has stalled, a number of economies have been picking up pace as a result of some concrete benefit from the conditions of globalization. African traditional values and norms, what we call ethos, have long been under siege by a European systematic attempt to simply bulldoze them. They were deemed irrelevant to what Europe had in mind. The African traditional value system and norms have proven resilient. Many modern educated and fully functional Africans in today's global world have kept their African ethos. This is to say that the African still apprehends the world and has an outlook that is particularly African and foreign to a Chinese or a European. It may be a matter of worldview. Africans have not ceased being Africans despite the European attempt to culturally reroute their ethos. While remaining Africans, many could adopt etiquettes and even grasp and master the expectations of the European implanted social system without clashing with the West. The recorded clashes between Africa and European colonizers have been, here again, in the context of political power, for instance, the Mau Mau uprising in Kenya (1952–1960), the Ndebele rebellion, the Tshaka Zulu–led revolution, the Hereros in South Western Africa (today's Namibia), the Asante of Ghana in the nineteenth century all the way to the early twentieth century, the Fon of Benin engaging the French in 1891–1902, the Hehe of Tanzania engaging the Germans in 1891, the Yoruba and the Sokoto Empire against the British in the late nineteenth century, and in Zimbabwe the war of independence between 1965 and 1979, to name just a few. These resistance attempts have failed to politically alter or halt the political control of European colonization, essentially due to the absence of centralized power structures of unitary states and the less than impressive military capabilities. The wave of independence movements in Africa at the turn of the twentieth century, and with the help of changing political tides internationally, have finally seen Africa liberated from the colonial yoke. It is, however, the more subtle and nuanced cultural front where the resistance seems to have remained solidly anchored. Despite years of colonization, the African core ethos has hardly been dethroned. The result is a sense of biculturality, and in some cases, even triculturality to which modern Africans subscribe, being essentially African in their core ethos while being conversant with the ways of modernity and those of the Islamic culture.

After all is said and done, this game of competing civilizational value systems is complex. It is both obvious and hidden—obvious because adhering to the values of a new or different civilization can manifestly be seen by some specific symbols, behaviors, attitudes, choices, and decisions, and hidden, because adhering to value systems is a personal experience and therefore can be appreciated only individually.

The Middle East, is the region where the amalgam between political interests and civilizational aspirations has produced the most striking and concerning case of civilizational value-systems' conflicts. It is the theater of tumultuous conflicts between the West and the Islamic civilization that endures.

Conversations around the subject of encounters of civilizations and the notion of competing value stems and norms soon gravitate toward the Islamic and the Western civilizations. The question that this gravitation toward just the Islamic and the Western civilizations begs is then how come the encounters of the West with other civilizations are less and less part of such a conversation? It is because the encounter of different value systems has been a source of enduring conflicts and nowhere have such conflicts been more on display in the case of Western encounters with the Islamic world. The Islamic civilization derives its values from a religion that lays claim to ordering public life, and therefore public space, which is the prerogative of politics. The teaching of the Prophet Muhammad and the traditional cultures of the Bedouin Arabs and to a lesser degree other cultures adhering to Islam have constituted the theological and sociocultural foundation of the Islamic world until challenged by development in the nineteenth century, namely, modernity, the nation-state construct and secular political ideologies.

Like other civilizations, the Islamic civilization has had to find a way to come to terms with dealing with the West and other occurring changes. Indeed, the Western influence has been felt in the Islamic world since the nineteenth century, leaving behind the earlier years (the Moors' conquest of Spain and the flourishing Islamic scientific activity in Bagdad during the Abbasid Caliphate (750–1258 AD) when Islam was in the driving seat and Europe was the civilization catching up one catching up before the Renaissance. The ascendency of the West in the Islamic world beginning with the Industrial Revolution reinforced by the discovery of oil in 1908, a better energy source for the machinery, as it attracted the British. Then came World War I, which brought about the demise of the Ottoman Empire, as the empire eventually sided with the losing party of the triple entente made of Germany, Austria-Hungary, Italy and the Ottoman Empire. The result was a dismantling of the empire and the Turks relinquishing claim to their Middle Eastern territories. The act was sealed in the Treaty of Sèvres in 1920. The treaty paved the way for the Europeans into the Middle East. Oil could now be exploited unhindered.

It is this history of Western presence in the Middle East that has come to constitute a primary starting point in any effort to understanding how Islam relates to the West. This relation was that of contention. It has attacked Islam and its believers to the core. The Islamic scholar Shaykh Muhammad Abduh (1849–1905) at the turn of the twentieth century, in this context accounting for the numerous invasion attempts by foreigners of the Islamic lands, wrote: "it was that the nations of Europe began to throw off their bondage and reform their condition (*their: of the Muslims*),[5] reordering the affairs of their life in a manner akin to the message of Islam, though oblivious of who their real guide and leader was. So were enunciated the fundamental principles of modern civilization in which subsequent generations as compared with the peoples of earlier days have found their pride and glory" (Donahue and Esposito 2007, p. 23).

This quest to understand how Islam relates to the West can even deeply and comprehensively be understood if we start a bit earlier than the nineteenth century and look at inner Islamic conflicts and tension before the Western involvement. Indeed, the history of Islam shows a period of tension between the rationalists such as the Kharijites and the Mu'tazilites on one hand and the traditionalists such as the Asharites on the other around the question of faith and reason. This debate ended in a way that opened space for advocating for a more purist practice of Islam and eventually its assertive resistance against forces that somehow dilute Islam, and science, the West, and modernity will count among them. Pervez Hoodbhoy (2010) revealed the tension in Islam around faith and reason as he wondered what happened to the Islamic civilization after spearheading science and intellectual enterprises between the ninth and thirteenth centuries to have fallen behind since and to have even developed an anti-intellectual attitude. Islam then encouraged intellectual pursuit. Islam has found value in linking faith and reason. The result was a flourishing intellectual activity and production from philosophy, art, architecture, science, technology, and literature from scholars in Bagdad from anywhere in the region. Universities were created, math and algebra were advanced and created, principles of optics were revealed, stars were named, the circulation of blood was elucidated, and Averroes and Avicenna sparked interest in ancient Greek philosophy and its entire body of knowledge. In his quest to find out what has happened, Hoodbhoy has mentioned a fundamentalistic interpretation of Islam that came to interfere with such intellectual endeavors. This current saw discordance between faith and reason and denounced the fusion of both. Hoodbhoy has argued that an Islam favorable to reason was supported by the Mu'tazilites. But the Mu'tazilites' rivals, the Ashrites were dogmatic and fundamentalist. The former argued in favor of free will, and the latter in favor of predestination. It is this tension that produced a competition, which was occasionally bloody. The Mu'tazilites were on the losing sides at the end of the dispute. With their demise, science was relegated to the margins. What follows did not help to revive the interest in reason and science. The Ottoman Empire subsequently in power did not extend to Bagdad the reverence and the status as being the hub of intellectual pursuit. The Ottomans presided over the erosion of the caliphate as the instance of higher authority in Islam. The process of disintegration of Islamic unity was in progress. In fact both the upper hand of the Asharites and the disintegration of Islamic unity have spurred a new wave of fundamentalism. This new wave saw fundamentalism is a remedy against the many cultures of Islam, both literary and otherwise. In the eighteenth century, indeed, various communities that had adopted Islam were practicing the religion with more or less loose dogmatism and with cultural connotations. The teaching of Sufism, as well more interpretative and less rigorously dogmatic, fit the times, to the dismay of fundamentalists. The fundamentalists saw in these developments a source of corruption to and the diluting of Islam. Purity was promoted. The Salafiyya led the charge. Their grand scholars and intellectual leaders were Muhammad Rashid Rida, Muhammad Abbdul, and Muhammad ibn Abd al-Wahhab, to name a few.

The challenges of Western influence, modernity, and Christianity faced by the Islamic world were now to be felt more directly. From the challenges of modernity and Christianity came the challenge of pure loss of political control. The West indeed has progressively grown its influence in the Middle East since World War I. The aftermath of World War I has paved the way for European colonization of the Middle East. The Ottoman Empire was on the losing side of the war. It had to relinquish its claim on the region, prompting Great Britain to move in on the ground of protecting its investment interests as Iraq was divided into three pieces[6] in 1917 and became a territory under UN mandate. France joined in and subsequently acquired Syria and Lebanon.

The influence of the West was now directly felt. Islam was now colonized by the West. This political reality of a post–World War I Middle East spawned Islamic nationalism, of which the North African Islamic countries became a part. The resistance movement of Islamic nationalism against European colonialism, led by the Egyptian Nasser, like all nationalism movements against a foreign power and much more so if and when the invader is culturally "other," drew on the values and pride of Islam to galvanize support. As in previous times where a sense of disorientation prevailed, the need for introspection was the consequence. The conservatives among the Muslims argued in favor of the need for a more purist and fundamental Islam as a way of countering the influence of the West but also as a way of ensuring resistance against a faith diluted by such influence. They sought and elevated to norm the life of early Muslims who in their eyes had practiced Islam in its purest way. The approach led to the revival of the Salafiyya teaching, and its leader in the late nineteenth century was al-Wahhab. A renewed revival in the 1920s was initiated by Abdul al Aziz, which produced the Muslim Brotherhood in 1929.

Not all[7] embraced the conservative current. The corruptive force against Islam and the dominating power that the Islamic world had to rid itself of was the West. Wahhabism was now a movement with a clearer purpose. It has never dominated the entire Islamic world. The Islamic world is too vast and too culturally diverse for that.

Just as Islamic conservatism focused on the purity of Islam, Islamic nationalism focused on the independence of Islamic nations. The theater of Islamic nationalism was the nation-state, not the religion of Islam. Such an Islamic nationalism movement has had both religious and secular underpinnings. Both the religion of Islam and secular ideologies have been used to fuel the movement, one used to galvanize support and the other to ensure that political power reflects the interest of political actors, not that of the religion. The movement itself was part of the overall anticolonialism and anti-imperialism movement prevalent in the Middle East, Africa, and Asia. These movements have gradually produced the emergence of political leaders. These movements finally succeeded at ridding colonized nations from European colonization and Western imperialism in the aftermath of World War II. Their leaders, those in the Islamic nations of North Africa and the Middle East, who although Muslims, claimed political authority in an authoritarian way, as was the case in Egypt, Libya, Syria, Algeria, Tunisia, and Turkey. And where Islamic monarchs remained in power, in the United Arab Emirates, Jordan, Morocco, Saudi Arabia, and Kuwait, they saw their power needing to negotiate with a new state institutional reality.

This new development was creating a political environment in which Islam was no longer the uncontested public space–ordering agency. Indeed, Islam was increasingly in a predicament caused by modernity, to use the terminology of Bassam Tibi (2009),[8] a predicament caused by modernity that he sees challenging Islam in the following key areas: cultural change and whether religious reforms should ensue, the Islamization process versus empowerment through knowledge, modern law or sharia law, Islam and individual human rights, religious tension and identity politics, secularization or desecularization, cultural pluralism or Islamic supremacy, Islamic rationalism or *fiqh*-orthodoxy. All of these areas are now issues thanks to modernity in the Islamic world.

This new development has not been welcomed by those among the Muslims who want to practice the purist and fundamentalist form of Islam and to whom Islam is that undisputed public life–ordering agency. They argue in favor of Islamic supremacy. They have remained the Muslims the most hostile to Western influence in the region and from whom resistance often comes, either in the form of protest or Islamist political parties. They are full of fervor for their cause and often louder than the more lukewarm or moderate Muslims. From their perspective, the history of Western presence in the region continues to provide reason for their grievances.

History, indeed, has been tumultuous over the years. In the 1940s Western petroleum companies, called the Seven Sisters (Standard Oil of New Jersey, Standard Oil of New York, Gulf Oil, Royal Dutch Shell, Texaco, Standard Oil of California, and the Anglo-Persian Oil Company), monopolized the oil business from exploration production, export, and distribution to pricing. After 1945, the post-World War II era, after its rise to superpower status, the United States managed to have influence in the region both in the context of the Cold War and for its own economic and oil interests.

Over the years, in the 1950s and 1960s, voices of dissent throughout the developing world were getting louder, arguing against forms of neo-colonialism and dependency. These arguments were fueled by a Marxist analysis both from the East and the West. The Arab world in the meantime created a league of its own, the Arab League, in March 1945, for purposes of common interest, and the OPEC in September 1960, in which arguments of exploitation by Western petroleum companies had become the main topic and concern. In the early 1970s they succeeded in regaining control of the oil industry.

The region has continued to be an explosive cocktail. In 1973, the Israeli-Palestinian conflict erupted, and the entire region was involved in a war that lasted six days, prompting the Arab nations to decree an oil embargo and sparking a world economic crisis. In 1979, there was a revolution in Iran in which fundamentalist Shiites led by the Ayatollah dethroned Shah Mohammad Reza Pahlavi, who was a friend of the West in general and of the United States in particular.

All these events kept the flame of fundamentalism burning. As a result, fundamentalists have remained a force to reckon with in the Islamic world even when kept silent by powerful Islamic potentates and authoritarian regimes the likes of Saddam Hussein, Hosni Mubarak, Anwar Sadat, and others. Their latent force and power have occasionally been displayed, for example, when they assassinated Anwar Sadat in Egypt or whenever there was a political opening in the form of elections and they won, such as in Turkey, Egypt, Algeria, etc., and where they are not acting, they have to be kept satisfied, as is the case in Kuwait or Saudi Arabia.

The region remains an explosive cocktail, capable of exploding any time. The cocktail is made of ingredients such as the Israeli-Palestinian conflict, the role of the United States in it, and Islam and oil. Indeed the US role in this context has been to manage a variety of interests that are not at first glance compatible. The United States entertains relations with Saudi Arabia, a Muslim nation sympathetic to the Palestinian cause and fellow Muslims. The United States entertains relations with Israel, seen as the villain in the eyes of many Muslims who pressure their governments for a stand. They know they possess oil, which can be used but has to be sold and therefore needs customers. The United States wants to be that customer and in addition provide assistance, protection, and security, which explains its military presence in the region. Even if disliked by many, the United States is a welcome ally to those in power in the region, including the Saudis and the Kuwaitis. They must please their people while maintaining their relations with the United States. Israel needs the United States for additional and welcome support in a sea of unfriendly nations, but must come to terms that its ally is as well a friend with some of its enemies. The United States provides to each one what it needs the most and gets in the process what it needs. This triangulation by the United States has been a cause of discontent to fundamentalist Muslims. The United States is a foreign, non-Islamic nation, infidels in their holy land, with too much leverage, and not opened to Muslim causes as demonstrated in the Israeli-Palestinian conflict, they argue. US triangulation in the region has caused some discontent. Among the discontents are fundamentalist Muslims. Their known arguments through various publications and their own pronouncements, among which Osama Bin Laden's own videotaped messages of October 7, 2001, in which he spoke of humiliation suffered by Islam in the hands of the West for almost a century. Other causes of grievance have been that the holy land of Mecca has been soiled and the double standard observed in the US attitude vis-à-vis Israel in the Israeli-Palestinian conflict, and of course that the West was essentially not Islamic, which is to many fundamentalists a reason more than good enough not to count, to say the least. This is an argument that clearly places the United States in a category that calls for consequence to a fundamentalist Muslim. What is the category? It is that of hindered or roadblock to the Muslim and/or Islam. From this perspective it becomes a baby step to declaring jihad, which is the consequence. Jihad is a requirement, a demand of Islam and therefore an expectation of the follower to execute. If the United States is viewed as an enemy to Islam or the fundamentalist Muslim it should become the subject of jihad. The United States is, however, a powerful foe. How is jihad to be carried out against a powerful foe? The question is not new. It is historical. A powerful foe cannot be fought *mano a mano*, or ad hominem. The chances for success are practically nonexistent. The strategy has been unconventional means used by the weaker party. Among such unconventional strategies, guerrilla warfare is one. Terrorism is another.

TERRORISM

Discussing terrorism at this junction of the text does not intend to associate intrinsically terrorism to Islam, nor should it suggest that terrorism is the sole domain of Islam. Like other "isms" terrorism is at first an idea of terror. The preference to inject, inflict, and cause terror is what we call terrorism. As such, terrorism can be found anywhere. As such, terrorists can be found everywhere. As a result, there are many terrorist groups around the world. They often have a grievance from which one can deduce their goal. Such grievances are political in nature, which leads us to distinguish between terrorism and political terrorism. We define more precisely the nature of political terrorism below. But in addition to being political, the grievance and cause of some terrorist individuals or groups can be grounded in their worldview, ideology, or religion. Because of that some terrorist acts are political and linked to religions. It is in this sense that consequently some terrorist acts have a religious connotation, and some do have an Islamic motivation just as they may have a Hindu or a Christian motivation. Granted these are religions, but we have established that the same religions are at the basis of the civilizations in whose value systems their motivations are grounded. Next to religions and civilizations, ideologies and other ideals provide as well such motivations in which political terrorist acts are justified.

Terrorism is introduced here because, indeed, there are acts of terrorism perpetrated in the name of Islam. It is discussed here because of the notion of competing value systems, namely, that of the West and Islam, and terrorism is a means chosen by some Muslims to combat the infiltrating value system of the West in the world of Islam. Indeed, terrorism is a preference for a means, not even warfare, since it does not presuppose war; in fact it avoids war and does not imply a tactic or strategy, which implies a thought sequencing of activity designed to approach a conflictual context and whose end is not immediate. It is simply an act. It is an act whose context is not war, and it therefore does not discriminate between armed forces from civilians. It is a means to achieving a goal.

This means terrorism has been prominently and in a more international politics' relevant manner utilized and carried out by various individuals or groups affiliated with different currents. The most infamously spectacular of the Muslim terrorists were those engaged and involved in the attacks on September 11, 2001, in the United States.

This segment will not discuss the variety of terrorist groups to be found around the world, each with their grievances, organization skills, and capacity to carry out acts of terrorism, their modus operandi, their religious affiliation within Islam. A number of publications have appeared since the event of

September 11, 2001, with that focus. In national security debates and other venues of public discussion, the topic of terrorism has been discussed with the focus on these groups and where they operate from. We provide, however, an inventory of known terrorist groups or organizations around the world in Table 6.1.

We limit ourselves here to understanding the historical and religious roots of the tension between the value system of the West and that of the Islamic civilization, at least as seen by some Muslims, as we have briefly discussed in the case of other civilizations, in the previous segment. In this segment, we dissect the notion of terrorism itself, its political dimension. We are therefore speaking of political terrorism as opposed to, let us say, a psychotic or maniacal act of terror driven by the mental imbalance of a perpetrator, such as in cases of sick criminals or tyrants. There may as well be criminal terrorist acts without a political dimension as in cases where the intentions or motive of the perpetrator is to simply cause terror or when the consequence of the act, without an intended motive of terror, produces generalized fear in the population or a group of people.

We therefore have to define an act of political terrorism more precisely here. We define political terrorism as any act of terror motivated by a political motive, which we call a grievance. From such a grievance derives the end goal of terrorist groups, which in many cases is simply the wish, need, and demand to satisfy the cause of grievance. Such causes of grievance may vary, from quest to or access to political power, influence, and from territorial claims to seeking to assert their ideology, etc.

Political goals can be achieved in many ways and through a variety of means and strategies. The question then becomes why some groups with a political grievance choose the strategy of terrorism to seek the achievement of their goal. This seems to be an odd choice given the fact that acts of terror do not entail any compelling plausible reason why it is a better means to achieving a political goal. Terrorism engenders negative reaction, retaliation, and determination not to surrender on the part of those victimized by terror. In addition, as stated in the previous segment, these groups resort to terror exactly because they are in no position of engaging in traditional confrontation, *mano a mano* with those they deem standing in their way, as those standing in their way are usually larger structures such as states or international organizations or norms. Terrorist acts therefore do come full circle, as they seek to achieve goals through means that seem to move them further away from achieving their goals, but the reason why they choose the means of terrorism is exactly because they have a sense, all along, that their goals may not be achievable through any other political means or venue. The logical end of this process transforms terrorism into a goal. The capacity of such groups to inflict terror becomes the finality of their reason d'être. Hence, we live to fear what new act of terrorism they will be able to successfully carry out, and we think less of how close they are coming to reaching their goal.

The peculiarity of groups with a political motive to becoming terroristic lies in the self-defeating choice of terrorism as a means of achieving their goal. All these elements taken into account, they inform our definition of an act of political terrorism. As a result we define it as:

> an act of violence by individual(s) born out of a sense of frustration and disillusionment for a successful outcome to a cause/grievance (political, economic, religious, cultural, etc.) aiming at inflicting suffering/cost to a real or perceived enemy who cannot be fought conventionally (based on its superiority).[9]

THE ANATOMY OF A TERRORIST ACT

Dissecting a terrorist act based on the definition supplied above we have before our eyes, the following elements: actors, cause, target, violence, goal (ideal and realistic), effect, and side effect. Let us proceed with elucidating each element further.

Actors of an act of terror may be loose individuals, part of a group or organization, often with a mastermind. The mastermind is the ideological leader who provides the idea, the purpose, and the benefit of the acts of terror to followers. As they are not the ones that personally carry out acts, they rely on courageous and most zealous brain, who becomes the strategist to planning and executing acts. These strategists often instruct willing souls how to execute. Executions may be carried out by zealous followers in isolated operations (the attack on the USS *Cole* in October 2000, the underwear bomber, the shoe bomber), or by a group in concert for specific tasks (the bombing of the train in Madrid, Spain, in March 2014), or for a larger operation in scale that necessitates many hands (the case of September 11). Besides all actors actively involved, there are many more in supportive roles who remain unknown and often unsuspected.

The cause of terrorist acts is the grievance as a result of an existing conflict, disagreement, or discord often between established and entrenched structures and a lesser powerful opponent. Such causes of conflicts are in nature political in a sense that they often are about a matter of interest to a larger group and its claim for either power, control legitimacy, recognition, etc. The imbalance in the rapport de force between the parties in conflict is why terrorism becomes a means of choice for the less powerful opponent, as the less powerful reckon with their inability to solve the conflict through any other means.

Target is an integral part of a terrorist act, as the success of the act depends on accessing the target, on the meaning of the target both for the perpetrators and their potential victims. Target determines the casualties and resonance or advertisement of the act of terror, as some targets have more resounding effect than others. Targets, when reached, are a measure of success for the perpetrators themselves, as it allows their confidence to rise and their establishment in the community of other terrorist groups and Islam as a whole. Such success becomes then an argument to recruit or entice aspiring terrorists to join the group. As a result targets are often people, as they are accessible, they are a soft target that allows for a "success." In addition people as casualties procure the highest resonance and bring the benefit that terrorist groups associate with such advertisement. Next to people, landmarks and public infrastructure are some such targets that meet the criteria of access, meaning, resonance, and casualties. Only here, the casualties are not human lives but material resources. If they cannot directly produce human casualties, making their victims bleed, terrorists are almost equally content to make them bleed through finances.

Violence, as an element of an act of terrorism, is a way of ensuring the bleeding of the enemy. Bleeding does not occur as a result of a tender touch but rather as a result of an aggressive act. Violence is an extreme expression of an aggressive act. Acts of terrorism as a result produce a harmful dimension, which explains the casualties they are designed to produce. Here, again, the higher the casualty count the more successful the act of terror has been from the perspective of the perpetrators. If violence is a measure of success, more violence guarantees more success. We then are astonished at the degree of what some in the US media refer to as "evil" that seems to characterize acts of terrorism.

Goal is the end result of any reasoned act. Goals however are the link to cause. There is a reason why we act a certain way. It is often because of a cause. Cause therefore motivates our actions. Hunger motivates the quest for food. Finding food is linked to hunger. Finding food is therefore designed to remedy hunger. An act of terror has a goal linked to its cause. And only if and when our action leads to food, then we can deem our action to have met its goal. Terrorist acts are therefore actions that have a goal, which is linked to a cause. September 11 was an act. Its cause was dissatisfaction with US policy based on its own interest and goals and presence in the Middle East. The goal was to rid the Middle East of US policy and influence. But Islamic terrorist groups, affiliated or not with al-Qaeda, have no chance of getting the United States to drastically change its policy in a way that suits them. This means they had no hope for their goal to be met. This leads us to distinguishing between ideal goals and realistic goals. The difference between these two categories of goals in this context is that the ideal goal is the actual cause of grievance that a group has. This cause of grievance can be political, as is the case here. And a political, logical way to dealing with it would be to engage the United States to get it to change its ways in the Middle East. This course however was not charted, because, as stated earlier, of its minimal, almost nonexistent, chance for success. These groups then resort to what we call the realistic goal of terrorism, namely, to vent the frustration of the terrorist group through ways that make the enemy pay. The ability and capacity to vent the frustration in order to make the enemy pay then becomes the more realistic goal.

Fear is an integral part of a terrorist act. It justifies the stem of the term terrorism. Beside the fact that acts of terror are carried out with violence and therefore produce casualties, they produce as well fear. Fear is an emotion. It can be instrumentalized to any number of ends, outcomes, and purposes. Here it can be instrumentalized for political purposes. Terrorist acts are thought of theoretically as a means to inject fear, hoping to instrumentalize fear by the enemy to get them to change their way. In this scenario fear would be instrumentalized for a political outcome. But we have established that such an outcome is often not what acts of terrorism inspire. They inspire the opposite reaction, namely, resilience. And because in such a case, a terrorist act and the fear it engenders cease to be instrumental for inducing change, it becomes a goal in and of itself. The fear that a terrorist act brings becomes then the end goal of the act. Terrorism becomes then about injecting fear. The terrorist group derives in such a case its reason d'être from the fact that it is feared, from the fact that the enemy reckons with it.

Side effect is an element of any act of terror that is inherent to terrorism. In its very nature an act of terror injects fear. Fear is a direct effect of terrorism, but the side effect of an act of terrorism is about the consequence of the fear, which is itself the effect of a terrorist act. In other words, the fear we have gained as a result of a terrorist act changes us, our behavior, outlook, and sensibility. It is the lingering effect of the fear itself caused by an act of terrorism. And because the ideal goals of most terrorist groups cannot be achieved through institutional political processes, these groups make the achieving of both the effect and the side effect of terrorism their most realistic goal. They therefore must rejoice at the thought and realization that their enemies are preoccupied with the idea that they might strike again. Such preoccupation has been indeed present in the United States since September 11, 2001. It has become increasingly part of the culture to worry about it and part of the cultural measures and practices have been put into place to reduce the risks. In the public sphere, public venues and event security measures that used to be geared toward possible domestic disturbances now have in mind even larger and potentially more deadly foes, namely foreign terrorism, essentially driven by a certain fundamentalistic interpretation of jihad against the United States. The screening at airports, the biometric fingerprinting, the Patriot Act, profiling of individuals who fit the profile of a prototypical terrorist, the requirement to hold a passport to travel to Canada, etc., are residual effects of the attack in 2001. They constitute a side effect of the attacks.

The harm from fear and its side effects is that it reaches a deeper level. It is the level of the psyche. A soldier in war or open conflict may have fear but it is fear of which the necessary elements are known and it becomes a material fear of simply losing the soldier's life. The enemy is known. The battlefield is geographically determined. The size, means, capability, and personnel of the other side; terms of the end game; the timetable; and even the standards of conduct of war are known in a classic conventional war. An open conflict or war, in which the counterpart is a terrorist group, loses the almost securing elements of the known factors. The unknown factors become an additional burden and cause of stress. The stress of the unknown needs to be managed just like in war or open conflict. The stress factor becomes a war in and of itself that needs to be won. And as long as the enemy is out there, there is truly no peace. This was made clear at the news announced by President Barack Obama of the death of Osama bin Laden in May 2011. The spontaneous expressions of joy around the country in the United States that the news sparked could partly be explained by the fact that the person made responsible for the attack of September 11, 2001, had been captured and killed, but also because the spectre of an Osama bin Laden out there simply meant a possibility of another sinister coup against the United States was removed. This unsettling thought of a living Osama bin Laden could be erased from the mind with the announcement of his death.

DESIGNATION OF INDIVIDUALS, GROUPS, OR ASSOCIATED ENTITIES AS TERRORISTS

The definition of terrorism we have provided, as well as the one from the US government, allows calling any act that fits the mold terrorism, not only those acts perpetrated by Muslim individuals, groups, or associated entities. It allows as well the designation as terrorist a number of individuals, groups, or associated entities from anywhere around the world.

The definitions also entail the dimensions of action, intent, and activity conducive to such terrorist actions as falling under the comprehension of terrorism. Based on these definitions, criteria used to designate and list specific individuals, groups, or related entities as terrorists are derived. The UN has a list of individuals associated with al-Qaeda but also entities and other groups and undertakings associated with al-Qaeda. The UN Security Council introduced Resolution 1267, establishing the 1267 Committee, in 1999, which is essentially a sanction regime initially pertaining to Afghanistan. There have been numerous other resolutions since, the last one to date was Resolution 2083 in 2012, reaffirming the imposition of such sanctions to names figured on the list. UN member states can propose names to be, listed just as they can request a delisting of names.

The listing that induces the sanctioning of individual terrorists, groups, or associated entities has since been common practice, more so in nations the most exposed to terrorist activity. The most important sanctions that listed names incur and that apply for both UN and US listed names consist of:

- The freezing of assets and funds
- Travel bans or restriction for entry or transit (of member states for the UN members)
- Prohibition of support, contact, membership, association, business (supplying, selling, transferring of arms)

The United States has been at the forefront in dealing with terrorism. The United States has more elaborate legislation on terrorism and a listing procedure. Names designated and listed by the United States reflect the legal criteria it has established. To be designated and listed as terrorist individuals, groups, or entities, they must meet the following criteria, under section 219 of the Immigration and Nationality Act (INA):

- It must be a foreign organization.
- The organization must *engage in terrorist activity or terrorism, or retain the capability and intent to engage in terrorist activity* as defined in relevant US government documents.
- The organization's terrorist activity or terrorism must threaten the security of US nationals *or* the national security (national defense, foreign relations, *or* the economic interests) of the United States.

As for the United States, a listing of terrorist groups or organizations around the world, according to the US Department of State, produced the names listed in Table 6.1.

Countries with a terrorist legislation have their own mechanisms and criteria of designation leading to listing and delisting of names of terrorist groups or entities.

Such listings, and because of the legal consequences they bring along, have been criticized for not giving to individuals, groups, or organizations

Table 6.1.

Terrorist Groups	Active in:
Abdul Nidal Organization	EU, Canada, Great Britain, USA
Abbu Sayyaf	Australia, EU, UK, USA
Al Aqsa Martyrs' Brigade	Canada, EU, USA
al-Gama'a al Islamiyya	Canada, EU, Russia, UK, USA
al-Qaeda	Australia, EU, India, Russia, UK, USA, Iran
al-Qaeda in the Arabian Peninsula	Australia, Canada, Saudi Arabia, USA
al-Qaeda in Maghreb	Australia, Canada, Russia, USA
Al Shabaah	Australia, Canada, UK, USA
Ansar al Islam	Australia, Canada, UK, USA
Aum Shinrikyo	Canada, Kazakhstan, USA
Boko Haram	Canada, UK, USA
Caucasus Emirate	Canada, Russia, UK, USA
Egyptian Islamic Jihad	Canada, EU, USA
ETA	Canada, UK, USA
Hamas	Canada, Egypt, EU, USA
Hezbollah	Canada, Egypt, UK, Turkey, USA
Hezbollah (external security)	
Islamic Jihad Movement in Palestine	Australia, Canada, Egypt
Islamic Movement of Uzbekistan	Australia, Canada, UK, Russia, USA
Islamic State of Iraq and the Levant	Australia, Canada, Saudi Arabia, USA
International Sikh Youth Federation	Canada, EU, India, UK
Jabht al-Nusra	Australia, UK, Saudi Arabia, Turkey, USA
Jaish e-Muhammed	Australia, Canada, India, UK, USA
Kurdistan Workers Party	Australia, Canada, EU, Iran, Turkey, UK, USA
Lashkar-e-jhangvi	Australia, Canada, UK, USA
Muslim Brotherhood	Egypt, Saudi Arabia, Russia
National Liberation Army	Canada, EU, USA
Popular Front for the Liberation of Palestine	Canada, Egypt, USA
Revolutionary People's Liberation Party Front	EU, Russia, UK, USA
Revolutionary Armed Forces of Colombia	Canada, EU, USA
Shining Path	Canada, EU, USA
Osbat al Ansar	Canada, UK, USA

Source: United Nations

designated as terrorist either the possibility to argue their case or a heads up. Indeed, they have been criticized for being the products of specific interest groups that have more influence with specific governments. In some cases, the same individuals and groups, or that in some case, the same individuals and groups that once have collaborated with a given government, may find themselves on the list simply because the interest or the policy of that state has changed.

A WORLDWIDE LIST OF TERRORIST
GROUPS AND THEIR THEATER OF OPERATION

Many terrorist individuals, groups, or associated entities operate in more than one country or region. Indeed some operate worldwide. Taken into account those operating in at least three different countries, we have the following picture.

THE CHALLENGES OF TERRORISM

Terrorism poses a number of challenges to the opposing party, the target of terrorist activity. These challenges derive from the elusive context within which terrorism and terrorists operate, the unknown factors mentioned above, namely, no clear battlefield or enemy line, no classic enemy, no way of knowing the size or capability of the opponent, no clear terms of the conduct of war, no standards to uphold, no timetable, etc. These loose ends open the gate for numerous adjacent factors, which all can be lumped into one word: elusiveness. Concretely, the elusiveness of terrorists is primarily their rapport with geography. Although the location, city, and region we operate in are known, terrorist individuals and/or groups remain geographically unbound. Their radius and circumference of action are large enough to remain illusive. Their modus operandi is informal enough to function principally underground. They blend with their environment to create the illusion of nonexistence. Although some are constituted in groups their groups and organizations do not function in a sedentary manner, whereas a state or any institutionalized sponsor of terrorism can be found. Aware of their illegal nature, their nefarious intent to the public at large, the operations of terrorist individuals or groups remain subtle and unsuspecting. Intelligence remains the only tactic to trace their subtle and unsuspecting ways.

There are on the other hand terrorist groups whose actions and goals are local. Such is the case of the Boka Haram for instance. Although local, and therefore their operational basis is geographically identifiable, they still operate undercover and with ambush-based terrorist acts. There are terrorist groups whose scale and reach are global because their cause may be shared by others elsewhere, as is the case of Islam-linked terrorist groups. They are even more elusive. Many are informal, as they split based on religious, ethnic, and other affinity bases. They can even become a one-man show. They are therefore sporadic and can be spontaneous, unbound by institutional rigidity or chain of command. They all have learned to become even more subtle since the United States under the Bush administration began what President Bush called the *war on terror*. As a result, there is no headquarters to speak of, and where there is one it is simply nominal. There is no battlefield where to expect them to be.

The elusiveness of terrorism can be secondarily institutional. Institutions are traceable. They are rigid, they are embedded in a legal, personnel, and infrastructural architecture, all of which render them a large target, easy to reach. Indeed some of such institutionalized groups with ties to terrorism have been targeted by tools made possible through institutional liberalism. Their financial transactions, assets, and other investments could be traced, stopped, or even ceased. The United States has identified and branded some of these organizations as sponsors of terrorism. Many terrorist groups, however, do not reflect this institutional mode described. When they rely on institutional means, these institutions are covert. They operate under pseudo names or cover of legal organizations, and certainly aware of the watchful eye of the United States.

Terrorism is elusive thirdly because it is uncontrollable through established means established by and known to the international system of states. One such means is the mechanism of hegemonic order. The US hegemonic power of the current international order has been itself the principle target of terrorism, which is to say that terrorism is not fazed by the hegemon. Warfare is another means through which to come to terms with a renegade state in the state system. Terrorist groups, although increasingly recognized as non-state international actors are, however, no such actors that can be dealt with through conventional interstate warfare. The United States has been involved in the asymmetric nature of engaging such a nonstate actor since September 11, 2001. The nature of such an asymmetric conduct of war against terrorism is one that does not know any end game. There is no such thing as a victory or defeat. The trophy to be held is itself undefinable. The entire endeavor of fighting against terrorism is by itself an open-end case with moments of calm and phases of calamity. The end game is ideally the end of grievance, or the end of adherence to terrorism as a legitimate strategic of engaging a perceived enemy.

Fourth, terrorism is a method, a strategy, or an option to apply. It exists independently of the social world. It becomes part of the social world from the reality of the existing social world. Such reality dictates the appeal of terrorism as an approach to embrace. As such, terrorism does not disappear or die with the number of dying terrorists. It disappears or dies in the social world as an appealing means to face a powerful opponent, if and when the conditions that make it appealing are no longer given. And because such conditions in the social world cannot be forever excluded, terrorism will remain a tool that can be utilized by groups that find it to be a viable option for their grievance, any time. We will not get rid of terrorism as an approach. We can only get rid of terrorists or of conditions that make terrorism appealing to some.

NOTES

1. Patrick O'Neil, *Essentials of Comparative Politics*, 2010.

2. Gramsci understood cultural imperialism as a process through which cultural institutions are instrumentalized to cement the structure of capitalism, whileFoucault sees in institutions the cultural instrument of power in which the socialization of the individual unfolds through an acquisition of a knowledge system that is itself designed to support the power structure. Institutions, power, and knowledge are Foucault's recurrent themes.

3. This has been a question much debated in the United States in the aftermath of September 11, 2001, pertaining to detainees held in Abu Ghraib in Iraq or those taken from the battlefields of Afghanistan and brought to Guantanamo Bay.

4. Rhoads Murphey, *East Asia: A New History*, 2004.

5. Italics added.

6. Bagdad, the North and the South.

7. Some Muslims have simply embraced secular political ideologies of nationalism or even socialism. The rest have found other ways. There are those embracing modernity, known as Kemalists, and there are those, known as reformists, who have voluntarily selected, filtered, and explored the possibilities of remaining faithful to Islam while living a modern life.

8. Basam Tibi, *Islam's Predicament with Modernity*, 2009.

9. Following is the official US government definition: "[An] act of terrorism, means any activity that (A) involves a violent act or an act dangerous to human life that is a violation of the criminal laws of the United States or any State, or that would be a criminal violation if committed within the jurisdiction of the United States or of any State; and (B) appears to be intended (i) to intimidate or coerce a civilian population; (ii) to influence the policy of a government by intimidation or coercion; or (iii) to affect the conduct of a government by assassination or kidnapping." *United States Code Congressional and Administrative News, 98th Congress, Second Session*, 1984, Oct. 19, volume 2; par. 3077, 98 STAT. 2707 [West Publishing Co., 1984].

Chapter Seven

The Global Space

From the Columbian Epoch to Globalization

A TRADE-DRIVEN INTEGRATION PROCESS

The global space as we have come to understand it is the product of a process of history. Our physical world is vast enough to entail a variety of constitutive geographic locales, locations and places, regions, and continents in which humans, since the Paleolithic era, fairly minded their own business in their own isolated communities. Large or small, their communities eventually developed their own societal systems and cultures (customs, value systems, languages) and adhered to various worldviews, belief systems, and religions. But they have not remained secluded nor do they exchange in just their immediate geographic proximity with their neighbors. They have eventually looked past their own communities and borders. Indeed, the history of mankind is characterized by a dynamic process not only qualitatively, as it produces different eras, epochs, and periods with their own distinct marks, but also geographically, as it produces a movement of peoples that we call migration or the colonization process, from one geographic area into others. Among such migratory and colonization processes, one in particular stands out, namely, the one at the beginning of the modern era, in the early 1500s. It was an era that in 1904 the British geographer Mackinder called the Columbian era. It has been characterized by a gained momentum in a process of linking the variety of peoples existing on the planet, triggered by the European quest to access markets in Asia Minor first and later in Far East Asia. The result, an unintended one at that, was more than just establishing trade with faraway regions. It was the beginning of an integration process that eventually led to a new paradigm we are currently in the middle of, namely, globalization. In the end, the history of mankind has been characterized by a journey of an integration process from isolated tribal communities to the consciousness of a global community.

History is indeed dynamic because human beings, who write and produce it, are themselves dynamic. Everything about them is dynamic. World history seems to be driven by centrifugal forces. We are constantly part of a process of history, as if we are on a journey leading somewhere, a question that pre-occupied the philosopher F. W. Hegel (2010). In this journey we move from any given epoch into the next, and we seem to lend credence to what the philosopher elsewhere (Hegel 1816) describes as a process (*prozess*), namely, that the essence of being is becoming.

Human beings are dynamic, as they constantly seek greener pastures, both literally and figuratively. Their political powers seek to expand their space of influence. Their religions seek new converts. And their commerce needs new markets to enhance the basis and potential for material welfare and security. Responding to this dynamic that seems to be inherent to human existence, we forcefully produce either by design or involuntarily, integration. The colonization process by European powers since the modern era has been the decisive precursor of globalization. Both these eras or paradigms, colonization and globalization, have allowed people to meet, civilizations to encounter each other, religions to reach new flocks, politics to expand its space of action and influence, and new markets and new products to be accessed. These two eras or paradigms were and are driven by commerce and trade. Commerce and trade have the ability to carry along, to condition, to transform, the rest of other areas of human endeavor, politics, society, individual lives, even religions, as they too, are grounded in the materiality of the social world.

We have come a long way from isolated, parochial, secluded, or regionally confined communities to understanding that we are all on the same journey, that of the human experience, and that the history of mankind is just one world history. We are now in the process of developing a global culture (institutions, values, and norms) that bind people and nations and in the process their fates. We have increased the scale and scope of our individual exchanges across nations. Our institutions of global governance have supranational competence. Businesses and corporations look at the world as a marketplace. Our national economies are intertwined. Our nations have fewer and fewer enemies and more and more partners.

All these events are recent developments. How then did we concretely get where we are today? To answer the question we must trace the history of world trade. The practice of trade seems to be an organic reflex. It existed as early as the human communities had become sedentary. It had reached a noticeable extent in the time of the Silk Road, since the Han Dynasty (206 BC–220 AD), commercially linking Rome to China. The more consequentially extensive trade has been that driven by an ideology of European mercantilism, consequential because although other trade routes existed prior to European mercantilism, namely, Chinese explorations up until the Ming Dynasty (1368 AD–1644 AD), they have remained without a self-sustained momentum. In fact the Ming Dynasty itself put an end to it. Initiated by Italian city-states around the eleventh century to the dawn of the modern era (1250–1453 AD), Venice's, Florence's, Genoa's, and Pisa's quest for products and goods from Asia Minor triggered an explosion of trade that far exceeded in scale and scope what any of the initially involved states and those that followed in trading could have imaged.

Indeed, after, and because of the success in wealth of the Italian city-states, other European states joined in. It soon became an all Western European phenomenon as Spain, the Dutch, the French, the Belgians, Great Britain, and Germany, to some extent, joined in.

Italian city-states had been trading for silk and spices from Asia; wool, metal, wine, and armor from the West; and slaves and salt from Dalmatia (the Adriatic Sea region, Croatia). The geography of the region dictated the crossing of the Black Sea, or at least access into the region through Turkey. This trade and its route were soon interrupted. The tensions between the Christians and Muslims over Jerusalem, which eventually produced a series of confrontations that Christians call the Crusades, eight all together from 1096–1270, were the reason for the first interruption of the Italian city-states' trade with Asia Minor. The tensions between Christians and Muslims made it difficult for the former to traverse the land of the latter. The interruption, however, was short-lived because of the incursion into the region by another imposing empire from the steppes of Mongolia, led by Hulagu Khan, the grandson of the great Genghis Khan. He conquered Bagdad, subjugating the Abbasid Caliphate in 1258, which allowed the reopening of the route to trade with Asia Minor. With the reopening of the route, trade flourished again, allowing the Italian city-states, with Venice having the most trading posts, to grow richer, a development that partially explains why Italy became the locus of origin of the Renaissance. The era of the Mongols in Islamic land did, however, not last and did not change in any way the character and weight of Islam in the region. Islam, the vanquished, had become the conqueror of the Mongols. The Mongols faded, as many of their descendants converted to Islam and were absorbed into the Islamic culture. Mohammad Abduh noted, "The Islamic lands were invaded by the Tartar peoples, led by Jenghiz Khan, pagans who despoiled the Muslims and were bent on total conquest, plunder and rapine. But it was not long before their successors adopted Islam as their religion and propagated it among their kin with the same consequences as elsewhere" (Donahue and Esposito 2007, p. 22).

Around 1250 the rivalry between Turkish tribes and their chieftaincies, among which were the Seljuks and the Mamluks, was in the process of producing an emerging regional leader. The emerging leader was a chief among the Seljuks, who would soon declare his independence in 1299, and his bravery would lead him to the creation of one of the historically recognized empires, the Ottoman Empire, in place between 1299 and 1922. As the power of this nascent Muslim empire grew, so did its claim and eventually its grip on the entire Islamic world. The Ottoman Empire was to rise to its highest glory in the mid-1450s. The only thorn in their eye was the existence of the Byzantine Empire, which naturally was a nemesis because it was so close, so rich, and so Christian. The valiant sultan Mehmet, known as the Conqueror, eventually, after several attempts and failed assaults, succeeded into sacking Constantinople in the year 1453. Reigning supreme there was no one to challenge the empire. The only rival would become Russia but only because the Ottomans would venture too far in their quest for more land to call their own. In the quest they entered the Balkans and tried in vain to enter Western Europe, as they were defeated in Passarowitz in 1718. Eventually, Ottoman rule would encompass the entire region from western Asia to Asia Minor and from the Middle East to Egypt. During that time, access to the Black Sea by the Italian city-states was blocked a second time. This time with the Ottoman Empire at the height of its power, there was no hope for a reopening of the route; a new route was needed.

In the meantime, since the Crusades, Europeans had learned about a more important market in the Far East. Access to the Asian market was even more enticing. Geography would dictate a possible alternative route, consisting of circumventing the Asian landmass, whose entry would have meant crossing paths with the Ottomans. Circumventing the landmass meant embarking on a sea route around the continent of Africa. It was a route not traveled before, meaning the risk factor was high. However, with the new technology of the compass and the pioneering efforts by the Portuguese in shipbuilding, allowing them to use caravels, two elements were available to reduce the risk factor: the maneuverability and speed of the caravels and a new navigation tool to provide guidance at sea.

Less enthusiastic and less adventurous, but also already wealthy, Italian city-states were reluctant to test the new route. The adventure was pioneered by the Portuguese, who were eager to capitalize on trade. They had been familiar with the sea, as their adventures in North Africa had served as training. They continued to reach the western coasts of Africa, with growing confidence, driven by prospects of new riches (such as gold), which they had heard of from the Arabs, who had already been familiar with Africa since the seventh century AD. The Portuguese and the rest of the would-be colonial powers would not stop until eventually reaching Asia with their many explorers, including Diego Cao, Magellan, Vasco da Gama, Pizarro, Cortes, Vespucci, and Columbus, to name just a few. With any major sea journey the interest and enthusiasm back in Europe grew, as the benefits were made tangible. A pattern was arising in this adventure. It consisted of a group of merchants, influential elite, or kings and queens who needed a few courageous explorers. These explorers organized expeditions. From these expeditions followed exploration of the geography of the new lands. From these explorations followed exploitations. From exploitation followed colonization. The above-mentioned European states gradually bought into the pattern.

A new paradigm was emerging: European expansionism, colonization, and colonial imperialism.

COLONIZATION ERA

Although the modern era started with the need by Europeans to reach Asian markets in the 1500s, to trigger what Halford Mackinder referred to as the Columbian Epoch, rendering homage to the Italian explorer Columbus in the service of King Ferdinand and Queen Isabella. It is the epoch that has produced a linkage of various regions and continents of the planet since the 1800s, from Europe to Africa, from Asia to the Americas, from Australia to the many Pacific Islands, prompting Mackinder (1905) to speak of the world as a closed system. The European colonization of these territories was a by-product of such a process. This by-product, in fact, turned out to be the main heritage of the epoch. It turned out to be the main heritage because the functional and infrastructural foundation of institutional liberalism, which is the global system we live in, would not have been possible without the prior effects of integration of different regions of the globe, trade, and adhesions to the growing number of international agreements produced as a result of the Columbian Epoch. But the road to where we are today has not just progressively evolved. The different parts of the closed system produced by colonization were first essentially protectionistic, as each colonial power jealously protected its territories and resources within to the detriment of liberalists pushing for a more free market since Adam Smith. The protectionistic mindset was to last until World War I and beyond. It eventually took until the end of World War II to build the institutional infrastructure to truly produce a closed system.

Seen from this perspective, one can hardly exaggerate the importance and significance of colonization. Regardless of whether Western colonization of non-Western territories is perceived as salutary or detrimental to the latter, a topic much debated for years and explored in many books (which we will not discuss here), it remains a fact that it has allowed the West to export some key features of its history and civilization abroad. Among such key features we count the nation-state model and its administrative infrastructure, international trade, Christianity, political ideologies, and the intermingling of the peoples, to name just a few.

TRADE AND MODERN ECONOMIC SYSTEMS

Trade is older than modern economic systems (communism, socialism, capitalism, dirigisme, social market economy, etc.). It precedes the existence of nation-states. It does not depend on government, as the needs of people precede the existence of government. Trade has been a potent driving force of history, as it has always been more than just about the exchange of goods and value. Trade has allowed the exchange of ideas and the spread of technologies, knowledge, cultural identity factors such as religions and languages, and even exchanges through intercultural and interracial marriages simply because trade is exercised by human beings who do not exist in a vacuum. And it is this all-encompassing dimension of trade that justifies its linkage to both economic systems and political systems.

Matters of economic activity were discussed by thinkers and theorists interested in suggesting the best way to improve the economic life of their communities. Theorists such as the physiocrats in France argued for a greater free circulation of goods and products in the 1600s and 1700s. They were followed by the British classical theorists, from Adam Smith (1723–1790) and David Ricardo to John Stuart Mill (1806–1873). These theorists and the economic system of liberalism they advocated carved out a prominent role for trade in their thinking (theory of trade), suggesting its promise and benefit to all participants. But a new approach to economics then emerged since the mid-nineteenth century, later labeled communism or socialism. The difference between them being the degree of radicalism of absence of private property, the former being the accomplished form of collectivism. Socialism or communism as argued by Karl Marx in his Manifesto published in 1848, one of the many collaboration products with Friedrich Engels, castigated trade in a role. Seen as an inherent consequence of the market economy he repudiated, Marx argued against both the arguments and mercantilists who practiced trade with protectionism and the liberalists who argued in favor of free trade. The only benefit that Marx saw in free trade was that it would internationalize the awareness of the proletariat class and hasten the revolution against factory owners.

Trade, Marxism argues, is the tool that reinforced and sustained the exploitative mechanism of capitalism. This market economy known as capitalism, a brain child of liberalism, as Marx saw it, was exploitative of the masses without means of production, allowing their labor to be alienated from their humanity. Marx's approach was stressed in the light of the social consequences of the Industrial Revolution at home in Europe and abroad in the light of colonial resources expropriation and labor exploitation by Europeans.

There will be other nuanced expressions of economic systems such as dirigist economies, social market economies, or corporatist economies.

These economic systems emerge because more than just being about trade, economics has an encompassing social material purpose, organizing production, ensuring survival, and generating prosperity. Economics is linked to society. And because collective social choices for the welfare and well-being of society are the prerogatives of politics, economics is political, and economic systems are congenitally political. Indeed, a high unemployment rate is both economical and political. Raising interest rates and the minimum wage are both economic and political phenomena.

THE CONGENITAL BIRTH OF MODERN
ECONOMIC AND MODERN POLITICAL SYSTEMS

These various economic systems therefore differ because each expounds a different idea or ideals around the notion of wealth and prosperity that economic activity generates. If economic systems are about wealth and prosperity, next is to establish the best way to generate wealth and prosperity; they ought to suggest who in society should benefit from it. And because economics is political in its essence, these economic systems ought to suggest what the role of the state or government should be in ensuring that economic activity generates wealth and prosperity that ought to go where society want them to go. The answer to the first question helps answer the second question. Indeed, the role of government or state in economic affairs depends on who society wants to benefit from economic activity of the nation.

Different economic systems provide different answers to these two questions. Mercantilism, which is an economic system no longer in practice, suggested that it was primarily the nation that ought to benefit from the wealth of the nation in what was known as economic nationalism in an era (early modern Europe) when political powers were contested. Liberalism argued that it is the individual worker and entrepreneur or corporations who should benefit from the fruits of their labor. The result is that the state should be minimalistic in what it does. It should just facilitate enterprise and investment in a laissez-faire fashion. Macroeconomic policy focusing on monetary policy (interest rates and money supply) and fiscal policy (taxation and spending), trade practices, and regulations are designed to meet that end goal. Communism and socialism argued that it is society that should benefit from the economic activity of the nation, and consequently the role of the government that derives from that argument is that the government should organize the economic life and activity to ensure the sharing of the national prosperity by all. Other economic systems such as the social market economy, in post–World War II Europe, suggested that society and the individual worker, entrepreneur, and corporation should benefit from the economic wealth generated by the nation. Here, as well, the consequence is an attempt to reconcile the disparity that the free market distributive process tends to produce and the need to service, through redistributive measures, those in society on the needy side of wealth distribution. The role of the government here is to accommodate both free entrepreneurship and society through social and public programs.

As these economic systems were in the process of making their respective cases throughout the mid-nineteenth and early twentieth centuries, Europe was in a state of constant political tension at home in the quest for continental supremacy and abroad to solidify their colonial empire status. In this context, the quest for power and the quest for wealth were intertwined. Protectionism became the preferred economic attitude until the end of the nineteenth and early twentieth centuries.

The early twentieth century came with the tumult that its early decades produced. Then came World War I caused by the unsettled and contentious Balkans, where the Russians, the Austro-Hungarian Empire, and the Ottomans had been rivals and competing for influence. The alliances formed in the war had produced conditions that only explained the post–World War I but also the time after. The Austrians were joined by the Germans and the Ottomans, who needed to be on the opposite side of the Russians, since Russia sided with the Serbs. Great Britain because of Germany's positioning joined the Russians. The first alliance was called the Triple Alliance and the second the Triple Entente. To these alliances came Japan, and Italy and the United States, respectively, to either side. At the end of World War I the alliance was on the losing side, which led to the collapse of both the Austro-Hungarian Empire and the Ottomans and the weakening of the rising Germany. Their collective demises were respectively sealed in the Treaty of Versailles in 1919 and that of Sevres in 1922. Both the Russians and the United States were on the winning side, and their time to assert themselves would soon come.

The aftermath of World War I was, by all accounts, not less tumultuous. It had produced increased protectionism, as partners shielded their markets and those of their colonies with tariffs as high as 32 percent in the United States in 1922 and as high as 41 percent in June 1930 on over 20,000 imported goods after the Smoot-Hawley Tariff Act was passed. Nations practiced a competitive depreciation, a deliberate depreciation of their currency value known as "beggar-thy-neighbor," which led to the collapse of the exchange rate mechanism and produced a world high unemployment rate (33 percent; Ravenhill 2011) and the Great Depression starting in 1929 and was prolonged as a result of retaliatory measures by US trading partners reacting to the Smoot-Hawley Tariff Act. The world economy was in bad shape. It needed rescuing. But who would take the job in a world characterized by the notion of anarchy and wherein states are expected to organize into creating the order they need? These states however were in a state of mistrust. It was a case for which hegemonic power is welcome to initiate the steps necessary to getting out of the crisis. The United States up until that time was, however, isolationist. Recognizing the need to intervene to stop the degradation of the world economy and the increasing broader interest of a growing world economic power, the United States would have a change of heart. The debate in Congress was shifting in favor of trade. In 1934 the Reciprocal Trade Agreement Act (RTAA), which gave the president the authority to negotiate foreign trade agreements without congressional approval and to promote trade liberalization, primarily between the United States and Latin America and European nations, Great Britain first, followed by the rest of the European nations. US foreign policy had been internationalist since 1934, but the willingness of the United States to act would have to wait. Germany, frustrated with living under the harsh and punitive terms of the Versailles Treaty, was starting to rebel. It had started violating one after the other of the terms stipulated in the treaty. Politically, the unsettling time of the interwar period had become a propitious and fertile ground for nationalistic ideology. Nationalism, which often combines political frustration and the cultural pride of a people in distress, became the theme of some forming political parties in Italy, Germany, Spain, and Portugal. This European nationalism also known from its Italian origin as fascism had some of the most effective leaders both in Italy under Mussolini and in Germany under Hitler. Their grand vision of strong totalitarian expansive and domineering nations led to World War II, as Hitler seemed not be satisfied with anything he had and kept going for more until he was stopped in the Russian winter in its Operation Barbarossa and by the Allies in 1945.

At the end of World War II, once again Germany was on the losing side, and both Russia and the United States were on the winning side. Russia and the United States had increasingly consolidated their standing, the United States through a thriving economy that had become the largest in the world and Russia through a rush of industrialization driven by the Communist

Party's need to provide labor to the proletariat and to assert the worth of communism and its ability to stand its ground in a hostile world.

But these two rising superpowers were on opposite sides due to their ideologies. Their political ideologies were at the same time reflections of their economic systems, on one hand, collectivitist, and the other hand, liberalist. These ideologies are both political and economical.

THE TWO WORLDS BEFORE GLOBALIZATION

These rising superpowers subscribed to different visions of the role of economics in society. These two different visions were naturally antithetical, as the philosopher Hegel would have called it, considering their opposing essence and maybe their inherent imperfections, which would suggest a need for a synthesis as a compromise model.

The ground was set for a rivalry after these two emerging superpowers successfully together managed the strategy of ending the war and secured the terms of coexistence in Germany and beyond through respectively the Yalta Conference (February 4–11, 1945) and the Potsdam Conference (July 17–August 2, 1945). It is this rivalry that characterized the post–World War II era, known as the Cold War Era, which lasted from 1945 to 1991. During the Cold War Era, the Soviet Union, Eastern European nations of the Warsaw Pact (a security regime, the likes of NATO, comprising the Soviet Union and its Western European satellite nations), and all those in the rest of the world, in Africa, Latin America, and Asia. The satellite nations who were sympathetic to communism would coalesce to organize their societies applying, as much as they could, Marxist teachings. They were the East. On the other side was the West, the camp of liberalists, at least, the non-communists, led by the United States, and in its camp, western European nations, members of the security regime, and the North Atlantic Treaty Organization (NATO), created for purposes of collective security.

Politically and economically, the world was divided into two major ideological blocks, claiming different geographic spaces: the Eastern and Western hemispheres. The world's geopolitics consisted of expanding the sphere of influence for either camp by making new friends and allies, preferably encroaching into the sphere of influence of the rival, or better yet, by flipping the allegiance of those nations that already belonged to one camp to moving into one's own. Under these geopolitical circumstances, any process toward a more integrative dynamics of world politics was stalled. The Cold War was, therefore, from the perspective of a world history dynamic, moving toward more integration was on hiatus. And like all hiatuses this one was to end eventually.

The Soviet Union had, in the early phase of the Cold War, a momentum with a series of events happening in its favor. What were those events? A number of newly independent nations from the developing world were finding some attraction to communist ideology for diverse reasons, such as anti-imperialism, anticolonization, and some even anti-Western. Among such nations in Asia were China, Vietnam, North Korea, Cambodia, and Laos. In Africa were the People's Republic of Congo, Guinea, Egypt, Zimbabwe, Mozambique, Angola, and Ethiopia under Mangistu. In the United States' own backyard were Cuba, Nicaragua, and Chile under Allende. The Soviet Union had successfully tested and acquired its atomic nuclear weapon in August 1949, cutting into the US monopoly since World War II. The communist bloc was making progress, which naturally meant reduced influence of the liberalist world and the United States spearheading its bloc. The progress of the communist world became a cause of concern to the United States. A strategy to apply in order not to lose the ideological rivalry of the Cold War was needed.

In the United States, the National Security Council had designed a foreign policy published in a document (Resolution 68, or NSC68), known as containment, to that end. Officially adopted by the Truman administration it became known as the Truman Doctrine throughout the 1950s. The Korean War, the Vietnam War, and the tension between the United States and Cuba and the missile crisis are the expressions of the application of the policy of containment. The ideological rivalry between the two blocs also explains the many involvements of both the Soviet's (KGB) and United States' (CIA) secret and covert operations throughout the world to support their respective causes in the 1950s, 1960s, 1970s, and 1980s.

In the West, the liberalist world, a debate had ensued in the aftermath of World War II. It consisted of finding ways to avoid wars in which Europe was essentially the theater, but also getting back at organizing international trade that had collapsed in the interwar period. But first, the causes of both wars and economic disintegration had to be found and eliminated. Two main culprits were soon identified, namely, the mistrust that reigned among these European nations, and second, was the protectionistic mode they had come to dwell in as a result of mercantile practices, which they had extended into their overseas colonies. To build the trust among European nations and to reignite international trade, more cooperation and more liberalism in commerce was emerging as the consensus. This consensus had the promise of killing two birds with one stone. Liberalizing trade among nations would promote growth in all participating partners, as Adam Smith argued and even explained how in his seminal work *The Wealth of Nations* (1776). The Cobden-Chevalier Treaty (1860) between Great Britain and France served as a model and proof but not convincing enough for all to emulate and allow it to become common practice throughout Europe. This was going to become the opportunity to institute the practice of free trade to promote wealth among nations. It was the proverbial first bird to be killed. The second proverbial bird to be killed was the promise that trade entails to building trust among nations that trade with one another. Trading partners are fundamentally not enemies. Their interests become intertwined. Their economic fate becomes linked. Consequently, they are linked via their respective political viability. Liberalism in international relations argues that trade among nations was the best means to peace as in the end, in the process, it promotes prosperity.

To reaching both these ends, peace and prosperity, liberalism relies on a few key principles or premises, namely, individual freedom and therefore free will and choice, and the equality of rights to exercise one's freedom and choice. To ensure that these fundamental rights are guaranteed, they must be protected. They are protected through binding documents and institutionalized practices. Liberalism in economics becomes, therefore, interested in institutionalizing the principles to guide the practice of commerce by enterprise, corporations, and nations under the conditions of its principles and premises.

As the consensus to promote trade emerged in the aftermath of World War II, the United States, now committed to internationalism and after becoming the largest economy in the West and beyond, was now gearing up to take the mantle of the hegemon. The United States took over the leadership role and the initiative, seconded by Great Britain. Under the leadership of the United States and Great Britain, the rest of the West undertook to organize international trade among those nations that had bought into the promise of liberalism. They designed the principle and institutional foundation of the international trade, during which process on the principle side two schools competed for ascendency, on one hand, one advocating a laissez-faire approach and on the other hand, another advocating for an interventionistic approach. The two approaches led respectively by the British negotiator John Maynard Keynes and the US negotiator John Dexter. The circumstances of post–World War II have rendered the need for more state supervision a necessity. The political mistrust leading to World War I, the economic chaos and dysfunction causing the collapse and even paving the way for World War II, left a trauma. The chaos and dysfunction have as well been partially explained by the lack of more authority of the governing institutions or the lack thereof. Under these circumstances, the interventionistic as the more suited to address the need for a supervisory authority of the governing had prevailed against the laissez-faire approach. On the institutional side, the International Monetary Fund (IMF) was created in July 22, 1944, to support a system of payment and receipt among nations, to lend money, and to stabilize exchange values of national currencies. In the same vein the World Bank was created in 1945 to encourage more trade. The need to lower or dismantle trade barriers and tariffs led to an accord known as the General Agreement of Trade and Tariffs (GATT, in 1947), which morphed into the World Trade Organization (WTO in 1995) to better respond to the complexity of trade brought about by a more open global trade and new products of the mind (intellectual property), often dealt with within the service sector, whose importance has grown exponentially in the last thirty years or so. There was the short-lived creation of the International Trade Organization (ITO, in 1948), whose provisions in favor of transfer into the developing nations met resistance from the industrialized nations and therefore never materialized.

The international economic order, known as the Bretton Woods Agreement, remained in place until the 1980s. A number of economic issues around the world provided the advocacy of a more liberal economic practice. What were these issues and who were these advocates of a more liberal economic structure?

The issues were chronic balance of payment in the developing nations, which compelled them to be constant clients of the Bretton Woods institutions of the World Bank and the IMF. The situation led to mounting debts and culminated with the insolvency of Mexico in the early 1980s. The industrialized nations were generously or under pressure to do more to help the developing nations. The interventionistic approach of the Bretton Woods institutions was now in question.

The advocates of a more liberal economic practice were the voices, primarily from academia, from Friedrich Hayek to Milton Friedman, arguing for an alternative to the interventionism approach. They argued in favor of an economic liberal state, that which let economic processes unravel without much intervening, whose monetary policy was restrictive and trade barriers dismantled. They trust the market. They trust the supply side economics. They put faith in liberalizing trade for a more and better distributive effect and wealth. They despise development aid, the welfare system, etc. Their arguments soon left the campuses to find the ears of political practitioners, the conservatives. In the 1980s, both the United States and Great Britain had the most ferocious and poignant advocates of this brain of academic liberalism that led the way for neoliberalism. William has come to use the expression the Washington Consensus—in 1982—to describe the convincing effort by these two conservative heads of state to getting other leading economies to agree with the need to change the way Breton Woods institutions were run, namely, abandoning interventionism for liberalization, deregulation, and even harmonization, a policy remedy more in tune with liberalism. Liberalization consists of liberalizing trade laws and practices, employment markets and prices, banking systems, and trade practices; reducing and removing trade barriers;

and reducing expenditures in the public sector. It advocates elimination of subsidizing and privatization of national enterprises, fiscal discipline, austerity, monetary devaluation, etc.

Deregulation consists of loosening trade laws and the exercise of political influence on market and trade activity. Harmonization aims at facilitating transactions among trade partners in the area of monetary policy. The era of neoliberalism had arrived not only for the conservatives in advanced economies but also to the rest of the nations subscribing to the Bretton Woods order. These were all nations of the Western hemisphere, as opposed to those that have aligned themselves with communism or socialism. Since the Washington Consensus, the influence of advanced economies in these institutions has made the difference in vulgarizing neoliberal policy measures way beyond these advanced nations. The institutions of Bretton Woods had been asked to introduce new economic structures into most of the developing nations, whose chronic balance of payment and debts were seen as a result of interventionism. As a result, these institutions had started tying their financial loans and assistance to a number of conditions that had been designed and packaged to remove state or government influence in economic processes. They recommended privatization, liberalization of trade, deregulation of commercial activity, and even harmonization of macroeconomics. These recommendations were sold as a packaged program known as the Structural Adjustment Programmes. The Bretton Woods institutions had become the bridge to divulge neoliberal remedies to the economic problems of the developing nations. Neoliberalism was now prevalent anywhere the Soviet Union no longer had an influence.

THE COLLAPSE OF THE SOVIET UNION
AND THE ADVENT OF GLOBALIZATION

In the early 1990s, the implosion of the Soviet Union was under way as a result of disagreements and in some ways the success of the reform initiatives introduced by Secretary General Mikhail Gorbachev. Fought by the communist hard-liners and well received by many, they were carried out by Yeltsin after the demise of Gorbachev and the ultimate collapse of the Soviet Union. The collapse of the Soviet Union and the communist bloc paved the way for an institutional liberalism and its free trade and market advocacy already practiced in the Western hemisphere and among those nations that had chosen the Western bloc to spread around the world, as there was no longer any other noteworthy contending political and economical ideology. The institutions of

Bretton Woods (IMF, World Bank, GATT/WTO) were instrumental in this spread of free market and trade gospel by implementing their Structural Adjustment Programmes designed to align the developing nations' economies with the principles of neoliberal economics. They then swiftly turned their attention to the nations previously aligned with the Soviets. The world was becoming a global market, a space wherein trade was to reign supreme without barriers. To these events came the advent of information technology or digital technology in the 1980s, with its ability to defy time and space through the use of the Internet. In the end, we define globalization as a process that allows an interconnectedness of all regions of the planet, not extensively as in the Columbian Epoch of explorations, but intensively as the quality of our exchanges has been improved exponentially and unprecedentedly.

The entire world is open to free market liberalism. States have become spaces of commerce. They have become markets. The economical, rather than the political, is increasingly driving relations among them. Although states remain sensitive and cautious about their security and strategic issues, they are equally eager to harvest the power of global liberalism. Each is preoccupied with ways to benefit from it and not to suffer the unforgiving consequences of a global competition and pressure they all face simultaneously. They must now open up to trade but remain wary of the implications of trade to their prosperity (wealth), and by implication to their security (might). Indeed states' distribution of capabilities is induced by economic wealth, and losing economic wealth simply leads to losing in the power ranking among nations.

Despites states' concerns and the implications of a wealth shift to the mighty, global liberalism has continued to run its course, like the wheel of history, which once in motion becomes difficult to alter its course or pace. Such motion of history is often altered only in its course or pace through new developments that we call paradigms. As for now global liberalism continues its course fueled by digital technology, which defies time and space. The entire process has heralded a new era, that of globalization. This term simply describes the spread of economic liberalism since the collapse of the Soviet Union with the consent of state-actors, which justify the institutionalization of liberalism and produce an interconnectedness of all regions of the globe. The Columbian Epoch allowed an extensive expansion of Europe and produced globalization, which today has allowed a more qualitatively intensive interconnectedness among nations through cyber space. Extensive expansion is aimed at reaching, exploiting, and even controlling new geographic spaces, whereas intensive expansion uses cyber space to exchange knowledge, ideas, images, sounds, etc. (see Figures 7.1 and 7.2).

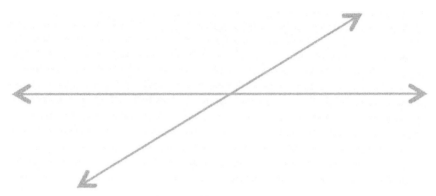

Figure 7.1. Extensive: Uses of geographic space

The globalization process, which was primarily driven by liberal trade as advocated by economic liberalism, has led to the creation of an institutional infrastructure, the World Trade Organization being part of that infrastructure, which has orchestrated the terms of a worldwide market economic system and rendered the nation-state permeable to foreign trade. This new reality in turn explains not only the growing interdependence among nations but

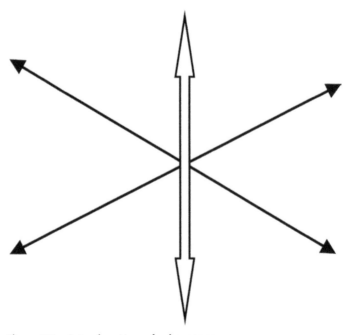

Figure 7.2. Intensive: Uses of cyber space

also explains the opening of the entire globe to becoming the theater, or the canvas, of not only trade activity but also all other activity revolving around trade, namely, production activity (businesses), individual lives (jobs), political activity (economic policy making), and even the culture of a society itself. Indeed, economic activity and economic systems have a way of determining societal processes in general. And globalization, in so far as it is essentially driven by economic exchanges, has increasingly affected the global society and its culture.

As a result, we are in the process of developing a global culture in which we are becoming familiar, through cyber space, with the intricate details of the lives of other people around the globe. They cease to be foreign and become inhabitants of this planet like we are.

The effects of worldwide liberalism are reverberating in all areas of human existence. Indeed the central role of economic activity in human life allows economics to play a key role in the organization of life itself and in culture in general. Karl Marx's analysis (1948) on the subject remains hardly refutable. The consequence of such assertions about the centrality of economic activity in culture explains why globalization, primarily an economic process, is producing such an epochal shift in all other areas of existence among inhabitants of the globe.

Chapter Eight

Globalization of Space and Its Implications

Since globalization, any activity has the potential of having a global scale effect as a result of the integration process started centuries earlier. The entire global space is now the theater of human activity. In this era of globalized activity we are left with just the liberal economic system as the economic system of choice by nation-states, with a couple of exceptions in South Korea and Cuba. All actors have since sought ways to best take advantage of this new reality. These actors are individuals, businesses, and aggregated actors, both governmental and nongovernmental. Adjusting to the conditions of a globalized world has brought about a variety of both opportunities and challenges that have affected the world of politics, the world of economics, and society.

WHAT DOES SPACE HAVE TO DO WITH IT?

Both opportunities and challenges of globalization are linked and understood through the expanding notion of space today. The myopic focus on ethnic communities has passed. The atavistic and nationalistic identification with a nation are challenged in many ways. The internationalization of supranational activity has intensified quantitatively through the flow of commerce, exchanges, movements of peoples, etc., and qualitatively because even without movement we reach faraway places thanks to the new information technologies. It is simply all about defying time and space. Time and space are the natural constrainers of human activity. Distances keep us apart, from communicating to seeing each other. To conquer distance requires time consumption through travel. If anything, the march of history has been up until today, slow because of the impediments of time and space. And then came the digital technology with the ability to considerably and effectively reduce their hindering effects on human activity. The result is an accelerated rate at which activity can proceed, and hence we accomplish more in less time and circumvent and overcome obstacles associated with space, among others, distance, better than ever before. The benefit to human activity is unquantifiable but enormous. All actors in this globalized era are benefiting. But just as they benefit, they must master challenges that come with changes. Such challenges are associated with the flow of activity, interconnectedness of national economies, and increased movement of peoples, and how people, governments, and businesses have had to adjust.

In this chapter we shall focus on challenges that the world of politics and its actors now have to reckon with as a result of doing politics in the era of globalization. We shall focus on the challenging implications of the spread of the liberal economic system, which now uses the globe as a marketplace, to its participants, namely, corporations, governments, and individuals. Finally, we focus on social and cultural challenges of globalization simply because society and cultures are shaped by economic systems of production in place on which they depend.

POLITICAL IMPLICATIONS OF GLOBALIZATION

The world of politics is naturally and congenitally linked to the world of economics. Although it is politics that determines the economic system, its practices, it is, however, economic systems that determine the role of government and politics. This is the case from mercantilism, communism/socialism to capitalism, whether in its interventionistic or social market or laissez-faire or developmental state approach.

This congenital fate of politics and economics also explains the fate of either. The fate of politics in the era of an intertwined global economic system has been essentially to face both the advantages and challenges of current times. Among the challengers, the world of politics has continually has had to take into account the existence, presence, role, and influence of supranational organizations created to deal with supranational issues, anywhere from trade, the environment, etc. Granted that these organizations do not function without the imitative, the vote, and the financing of individual nation-states, but their relevance has continued to increase as more and more activity of global citizens, corporations, and even states themselves grows interdependent. This interdependence, which also benefits individual nation-states, justifies the growing need for global governance tools and mechanisms.

Such a need for global governance mechanisms and tools explains the first implication to the political supremacy of nation-states in the era of globalization. To run efficiently the globalized world states and their increasingly complex web of interdependent activity states must find and create organizations and institutions that focus and specialize in the relevant issues of our time. To live up to the reason why they exist, these organizations design functional conditions to take care of the issues for which they exist. They create international regimes to guide the behavior of individual states. These international regimes establish rules, norms, principles, and decision-making processes for any international issue at hand. They establish a common ground for behavior in areas of trade practices, environmental carbon dioxide gas emission, and proliferation of nuclear weapons, to name just a few. These international regimes become norm providers for nations. In their capacity as norm providers, they supersede nation-states. Indeed, they sanction member states that deviate or fail in their practices to reflect the rules of these international regimes. Of course, nation-states remain sovereign, and the issue has always been what to do if the powerful among them simply do not budge. Nevertheless, nations relinquish in concrete ways a few of their normative prerogatives such as to apply unilaterally a trade policy that contradicts the rules of the World Trade Organization. Indeed, international organizations and regimes are the manifestation of a need to look beyond nation-states for legal jurisdiction and functional competence and authority. Although the process remains controllable by states and unfolds through states' initiatives, the demands of the current global paradigm often leave no other choice to states but to ride along the wheel of history and go along with the will of the rest of the international community. In the process they erode some of their sovereignty. Regionally, groups of nations have come together to join forces, integrating their economies. Such a process is a liberal economic–induced phenomenon, which looks beyond the state for its most effective outcome. This need underlines the inadequacy of the nation-state to organize global economics and in the process exposes the need for a new locus of jurisdiction beyond the state. This process cannot materialize without the creation of a supranational structure and infrastructure. In some regions of the globe, the economic integration process has continually eroded such political prerogatives of decision-making competence up to the point where some are becoming political unions. The process is currently the case of the European Union, with all the difficulties it implies.

The second implication is the one that globalization addresses to the notion of territorial integrity and the idea of national sovereignty linked to national borders. The hermetically controlled national space, seen as a space wherein governments organize national security and national prosperity, is now, in the era of globalization, seen as a market space. Whereas the world of politics sees nation-states as a space wherein both national prosperity and national security must reign and the latter over the former are privileged, the global liberal economic system sees the state as a market that needs to open up. It privileges prosperity and argues, from the perspective of liberalism, that national security and peace come as a result of prosperity. As the global liberal economic system pushes for the dismantling of trade barriers, the political world must come to terms with all kinds of infiltrations that free markets may bring. This simply means that the model of tight and hermetically sealed and controlled borders must give way for more opening of territorial national borders to allow access to the state market. It does not mean that states no longer have borders nor does it mean that these borders are no longer controlled. It simply means that governments should accommodate markets and politics should accommodate economics. In this accommodation need, it is the state that is doing the adjustments necessary.

The third implication derives from the second. As markets, states must be competitive to attract investments and funds. They think twice about their fiscal policy, corporate taxes, regulatory policy, banking practices, trade laws, reducing their employment costs, etc.

In this need to render attractive a national market space, nations utilize different tools. They are of different size, different levels of economic development and wealth, different amount and size of multinational corporations, different rate of technology use, different absolute or comparative cost advantages, raw materials, financial and human capital, different labor costs, different supporting institutions, different legal grounding, different policy grounding, etc. All these factors, unevenly distributed, render individual nations differently sensitive and vulnerable to challenges of globalization. Nations are differently competitive. Each uses its competitive advantage. As a consequence, those adjusting the best have been thriving. China, India, Brazil, Turkey, Vietnam, Sweden, and Norway are among them. Some nations have specialized in key sectors of liberal economics such as finance. They have come to be known as safe havens, fiscal niches, beneficiaries of capital transfer, some of it legitimately, some of it illicitly, serving as money launderers. Among them we count Switzerland, Luxemburg, the Bahamas, Monaco, Panama, Cypress, and the United Arab Emirates. Others specialize in fiscal policy to attract foreign direct investment and attract relocation of multinational corporations. Among them we count Ireland, Great Britain, and Iceland. The success at rendering a national market attractive to the competitive conditions of the global economy has proven to be a factor of economic growth, as it is linked to investment and trade. The empirical proof has been evident, and one of the most potent arguments of neoliberalism is, namely, that those nations more open to investment and trade, through neoliberal principles (deregulation of economic activity, liberalization of trade and its consequences such as the minimal state, privatization, low tariffs, etc.) and their macroeconomic policy tools (monetary and fiscal policy), have been as well nations with the most vibrant and thriving economies.

Many other nations have been struggling to find the appropriate responses. France, Spain, Portugal, and Greece are some of the nations failing to render attractive a national market that produces effects such as low foreign direct investment inflow, outsourcing, delocalization of businesses, or offshoring. These consequences are among the causes of unemployment,[1] even in advanced nations long established in the practice of the free market economic system. Those failing to adjust have increasingly been feeling the level of their influence diminishing.

Nations in the political world in the era of globalization face common pressures of the market. The differentiated responses and the different competitive predispositions have started to produce some winners as well as some struggling nations. Winners, of course, are reaping the benefit of a liberalized global trade. They are becoming the status quo nations, supporters of globalization. On the other hand, it is from the struggling nations where we have heard voices of revisionism and denunciation of globalization. The picture of winners and struggling nations has been the surprise of globalization to nations around the world so far. Indeed, since 1500 AD, the beginning of the modern era, Western nations have been on the winning side of changing international paradigms. Today, some of the most thriving and competitive nations come from the South and the non-Western world. They average, in general, an annual economic growth rate of anywhere between 3 percent and 9 percent. They have names such as Turkey, Indonesia, Brazil, Vietnam, the Philippines, Botswana, and Mauritius. They are members of the G20, the group of nations with the most economic growth. In fact, among these nations, most of them (eleven) are from the global South and are non-Western. In this category of nations with an annual growth rate above 3 percent, we do not find France, Portugal, Spain, or England.

The voices calling for protectionism therefore have come not necessarily from poor, developing nations but from struggling advanced economies. In fact, it is from nations with advanced economies where protectionism has been strikingly blatant. Advanced economies of the West use protectionism against clothing, textiles, and agricultural goods from the developing nations. It just happens that these are the areas in which these developing nations are the most competitive. Thomas Hertel and Will Martin[2] have even pointed to high tariffs imposed on manufactured goods from the developing poor nations by advanced economies, as much as four times higher than tariffs imposed on rich countries.

The fourth implication derives from the fact that globalization is producing a new distribution of wealth and therefore a new hierarchy of wealth among nations. Considering the fact that economic wealth breeds political influence, the logical assumption is that this new distribution of wealth will produce in due time a new hierarchy of world powers. This also simply means that globalization has the potential, and therefore a challenging potential, of inducing a relative loss of power status for struggling nations.

The fifth implication is that the macroeconomic tools of monetary (money supply and interest rate) and fiscal policy (taxation and spending) of individual nation-states become, if not conditioned, limited but at least influenced by the overall global economic environment. The ability of countries to access capital in the global financial market depends on the policies and political climate of individual states. International rating agencies may suggest confidence or the lack thereof of any given state.

The sixth implication resides in the orthodoxy of the practice of a sole and unique economic system and the policy choices it prescribes. Although there is a nuanced spectrum of policy choices and alternatives within the free market neoliberalist economic system, it remains a choice within one ad sole economic system. What room is there in politics for those who want to apply, try, or simply bend the prescribed policy measures of laissez-faire of interventionism? What room is there for those with a new idea that seeks a different outcome to societal issues than those ultimately proposed by neoliberalist policy measures? Indeed, the finality of any economic system is as well societal. Economic systems are driven by a societal vision. The outcome of economic process is more than material. Economic systems have an idealistic outcome in mind. Neoliberalism as an economic system has a societal vision. It is that of individual pursuit of happiness materially induced by free entrepreneurship. If there is no other competing ideology or economic system, does it mean that humanity agrees with the neoliberalist societal vision? And have we reached Fukuyama's metaphorical end of history? This question is not intended to deplore the absence of a competing economic system for a societal vision that might be morally superior to that of neoliberalism, but it intends more to underline the limitation in the world of politics in which all national actors, with a couple of exceptions, function with the same user's manual, in which you find prescribed liberalization, privatization, deregulation, and harmonization. Their differences become more and more nuance based but not substantive. It is true that Japanese and German liberalism differ from that of the United States or British liberalism. These differences are nuanced differences. This is a political world in which globalization has constrained a number of ideas and policy moves that could otherwise appear on the marketplace of ideas and compete for the approval of the public.

ECONOMIC IMPLICATIONS OF GLOBALIZATION

The primary evident and significant effect of globalization to all economic actors, states, corporations, and individual consumers and workers is that it has opened most markets, with still a few exceptions, to a worldwide competition. Hence, the challenge of today's market participants is how to be and remain competitive.

We have discussed the challenges that nation-states face. Such challenges are implications of globalization. Now, let us look at those that other economic actors such as corporations and people in general face.

CORPORATIONS

The principles and institutional arrangements of an economic global liberalism put in place by relevant institutions such as the World Trade Organization (WTO) and with the support of member states have encouraged global trading, global investment, and mobility of factors of production. The process has allowed a greater synergy between financial capital, human capital, and resources around the world. Naturally, the primary beneficiaries of this process have been businesses and multinational corporations. As the market went global, so did businesses and corporations that could. This new reality has brought about the conditions for a fierce and ubiquitous global competition not only in terms of geography but qualitatively. To prevail, corporations had to apply new management strategies to ensure competitiveness. Those companies that could have made acquisitions (Mannesmann by Vodacom, MCI by British Telecom, etc.). Others have merged. Others again have formed alliances (the Starr alliance in commercial aviation, etc.). Many corporations went big, increasing the scale and scope of their production. They increased productivity. They relied on innovation for a competitive edge. Others sought to access new markets more efficiently and reduce production and transportation costs through outsourcing, relocation, offshoring, and securing a market share wherever they went, with low entry barriers. Once they did, operating management still had to figure out how to organize their supply chain, find skilled labor, ensure financing through a globally competitive financial market and logistics, and continue innovating.

Advanced economies and their corporations had to compete against a growing number of corporations from the South. These corporations of the South have their own competitive advantages through operating in conditions with low environmental and labor standards and a cheaper workforce, allowing them to benefit from low production costs thus offer products at a lower cost. This situation caused worries of what was called the race to the bottom. The worry expressed the fear of a consequence of a global competition in which corporations from advanced economies and their high standards in the use of technology, labor standards, and environmental regulations could be forced to "cut corners" in order to remain competitive with corporations and products from nations in the emerging markets and the developing world in general. The fear, however, has been rejected as unfounded, by among others, the Organisation for Economic Co-operation and Development (OECD), which found, at least with respect with labor standards, that low labor standards were not necessarily an argument to attract investment and that there was no such thing as multinational corporations lowering their standards to remain competitive with their counterparts or products from the developing nations.[3]

The notion of competition is inherent in the free market economic system. It is therefore not a new challenge. What is new is the pool of competitors, which has expanded. Its consequence has been the demise of uncompetitive corporations, large, such as Kodak, Nokia, Swissair, Lehman Brothers, and ABN-Amro, to name just a few, or the documented high rate of failed small businesses, which can be counted in the thousands.

PEOPLE

Economic systems and processes are man-made. Society primarily needs to organize production for survival. It eventually uses economic activity to prosper and to pursue happiness. This makes human beings the primary actors, consumers, organizers, and beneficiaries or victims of economic processes. They prosper as a consequence of a good functioning economy, and they suffer as a consequence of a depressed economy. This means that the fate of individuals in many ways is linked to their economies. The globalization process is producing a global economy. The global economy is, as well, an economy system on which the fate of many individuals on the globe depends.

Globalization affects people differently. It affects them depending on where on the globe they live, whether it is in the developing nations or advanced economies, whether in rural or cosmopolitan cities. It affects individuals based on their lines of work, their skill levels, whether software engineer or forklift driver in a warehouse.

The more exposed to globalization effects, the more directly affected people are. Many in the financial market prosper because the global economy allows for global investment opportunities, and others find themselves losing their jobs, being laid off as a result of failing investments or corporate restructuration, or lack of a competitive edge in the global market. These outcomes point to the fact that people living in the era of a globalized economy must readjust. They must readjust to remain relevant workers and consumers. To be a consumer depends on work. To work, one must fit the profile in demand in the labor market.

One feature of the global economy is that it is increasingly driven by the service sector and information technology. This means that, contrary to the manufacturing era, elementary, mechanical, assembly line and low skill labor are more and more scarce due to both delocalization and high productivity. This implies for jobs seekers the need to fine-tune their skills to meet the demands and expectations of today's labor market. This demand and expectation of today's economy is a challenge to individuals in these nations. Next to the challenge of acquiring new skills, there is the competition among job seekers in the global economy. Many businesses, corporations, and entrepreneurs do not shy away from recruiting anywhere on the globe. This sharpens the competitive landscape in today's global economy.

Although globalization has been an economic success story, it has started to produce casualties in the advanced economies. The deregulation that has been part of neoliberal policies of globalization has allowed for a number of corporations to increase their revenues by the billions. Just as corporate wealth has increased, the wealth gap has widened, leading to recent statistics, such as in the United States, showing that 10 percent of wealthy Americans control 75 percent of the wealth (Economic Policy Institute). Although the income gap exists, it is much smaller than the wealth gap. Still, in the United States, these facts coupled with the downturn of the economy since late 2008 have taken a toll on the middle class. It has been shrinking, and the recently published (2014) finding of a survey by LIS[4] confirmed this, showing that it was no longer the most affluent. The consequence of a shrinking middle class simply implies a growing number of people in poverty.

In the developing world, low-skill jobs are still the norm, as manufacturing has yet to reach mass production levels, and in many of these developing nations, the economy is still driven by the agricultural sector. This state of underdevelopment has become an asset to some nations that have started to open up to trade and attract foreign investment. Nevertheless, globalization has not altered the poverty statistics we have become familiar with. The UN Millennium Project still speaks of over 1.2 billion people living in abject poverty (less than one dollar a day) or roughly 3 billion living with less than two dollars a day. Some of the firms that relocate into the South to take advantage of low production and labor costs also take advantage of low environmental regulations and working conditions, causing all kinds of environmentally related illnesses, accidents, and sweatshops, and even child labor. Their investments have been the cause of all kinds of dangers.

Generally, however, one way that globalization is affecting people, and essentially with respect to the economy, is through increased flow of mobility. Indeed, globalization not only fosters and induces increased flow of trade, capital, and goods but also movement of people. People seek labor across borders, and they travel more for business, and as they earn more, for tourism and other stimulating reasons. The result has been a high mobility in the labor market. Bright minds in the developing nations have even started benefiting from the possibility and ability of multinational companies and others to invest globally. These companies tap into high-skilled labor anywhere on the globe. The presence in multinationals firms of software engineers, number crunchers, market analysts, mathematicians, and radiologists from India and anywhere in the global South is becoming a feature of globalization. Anywhere else, other high-skilled job seekers have found themselves working miles and miles away from home, as companies now, in need for such skills, do more and more to attract them. For instance, high-skilled job seekers from Spain are now being recruited in Germany, where a high-powered economy needs skilled labor. In Angola, the oil boom and Chinese investments have opened opportunities in the labor force. Indian software engineers are needed in the United States, Switzerland, and Germany, where highly specialized economies need a sophisticated workforce to remain on top.

Overall, conditions of globalization encourage social mobility. The mobility of factors of production allows for a greater synergy that has helped propel the process of globalization.

SOCIETAL AND CULTURAL IMPLICATIONS OF GLOBALIZATION

The process of globalization is characterized by increased exchange and flow of capital and goods. These exchanges of capital and goods are through new investment opportunities brought across borders. Increased economic activity across borders is carried out by people who communicate and eventually meet. Increased investment brings along employment opportunity. As a result, globalization has increased international communication and mobility. And mobility is linked to opportunity as people seek greener pastures. These greener pastures are found more in some areas than in others. This explains why high mobility in the era of globalization, namely, increased immigration, is a phenomenon that affects global megapolises and cities, and specific regions of the globe more than others. Globalization has produced new challenges and issues caused by the coming together, in specific spaces, of many individuals from many different places and from many different cultures. This phenomenon is allowing new sociological and cultural amalgamation and proximity we have come to call diversity, which in some spaces breeds its own set of issues. These cultural diversity–induced differences must be negotiated for a peaceful coexistence.

The kinds of issues we find in different spaces as a result of globalization differ depending on which space we consider, as they are affected differently based on their levels of exposure to the impact of globalization. We consider next each one of these spaces: rural spaces, suburban spaces, urban spaces, and cosmopolitan spaces (megacities, or global cities).

Rural Spaces

The rural space is the space among those in which human communities live that have been culturally the least affected by globalization. Rural spaces are generally geographically isolated, in infrastructurally less developed land, and therefore they are characterized by forests or deserts. They are sparsely inhabited. The US census provides the following quantitative criteria, namely, that they are inhabited by a population of between 1,000 and 9,900. They contain a lot of space for agriculture, hunting, and other outdoor recreation and activities. The remoteness of such rural areas from any centers of city attractions explains the fact that they have the tendency of being inhabited by generations that have lived there for years; they lose many of their younger generations to the cities, while not attracting new ones. They have a low pull factor effect. They are spaces where processes run their course in a traditionally established way. Habits are entrenched. There are negligible deviations. They are cautious, if not skeptical, with the idea of change. There are not many social changes, and as a result, they are not a harbor where one might see signs of global issues manifested. The result is a high rate of cultural homogeneity in rural spaces.

Suburban Spaces

Suburban spaces have become a new space of attraction in response to the influx of new immigrants in urban spaces and metropolises. They tend to attract a certain kind of resident. They are in the middle to upper classes, conservatives in their outlook on social issues, worried about the negative social influences of big urban spaces, worried about crime and violence, and attracted by the space that suburbs offer, and they mostly live in houses with backyards, as opposed to the confinement of metropolises and urban space apartments. They use cars for transportation as a result of available space and spread-out facilities. They may seek to that effect, a high quality of life in terms of the natural environment, schooling, and outdoor activities. The US census provides the figure of 10 to 49,000 inhabitants in its suburban spaces.

Suburban spaces offer some features of urban spaces and some features of rural spaces. The features of urban spaces are availability of infrastructure, resources, human capital, and opportunities. The features of rural spaces are more natural space, low population density, more cultural homogeneity, more controlled and controllable social environment, more one-on-one attention and focus on children in school or at home, less hectic life, and more sense of safety and security. As a result, many conclude that the suburbs are a good space to raise children.

Urban Spaces

Urban spaces are those that may be located within metropolises or in the middle to lower income social class residential areas of the metropolises, or the outskirts or peripheries of the metropolises. They inhabit populations attracted by the opportunities of the metropolises. These spaces within metropolises have relatively affordable housing access, usually apartments. These urban dwellers use mass transit means of transportation. Their activities may be restrained by spaces, and therefore many such activities take place indoors. They attract large enough populations, which in the case of the United States, the census bureau provides the figure of 50,000 and higher by each one of such spaces. The figure includes a heterogeneous cultural mixture, from autochthonous populations to various migrant populations. The mixture of high population and proximity and heterogeneity of cultures has been known, according to sociological studies, to breed tensions and violence in urban spaces in times when economic opportunities are scarce.

They attract people who want to stay close to metropolises and therefore are characterized by a more or less cultural heterogeneity found in metropolises only on the lower spectrum of social income.

Urban areas have continued to grow larger as a result of immigration and globalization. They have brought about subsequent phenomena. The first is that of shrinkage of cities around the world. Just as some areas grow in populations others shrink. The same factors, which are pull factors causing the arrivals into an urban or other space, do cause the departure from others, and therefore the shrinking. Among such factors causing the shrinking are lack of opportunity and shifts in industry or business practices and in demographic and environmental quality. In the process, migrant populations are a key driving force. Migrant populations gravitate toward large cities. And because these migrant populations gravitate toward big cities but do not have the financial resources necessary, urban environments become the closest they can get to metropolises. The second phenomenon is that of retreat into gated communities, which happen to be located in big cities, metropolises, and sometimes in the suburbs, where a housing location of those often sharing the same social class or a collective cultural identity feature consciously or subconsciously seek the company of their likes and congregate toward a homogeneity, to escape the heterogeneity of the metropolises cosmopolitan spaces, or sometimes just for more safety or a sense of security.

The third is the retreat into the suburban spaces for those to whom the influx of new immigrants alters the status quo social order, and worried of the impact of changes in the neighborhood. They move away from the urban spaces into the suburban space, where they find peers who have the same worries and want to hold on to the status quo social order, and are often of the same social class, which helps consolidate their interests and outlook on existence. These two phenomena of retreat, into gated communities and into the suburbs, are spread around the United States. They are beginning to spread elsewhere, such as around Paris, France, or Rio de Janeiro, Brazil, responding to the same sociological phenomenon.

Cosmopolitan Spaces

Cosmopolitan spaces are simply spaces wherein congregate a high and diverse population for various reasons. The diversity of population offers the possibility of encounter and familiarity with a variety of cultural and social differences in a given space. The reasons why cosmopolitan spaces emerge are dictated by the various opportunities that some areas offer. These opportunities constitute the attracting force, which we discuss in the next chapter on immigration, justifying the millions of people who live, work, and socialize in such spaces. Cities that attract a variety of people naturally increase their likelihood of becoming cosmopolitan, as they host visitors, tourists, or business executives, and/or become a place of residence to many. Some of such cities are known as metropolises, or megacities, as their capacity to absorb newcomers seems endless. Many have reached over 10 million residents, such as in Tokyo, São Paulo, Seoul, Mexico City, Osaka, Manila, Mumbai, Jakarta, and Lagos.

Although their populations remain essentially made up of historically traditional dwellers and indigenous or native peoples, they are characterized by a high degree of cultural and sociological heterogeneity compared to urban, suburban, and rural spaces. Such a high degree of cultural and sociological heterogeneity has widened as a result of growing mobility facilitated by the process of globalization. It accounts for a growing new phenomenon of trans-ethnicity, transculturality, and transnationality. These terms have in common the prefix "trans," which simply suggests "a move through spaces, a move across lines (Ong 1999, p. 4).

The growing relevance of these terms in global issues calls for the need to define them clearly. We define transethnicity as the product of exposure to and experience with features and expressions of another (ethnic) culture and their adoption by someone. We define transculturality as the bridging of a familiar culture with an unfamiliar or a foreign culture. As technology increasingly expands the bridge, the distinction familiar and foreign will grow obsolete, as Welsch (1999) noted. We communicate and interact more. We exchange and travel more. And as the process continues, we may very well be establishing the basis for a global culture. Finally, we consider the term trans-nationality. The term describes a complex phenomenon linked to globalization. It is linked to globalization in the following manner. The global liberal economic system in its current phase, argues David Harvey (cited by Ong 2004, p. 3), is centered on production, distribution, consumption, and profit making. To achieve these goals in the era of globalization, characterized by the mobility of high finance, the labor market, and consumption, economic actors must be flexible. They must decentralize the decision-making process, adapt and tap into the world labor market, etc. It all comes down to flexibility of involved factors, people included. This people flexibility means that they must be where the market or labor market has room for them. They have to be able to "trans" across spaces, which are nation-states, and across lines, which are national borders. The result is increased mobility across nations, which we call transnationality. The phenomenon includes businesspeople, skilled labor seekers, unskilled labor seekers, often part of the immigration debate, and even those needing to leave their nations because of various reasons such as wars, civil wars, or cultural conflicts and therefore must find another nation. They all do not shed off their past. They carry it into the host nation. They are part of the transnationality phenomenon. The phenomenon explains the growing numbers of diasporadic communities around the world. The phenomenon ultimately contributes to cultural heterogeneity.

We understand cultural heterogeneity to be the various expressions of the different cultures of people who reside in cosmopolitan cities. Such expressions logically dictate the notion of cultural pluralism inherent to cosmopolitanism. This pluralism exhausts the full extent of the notion since it does not simply allude to a few differences that may exist within a culture or a civilization, for instance, adhesion to progressivism or to conservatism within Western democracies, or for instance preference for an interventionist state or for small government. Heterogeneous cosmopolitan space implies a vast spectrum of expressions of cultural pluralism, as such spaces receive and host the habits, customs, religious faiths, languages, diets, attires, folklore, and value systems of diverse incoming populations or new immigrants. They do not necessarily change the status quo, which is the existing culture they encounter in the host city, but some aspects of these new incoming cultures end up becoming part of the cultural fabric of the city. And so for instance, some words from a language of the incoming cultures may infiltrate the host space's vocabulary. Some dietary dishes from incoming cultures may become part of the host space's dietary culture. Cultural practices of some may become familiar to others, etc. Such adoption by the host cultures of input from the incoming cultures, of course, depends on how significant the people of the incoming culture and their capacity to immerse themselves is through their activity in the social life of the host space. In the end, the incoming cultures, even when they do not dethrone the existing culture, become part of the character and fabric of a space to some degree. This absorption of new cultural features into the host culture and the familiarity they induce explains the heterogeneous character of cosmopolitan spaces.

Indeed expressions of incoming cultures found in New York City are a part of the character of New York City. Such expressions may be found at a microlevel in urban spaces of Brooklyn, New York, less probable in a suburb of Cheyenne, Wyoming, and much less in the rural space of Albion, Iowa. The name of the city, urban, and suburban spaces we mention here can be interchanged with any other city, urban, and suburban spaces in so far as spaces exude similar human and economic geographic features in terms of their sociological makeup.

Adjustments of Incoming Cultures in Host Cosmopolitan Spaces

We have established that cosmopolitan spaces are culturally heterogeneous. But how does that cultural heterogeneity manifest in those spaces? Knowing that there is an existing and dominant host culture that new immigrants encounter in host cosmopolitan spaces, and although they culturally enrich these spaces, how do new immigrants negotiate their cultural existence with the dominant culture of host cities? In other words, do all new immigrants in New York City equally become New Yorkers? Are there many ways to live in New York City for new immigrants? As we explore these questions, we observe that new immigrants adapt differently.

They have an array of options to choose from as they consider how to culturally exist in New York City or in any other cosmopolitan space. They can assimilate. They can hybridize. They can form ghettos. They can be selective, picking and choosing which values and traits of the dominant culture and others of their fellow new immigrants to take in and internalize and which ones to leave out. What do these options come down to? The first, assimilation, is simply opting to immerse oneself totally into the ways of the host space. It is leaving behind whatever preexisting cultural identity prior to entering the new cultural space, as far as possible to speak the language, to dress, to adapt to the folklore, customs, and value systems of the host space. The process allows oneself to become part of the mainstream. The second option, hybridization, consists of maintaining, and even continuing to entertain, the substance of the preexisting cultural identity of oneself, while adding and learning the ways of the new host culture. It is a process whereby the identity of an individual becomes dually constituted. They develop two frames of cultural references in which they must navigate depending on circumstances. The third option, the forming of ghettos, consists of creating a space of communitarian identity. It is an old anthropological reflex of minorities that either voluntarily ensues when in need of mutual comfort or forcefully ensues, as it was in the late Medieval period in Europe and formally described as such since the Venetian Republic in Italy, in the early AD 1500s, and since, in the case of Jewish minorities throughout Europe. It is a recurrent phenomenon for which the term ghetto is used as a descriptor, when, even today, a number of factors bring a congregation of members of a cultural minority into one space. A similar phenomenon involves members of an economic minority, who as a result of economic precarity find themselves in specific areas around metropolises wherein economical, infrastructural, sanitary, and safety requirements and conditions are not met. It has produced slums and shanty towns. In that sense, there are ghettos around the world, from the *favelas* of Rio de Janeiro to the outskirts of Nairobi, Kenya; from some cities around Detroit or Delaware in the United States to Neza-Chalco-Itza in Mexico City, or Orangi Town in Karachi.

The fourth option of selection consists of immersing oneself into the new and host culture, but with a self-conscious attitude and mindset. The self-conscious mindset and attitude serve to filter experiences as they unfold in the new culture through the lenses of one's appreciation and evaluation, to finally internalize, accommodate some, and reject some others. The process is individual and may manifest differently for different people. Some new immigrants participate in some activities of the host and new culture and stay away from others. Some new immigrants blend in with the rest in public but privately observe and still practice and function according to the value system of the culture of origin. Their private sphere remains a space in which their old ways remain relevant. These old value systems remain the referential norms of behavior, practice, and expression. They do as the Romans in Rome in a public sphere, but as themselves in the private sphere. In such individual cultural arrangements, for instance, one may live according to Islam, as Islam orders the life of its believers privately, but live like Americans when outside. They may not object and may even understand the claim of equality of genders of the public sphere but do subscribe to arguments of gender hierarchy in their personal life. Furthermore, because one new immigrant culture is not the only new culture, the immigrants encounter other new immigrants. They sometimes live in the closest proximity to them. They become aware of other cultures that all are part of the heterogeneity feature of the cosmopolitan space. Here as well there is a necessity for a Ukrainian or Pakistani American to become aware of the ways of the Italian American or Jewish American. There is an additional degree of cultural sensitivity, beyond simply being an American citizen, necessary for a peaceful intercultural communal life in New York for instance. These are imperatives dictated by cultural heterogeneity and therefore call for adjustments that a cosmopolitan life requires.

Heterogeneity of Lifestyles

The heterogeneity of cultures induces the heterogeneity of lifestyles. In a context where differences are part of the character of a place, the various forms of cultural expressions tend to flourish. The context of cultural pluralism in cosmopolitan spaces therefore encourages different expressions of lifestyle. These different expressions of lifestyle often reveal the essence of individuals; it suggests what is important to them, what they want to project, and how they want to be identified, etc. Consequently, cosmopolitan spaces become theaters of individual expressions. It is a space where the idea of "normal" is questioned or tempered. Deviations from the norms, social experiments, and new initiatives are likely to bourgeon there more than anywhere else. In the end, it becomes almost a nonevent in New York City to see a man wearing a dress, whereas the same act in Twin Falls, Idaho, may be a big deal. Cosmopolitan spaces are spaces of heterogeneity of lifestyle in contrast to the conformity of the suburban spaces and to a greater degree of uniformity of rural spaces.

As a result cosmopolitan spaces are spaces in which different cultures but also different lifestyles are found, tolerated, and even accommodated. The consequence is emerge.

Adjustment of Different Lifestyles in Cosmopolitan Spaces

The same way we see different cultures adjusting their existence in cosmopolitan spaces, we find as well different lifestyles adjusting to the cosmopolitan space. This adjustment is primarily driven, once again, by the anthropological and therefore natural tendency of those that are the same, sameness to congregate. The sameness is based on cultural identity, which produces a certain lifestyle. Such adjustments are necessary because there are so many different cultural identities. One's identity may get lost in the sea of many others. The tendency is, therefore, for those sharing the same lifestyle to congregate. Beyond that natural anthropological tendency to congregate, the adjustment is driven by the need for mutual reassurance, for comfort and even safety. Yes, indeed, the reality is that not all lifestyles are accepted or even tolerated, even in cosmopolitan spaces. The adjustment therefore is in many cases also driven by the need to escape harassment or to form a better resisting block. It produces the manifestation of identity communitarianism, as those sharing the same cultural identity feature or features, which they need to live, share, and express, form a community of lifestyle. These communities of lifestyles can be gays and lesbians, bikers, skinheads, transgenders, drag queens, etc.

As they adjust, their adjustment can take many shapes. They may create safe havens, which are primarily places where they may be in large numbers to signal their claim to space. This adjustment has produced places that are cities where gays and lesbians for instance are in considerable numbers such as San Francisco, Atlanta, in the "Village" in New York, etc. In these places, they may have their own locales, shops, stores, bars, or nightclubs that cater to their needs and aspirations. They may reside in locations, such as a neighborhood, where they are predominant.

And because any lifestyle in any given cosmopolitan space is likely to be found in any other cosmopolitan space around the world, such a phenomenon of community of lifestyle may go global. When it does, it produces a phenomenon of globalization of communities of lifestyles. We then have skinheads of Tennessee, for instance, or any other city that connects with skinheads of London or Barcelona, etc.

Issues of Cultural Heterogeneity in Global Cosmopolitan Spaces

In cosmopolitan spaces of pluralistic societies, such as in New York City or London, cultural particularities of new immigrant populations should theoretically not constitute or become a cause of issues. The reason is a certain understanding of the concept of the republic in which citizens and residents are subject to constitutional expectations and this means the rule of law. The rule of law is designed on the principle of equality of rights and addresses citizens and residents in terms of their responsibilities in the public space, and is not concerned with private practices, behavior, and expressions, with some exceptions, if and when they infringe on other people's safety or exercise of their freedom. This simply leaves room for cultural practices, behavior, and expressions of individuals of any background, as these generally proceed in the private spheres, provided they follow the law. Just as it is theoretically not problematic to live under the regime of cultural pluralism, it is theoretically conceivable that issues are more likely to arise in spaces where there is little or no tolerance for behavior, practices, and expressions of cultural particularities if and when they deviate from, are incompatible with, or contradict the dominant norm. Beijing, China, is yet to be fully culturally pluralist, and Catholicism, at least the underground Roman Catholic Church,[5] is the deviating cultural norm. Tehran, Iran, has a dominant cultural norm emanating from its interpretation of Islam and therefore is nonpluralistic, as some private choices such as an attire of one's own taste may not be tolerable to the cultural taste of the brand of Islam practiced. The lack of cultural pluralism here is evident not only because there is lack of plurality of cultural norms but also because laws of the republic applied to regulate these nonpluralistic spaces are designed with a specific culture of citizens and residents in mind; it therefore constrains the cultural behavior, practices, and expressions of all other kinds of citizens and residents. As a result, such laws do not reflect the principles of equality of rights to all citizens and residents.

However, in both cases, in pluralistic and nonpluralistic spaces, there are practical issues that arise because of behavior, practices, and expressions of particular cultures of incoming new immigrants. Indeed, some of the behaviors, practices, and expressions of various incoming new immigrants either strikingly contrast with those of the historically autochthonous populations or are incompatible with them or sometimes even mutually exclusive. Often the behavior, practices, and expressions of incoming cultures simply challenge the laws of the host nations. Following are illustrative examples. Examples contrast between autochthons and new immigrant cultural practices are gender rapport, dietary products, or things eaten in one culture but unthinkable in another. A case of incompatibility between autochthons and new immigrant cultural practices is monogamy versus polygamy. Cases of mutual exclusion between autochthons and new immigrant cultural expressions are honor killings, underage arranged marriages, Sharia law versus rule of law, etc. Cases in which the cultural expressions of new incoming immigrants challenge the laws of the host nation are the wearing of the *burqa* by some Muslims in France and the debate on the building of Mosques in Switzerland.

Two key concepts have been used to depict the nature of issues that a new influx of immigrating populations bring along are diversity or cultural pluralism, also known as multiculturalism, and integration.

Starting with the concept of diversity, cultural pluralism, and multiculturalism, these terms suggest the variety of cultures that coexist and constitute a social good. This implies that there is a certain richness that cultures can bring as they feed each other some of the best of their respective features, that is, if one buys into the premise that the coexistence of cultures must be encouraged, cherished, and promoted. This leads to the belief in multiculturalism. The intent is the hope that such multiculturalism softens the rough edges of individual cultures. It breeds tolerance in the light of so many expressions of intolerance observed since World War II, many of which have had a cultural cause. The quest for cultural recognition was privileged, as, indeed, around the world, such a quest was a *casus belli*, explaining the many civil wars. Multiculturalism was aimed at fighting against cultural intolerance. It was thought to be the way forward in the light of growing cultural heterogeneity in metropolises and its potential to breed tensions. It was promoted in Germany and among such nations up until recently, in the early 2000s. Its merits were questioned from the conservative ideological spectrum of European politics. Their arguments were, among others, that multiculturalism works against integration. It was accused of promoting identity communitarianism to the detriment of the social and national cohesion. The growing integration problems of young immigrants and their run-ins with the law have been brought forth to argue against multiculturalism.

Speaking of integration, the concept suggests as well a social good and strength resulting in the many cultures of incoming new immigrants to join hands with the host culture for a better, more prosperous, and stronger society. This could be achieved only if such incoming new immigrants and their cultures were tied to the existing cultures through their lives, work, and education. This proposition, of course, is a two-edged sword. It requires, on one hand, the host's politics to develop policy, strategies, and ways to facilitate interactions with the newcomers. Their communities, businesses, and government itself would have to make room for them. This part challenges the host nation to make integration happen. It is not a done deal, as there is political divergence on the issue among political parties around the nations that receive the most influx of new immigrants. There may be resistance from populations to accommodate new immigrants, as they are seen as takers of pieces of the economic pie or even seen as taking advantage of generous welfare systems across Europe and in many other Western advanced economies with adequate social security programs in place. Such a view may trigger active resistance, which often is manifest in the political discourse of extreme right parties. These parties are politically closer to the ideology of nationalism driven by a focus on national identity and pride. These parties see that focus diminished by the influx of culturally diverse immigrant populations. The resistance from some political parties often leads to changes in the law reducing opportunities of new migrants in host countries. A portion of the autochthonous population at large may, as well, see unfavorably the influx of new immigrants, which triggers passive resistant attitudes. Such attitudes lead to discriminating practices in housing, labor markets, and other subtle ways.

On the other hand, new incoming immigrants are expected to do their part. What is that part? It is their willingness to fully integrate. Some may not be willing. Others may be willing only to find themselves having to jump hurdles that may be too high. Many immigrants come from the developing nations wherein a number of standards are different, judged as below host nations'. Sometimes it is their degrees and diplomas that are not recognized and acknowledged. Sometimes there are hurdles of social and cultural natures. They have to learn new customs and the subtleties of doing things in host countries. This often leads to the fact that they end up not trusted with positions of trust, real competence, decision-making power, etc. Many do not bring along high-skilled labor credentials, which in the end allow only minimal or peripheral degrees of integration.

Geographic Scale in the Era of Globalization

An act that is posed in any local geographic space used to have a local reach. That reach is the scale. The scale, which is the reach of any act or action, has a natural limit. Calling a kid playing in the backyard is going to have a reach. The reach is the extent to which the voice of the caller can be heard. There will come a point beyond which the voice cannot be heard. The point can be geographically localized. It is the geographic scale of the voice that is an action. And that geographic scale of the voice can as well be localized in a given space. Today, the notion of space is globalized. This means that geographic scale of actions is easily globalized. This has been the result of two phenomena that have helped to produce globalization. The first is digital technology, and the second is the liberal world economy. These two phenomena have produced an interconnectedness of spaces and their peoples. They account for the fact that there is more and more interconnectedness of actions.

The voting of a US citizen in Rochester, New York, is connected to what happens in Rochester (locally), in Washington (nationally), and in Afghanistan (internationally/globally). The money deposited into a savings account anywhere on the planet is linked to the fate of your bank, the national economy, and global investment. And so does the hiring of a franchise's quarterback in the American National Football League or of a soccer player. The likes of the Portuguese soccer player Christiano Ronaldo will have ripple effects from ticket sales, to franchisee stock, local suppliers, the city economy, the national league, and beyond. This ripple effect is possible through interconnectedness, which is entrenched into a hierarchy of scales.

Ergo, just as interconnectedness is facilitated through software in the meta-geographic world of cyber space, which is a global space, the same

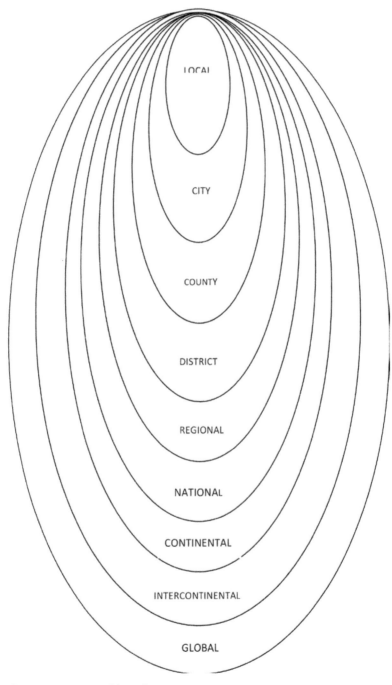

Figure 8.1. Geographic scale

interconnectedness is facilitated in the geographic world, the real world, through economic exchanges, ramifications and implications. The interconnectedness in both spaces allows for an act posed by an individual to cross geographic scales, from local to city, all the way to the global.

The Antiglobalization Movement

The ubiquitous effects of globalization have not always found the approval of all, everywhere around the world. They have been despised, rejected, and even fought by a number of those who have been persistent enough, consistent enough, articulated enough, and many enough to constitute a social movement. There is indeed a social movement that has emerged against globalization around the world. It is the antiglobalization movement. This movement, like any other social movement, reacts to changes brought about by the globalization process, as discussed in the previous section. Social change is indeed the driving paradigm of any social movement. Social changes affect different portions of the society differently. They may leave some people indifferent. They may please others, who then applaud them and support them. They may be a source of discomfort for others, who then are the ones from whom a reaction can be expected. They may choose to resist incoming change. They may choose to dismantle occurring change.

Sometimes, however, it is change that is sought by social movements. This is the case when the status quo social order is or is becoming unacceptable to those suffering from its discomfort. In such case, they seek to change the status quo, to induce change. The following historical examples are illustrations of such a phenomenon: revolutions (the French, Russian, American), independence movements (Gandhi and the decolonization of India), the civil rights movement (Martin Luther King, Jr. and the quest for equal civil liberties), etc.

Those joining hands for a cause around the change factor, who organize to achieve the purpose of their gathering, constitute a social movement. In the case of the antiglobalization movement, they come together to fight the changes, but by so doing they must fight the agents, institutions, and manifestations of the globalization process. However, all those attempting to resist the effects of globalization, and globalization itself, do not all speak with the same voice. They do not all focus on one thing for their resistance. Many focus on different effects of globalization, such as international trade or the dominance of the multinational corporation. Others focus on the institutions of globalization, and still others ideologically or philosophically reject a mercantilistic, materialistic, homogenized world that has become a hunting ground and prey for the global financial market to the detriment of the regular folks. What they have in common is their critical attitude vis-à-vis globalization. What they have in common is discontent. They differ in ways through which they criticize globalization. They differ in their approaches to resisting it.

As a result, we have various expressions of the antiglobalization movement, as described below. First, there are those who generally see the benefit of a globalization process but want to reform it to allow more redistributive effects of the liberal market toward the developing nations. They are called reformers (Ravenhill 2006, p. 68). Joseph Stiglitz[6] is one such voice of reform within the institutions of global liberalism. He argued in favor of a balanced approach in implementing liberal policies in developing nations. Developing nations themselves have been reformists as they participate in the globalization process while demanding changes to suit their respective sensitive economic situations and needs, primarily with the World Trade Organization.

Second, is the voice of the antiglobalization movement that focuses on the defense of the welfare state. They argue that liberal economic policies, which drive the globalization process, push unreasonably and irresponsibly the state out of the lives of its citizens by demanding small government in favor of privatization. These policies push for reduction of public expenditures, which leads to cuts in subsidies, subventions, and social programs and question the entire social safety net that has come to characterize Western European societies, practically since the time of the Industrial Revolution in England. Liberal economic policies, they argue, are an assault on the welfare state with its universal health care system, school and education subsidies, paid leaves and vacations, retirement packages, etc. These critics of the globalization process arguing from this perspective are often heard in Western Europe and in the Scandinavian countries, where such programs are part of the political culture and even the national psyche.

The third voice of the antiglobalization movement is that of the critics of the international trade. They argue that globalization produces outsourcing, relocation, and offshoring in search for cheap labor and favorable production cost conditions, which leave behind growing unemployment. Those arguing against globalization from this perspective also argue in favor of more protectionistic measures to protect their national economies and their low skills workforce. The argument has been utilized often by politicians whose districts suffer from such effects of the globalization process. Next to politicians, unions, as well, have joined this argument to pressure political decision makers. These political decision makers are often trapped between a rock and a hard place, as they cannot remain insensitive to their constituents' needs, but there is however the larger pressure of a global economy that is not going to stop because a particular district wants to protect itself. Such trade effects of globalization not only affect individual districts, but they also affect in the end entire nations, as many find themselves on the losing side of international trade competitiveness. Many are those nations whose trade balance is chronically in deficit, as they suffer the consequences of delocalization and outsourcing. This effect tends to affect wealthy industrialized nations, while those nations in the developing world who have learned to capitalize on their comparative advantages have now started to reap the benefits. In this regard, the example of China and the United States is the most striking.

The fourth voice of the antiglobalization movement is that of the antimercantilists. They are those who see entire societies of the globe being reduced to their status as consumers. They denounce the outrageous materialism that supplants and even suffocates noble aspirations of humanity and global humanity at that. They argue that not everything should be about money and not everything should have a price, and that some of the most precious things in life are priceless. They count among them traditions of peoples around the world and their cultures. Both traditions and cultures are dying or are under attack by the tendency of multinational corporations and their chains of stores to make products uniform, which they can produce en masse and therefore at lower cost, to the detriment of "mom and pop" boutiques and stores that reflect the various local expressions of material productivity of cultures. These "mom and pop" stores and boutiques are either bought out or are simply no longer viable in the sea of goods of mass consumption. These chains of stores have virtually succeeded in monopolizing some regions, where they become the primary suppliers and often dictate what today's consumers will buy. The result is a standardization of products and taste. It leads to often having around five to six different choices and to the phenomenon of seeing almost the same furniture style anywhere one goes, the same cell phone brands, the same GPS devices, etc.

Individuals' tastes are subject to markets. The products more or less determine what the buyers will get. The competition does not necessarily have different products but similar products. In the mercantile society these products keep changing, improving. Hence, it is the shelf life of products that is becoming purposefully shorter and shorter. Consumers are more and more compelled to keep buying so they do not miss out or get behind and to benefit from the newest features offered. It is the need to innovate in a competitive global market that drives the process and the growing social psychosis not to stay behind that drives the purchase of newest products. The culture as a whole responds to the need. It becomes mercantilist. Any calendar holiday, from Christmas to Valentine's Day, becomes an opportunity to sell and to buy. Society becomes, at varying degrees, and more so in advanced economies than elsewhere, subject to the market. Antiglobalization voices that decry this situation argue that we are gradually becoming a species of suppliers and customers, reduced to what we can afford and cannot. We are becoming people whose names are linked to serial numbers, account numbers, credit scores, etc., which now increasingly tell all the public needs to know about us and not about the wealth or the lack thereof of the humanity behind them. It is indeed the dwindling values of humanism that are being replaced in favor of those of materialism. In this materialistic culture, the antimercantilist movement argues that we are misplacing our priorities and that globalization is nothing but the process that accelerates and exacerbates the decay.

The fifth voice of the antiglobalization movement is that of leftist ideologues. Ideologically, they stand in opposition to the globalization process, as far as they driven by liberal economic principles that are part of the free market economic system, which uses capital as fuel. It is nothing but a predatory system, they argue, that not only alienates the worker for his labor but also privileges those in possession of the means of production, the most driven among the capitalist nations; hence, they used political imperialism to access resources from the developing nations, and now they use global institutions to do so. They practice liberalism as a religion. The World Bank is their Vatican (Strange 1986),[7] and they are producing a liberal orthodoxy that leaves no room for any deviation; therefore, they have become adept at market fundamentalism.

The seventh voice of the antiglobalization movement is that of anarchists, as a matter of principle, as *anarchos*, those without rulers/government or order; they despise any dictates imposed by governments and institutions and the order they impose. The globalization process is dictating the rules of commerce and the behavior of all those involved. It is embodied by specific international institutions (IMF, WTO, and the World Bank). These institutions have become the targets of various expressions of their disapproval of globalization. They protest. They disrupt the gathering of these institutions, such as the WTO in Seattle in 1990, in Prague; IMF and the BANK in 2000; and in Genoa, Italy, the G8 summit in 2001. They have organized expressions of protest such as the one against genetically modified food in France, led by Jose Bové.

The globalization process, therefore, reflects everything they reject. They see in globalization an intangible structure. As such, it restrains individual and other actors' freedoms to act as they please, even in the realms of economics, without a prescribed system for how to proceed.

NOTES

1. The leading unemployment cause in nations with advanced economies is "rising productivity," according to Daniel Griswold, 2000.

2. "White Man's Shame," *The Economist*, September 25, 1999, p. 89. http://www.economist.com/node/325062.

3. OECD, 1996.

4. A survey conducted by the Cross-National Data Center (LIS) in Luxembourg compiling data since the 1970s in twenty advanced economies in households of 5,000 to 120,000.

5. It is the branch of Catholicism with allegiance to the Vatican. There also exists in China the Patriotic Church, which is more openly practiced. It also recognizes the authority of the Vatican but has not officially proclaimed it.

6. Joseph Stiglitz while working for the IMF.

7. This is a recurrent and critical argument leveled by Susan Strange against liberal economics.

Chapter Nine

Globalization Issues

The Environment, Immigration, Global Health, and Human Trafficking

As a dominant paradigm of our epoch, globalization is essentially characterized by the interconnectedness of nations and peoples of the planet. The result of such interconnectedness is that the actions of people now, more than ever, have transnational implications and repercussions. Globalization has increased the flow of transnational activity. With the increase in the flow of transnational activity has come a magnification of specific transnational issues. There have always been transnational issues such as wars among nations, trade, navigation in international waters, uses of space, etc., but such activities have intensified as a result of globalization. There is, in addition, a number of other transnational activities whose relevance and impact have become considerably significant as a result of globalization. They are activities originating from one location anywhere on the globe but whose scope and scale reach faraway places. Such activities have brought about a set of new challenges that the globalized world must deal with. They have brought about transnational issues, as those issues that are of concern to all nations across borders, simply because they defy the traditional geopolitical bordering of nation-states. Among such transnational issues we count and will take a closer look at the following: environmental issues, immigration issues, global health issues, and human organ trafficking issues. As diverse as these issues appear to be, they are reflective of the state of our globalized world in its intensified communicative, commercial, scientific, technological, intellectual, relational, cultural, and political exchanges. All of these activities, despite the good they bring, also explain the intensification of global health concerns, immigration, human trafficking, environmental issues, and new technology-related issues, which we address in chapter 11. They have in common the fact that they are the result of today's human activity. Their commonality to space is that they all defy national borders. The challenges they cause, therefore, concern all human beings on the planet.

THE ENVIRONMENT

There is a link between globalization, the environmental space, global issues, and ultimately human activity. The link between globalization and the environmental space is that under the conditions brought about by the current state of globalization, economic activity of production has accelerated a number of environmental phenomena that are now developing or have already become a global issue. Among the phenomena are the sustainability of the balance between population, resources, and production; enhanced greenhouse gases effect; thinning of the ozone layer; climate change; pollution; depletion of nonrenewable resources; overuse of renewable resources; deforestation; and overfishing. Each one of these effects also produces its own set of consequences, which we address a few paragraphs below.

The link between the environment and global issues lies in the fact that any issues resulting from pressure, stress, or abuse to the environment such as pollution or rising of sea levels are naturally global issues due to the fact that environmental issues know no boundaries, no borders. Hence, the consequences of any environmental issue have the potential of endangering the security of the planet's inhabitants and of disrupting life itself. Ultimately, the link between environmental issues and human activity lies in the pressure, stress, or abuse to the environment dictated by the need to exploit its natural resources.

Environmental global issues therefore start with the exploitation of the natural space. It is a natural space abundant with natural resources. Such natural resources serve as the basis for production activity in order to sustain human existence. The use of natural resources has not always been a critical issue of interest to the international community from a global perspective. It has gradually become an issue, as production continues to exponentially increase to sustain the existence of soon to be 7 billion inhabitants of the planet. With globalization, which is essentially economical and therefore about production, and based on natural resources, access to resources anywhere on the globe has been made easier, and businesses are willing to reach and exploit any for which there is a market. This production activity has raised a number of concerns that justify the increasing significance of environmental issues as an issue area in international relations.

What are these concerns associated with production? In light of the seemingly ever present need for new resources comes the questions about whether the process is endless. It is the question of sustainability, which brings into account the Earth's growing population, the need to produce to support lives, and the continual availability of resources from nature. Sustainability therefore is "The level of ability of an ecosystem to maintain stable and remain functional" (World Resources Institute 2000, p. 16). And ecosystems are "not just assemblages of species; they are systems combined of organic and inorganic matter and natural forces that interact and change. The sun and water are crucial elements to make these systems flow" (World Resources Institute 2000, p. 11). Taken from a global economic perspective, sustainability is the needed equilibrium between world resources (nature), economic exploitation (economics), and consumption (population).

Sustainability is possible only if the equilibrium between these three factors (population, production, and nature) is maintained. This means that the ability of Mother Nature to provide natural resources must be measured against the rising curve of the world's exploitation of natural resources, which reflects the pressure of world economies driven by the increased demand from the rising population. The question of sustainability is pertinent in light of the fact that some resources we utilize are nonrenewable (oil, for instance) and therefore depletable, and those that are renewable (water, for instance) may not always have time to recover and regenerate due to sustained production assaults, as is the case for some fish species or repeated agricultural land uses, etc. These questions compel the need to reiterate the distinction between the use (*usus*) of natural resources, which is expected and legitimate, and the transformation (*fructus*) of nature for gain but not to abuse (*abusus*) it. The aggressive exploitation of natural resources around the world has shown signs of *abusus*.

The natural resources in question that are used, abused, or transformed are multiple and of various kinds. They are water (freshwater and salt water), land, minerals, biotic resources (living resources), energy resources, and air (atmosphere). They are used, transformed, or abused through human activity, namely, production. This human activity of production uses machines that burn fossil fuels (oil, natural gas, and coal), which power transportation systems and generate steam and electricity, a process that emits carbon dioxide and other elements such a methane, nitrous oxide, and sulfur dioxide. All of this is in addition to natural emissions (decomposition or decay process and ocean release and respiration). Of the human-produced carbon dioxide, 87 percent is the result of fossil fuel burning, and the rest is from forest clearing and land usage. Together with other greenhouse gases, water vapor (36–78 percent), carbon dioxide (9–26 percent), methane (4–9 percent), ozone (3–7 percent), and absorption and emission of clouds of infrared radiation, the burning of fossil fuels begets a series of other consequences. They are issues resulting directly from the burning of fossil fuels. Among them we count the issue of greenhouse gases, acid rain, carbon footprint, thinning of the ozone layer, climate change, and pollution. We look at each one next.

About greenhouse gases effect we naturally imply the enhanced greenhouse gases effect, the one that in addition to the natural interaction between Earth's atmosphere and its surface is made produced to affect such interaction that consists of absorbing, transferring and emitting heat energy in a cyclical process through the atmosphere and back to the surface. The issue is consequently about the balance of the cycle, once man-made interference increases the amount of circulating greenhouse gases through fossil fuel burning to disrupt the natural cycle, and therefore causing issues of the Earth's incapacity to absorb the circulating carbon. "A variety of human activities can disturb the carbon storage capacity of vegetation, especially grasslands. These include conversion of grasslands to croplands, removal of vegetation and subsequent cultivation, degradation of grass cover and burning grasslands" (World Resources Institute, p. 130). The phenomenon brought about the issue of climate change but also the need for solutions about the recuperation, transportation, and storage of produced carbon to prevent its spread in the atmosphere.

Acid rain is the result of higher concentrations of nitric and sulfuric oxides, due to the burning of fossil fuels, which pollutes cloud water and precipitation. As pollutants they damage water sources, lakes and streams, and forests. Carbon footprint is the notion and the intent to have a degree of awareness on how much individuals, organizations, or just activity contributes to the emission of greenhouse gases, since the higher concentration of such gases has become an issue. Obviously, the complexity of such intent makes it almost impossible to grasp, as there are many ways through such gases are emitted, which cannot always be measured, contained, or controlled. Nevertheless, the growing consciousness of the issue has led many to reduce concretely in small measures activities that clearly lead to emission of greenhouse gases.

Pollution occurs in many ways in different environmental sectors and is caused by many pollutants. The environment sectors where pollution occurs are everywhere, from air and atmosphere, to soil and forests, from water to food, etc. The pollutants are anything from emissions and concentration of chemical compounds such as greenhouse gases but also other sources such as the use of pesticides.

The thinning of the ozone layer is due to the use of ozone-depleting substances (atomic halogens such as fluorides, iodine, chlorine, etc.) found in homes and the products of manufacturing economies. The ozone layer shields the atmosphere from ultraviolet radiation from the sun. This is made possible because of the ozone molecule containing three oxygen atoms, which allow it to partially absorb radiation from the sun and by so doing prevents such radiation from reaching the lower layer of the atmosphere, namely, the Earth's surface. The thinning of the ozone layer consequently allows the penetration of ultraviolet rays into the atmosphere. Such penetration has been linked to increased cases of skin cancer. Due to the thinning of the ozone layer in the past few decades there has been an increase in ultraviolet ray penetration. Compared to the 1970s the level of ultraviolet ray penetration is about 130 percent greater in Antarctica and 22 percent greater in the Arctic. This heightened exposure can lead to the increase of cataracts and eye and skin cancer, along with adverse effects on plant life (World Resources Institute 2000, p. 138).

The production of chlorofluorocarbons (CFCs), the world's first nontoxic and nonflammable refrigerants, was linked to the beginning depletion of the ozone layer. The discovery of this hole in 1985 led to an international effort to phase out the production of CFCs (World Resources Institute 2000, pp. 7, 138).

We understand climate, like all geographers today do, as the result of the multiple interactions between distinct physical entities such as oceans, the atmosphere, the biosphere, and polar regions (Schimdt and Wolfe 2009, p. 1) and not just temperature. Hence, climate change is a complex reality that is evoked in cases and situations of rising sea levels, extinction of species, and, yes, even the rise of temperature, etc. Climate change is about weather patterns over a period of time and the balancing that it necessitates. as well as the need for adaptation it sparks for all species affected. The implications of changing weather patterns, therefore, become of interest and possibly an issue. The health of the human species itself, which is linked to food and water, which in turn are part of weather conditions, is affected by climate change. Extreme weather and weather disasters, heat waves, drought (as warmer temperatures cause more evaporation and transpiration of water from the Earth and plants into the atmosphere), wildfires and wildfire smoke, rainstorms, flooding, hurricanes, rise of sea levels, and rise of temperatures, etc., are more and more costly for human lives and the food and water supply.

These changes in the weather patterns are driven by the water circulation of the Earth's oceans, which is driven by Arctic marine ecosystems. Due to the gradual increase in the Earth's temperatures, these Arctic ecosystems are being depleted; this increases the level of the oceans and leads to a shift in water temperature and currents (World Resources Institute 2000, p. 137).

According to NOAA (National Oceanic and Atmospheric Administration), the average temperature on the ground and on the oceans' surfaces was 13.68 degrees Celsius (56.624 degrees Fahrenheit) in November 2013, which is 0.78 degree above the average of the past century (since 1880). Again, from the same source, there have been 345 consecutive data temperature samples (land and ocean surfaces) that have all been higher than those taken in the twentieth century.

Production activity aimed at using and transforming natural resources, sometimes abusing them, has caused another set of environmental issues, next to those directly linked to the burning of fossil fuels. They are issues of the depletion of nonrenewable resources, overuse of renewable natural resources, deforestation, and overfishing, and each of them with its own set of subsequent side issues.

The depletion of nonrenewable resources has been a subject mentioned in the context of sustainability. There has been much talk about oil, prompting research in alternative energy sources. Such a depletion, the result of human production activity, is in itself a complex reality, as any resource is part of an ecosystem, and consequently if and when negatively affected, it tends to have implications for the entire the ecosystem. "The massive production of human goods has led to the degradation of ecosystems throughout the planet. These include: overfishing, deforestation, destruction of coral reefs, soil degradation due to agriculture, etc." (World Resources Institute 2000, p. 16). There has been a lot of talk around oil, a nonrenewable energy source, and the prospect of its depletion "soon."[1]

The overuse of water as a renewable resource has been the most talked about recently. A UN report published March 2015, in the context of World Water Day, speaks of underground reserves running low and rainfall that may become even more unpredictable as a result of climate change. The projected 9 billion global population in the year 2050 will mean that more groundwater will be needed in the three main areas of use, namely, in farming, industry, and personal use, which also means an increase in demand of 55 percent, while reserves dwindle. The report further states that "If current usage trends don't change, the world will have only 60 percent of the water it needs in 2030" (Associated Press 2015).

Here, the issue is not that of use, but abuse. And it is the abuse that risks making a renewable natural resource scarce, but hopefully not totally depleted. A variety of uses of water, among them use of water in agricultural activity, more precisely in irrigation, which makes up 70 percent of water usage, and the rest for power generation and a variety of other purposes, can stress out the ability of this renewable resource to regenerate. This could occur with the extensive use of aquifers. The same aquifers are additionally in stress due to pollution of groundwater through the use of pesticides and the increased nitric and sulfuric acid in acid rain. The depletion of water is possible considering the fact that although Earth's land is surrounded by water, most of it is salt water and therefore not potable. Salt in the water not only affects its proprieties, density, salinity (high salinity of about 35 g/kg on average), behavior with respect to disintegrating effect, and even temperature, but also salt water is not suited for many immediate human usages of water. It needs therefore to be desalinated, which explains the growing number of desalination plants to alleviate the growing water scarcity. This led Pielou (1998, p. 1) to write: "Only the water temporarily withdrawn from the ocean is fresh." Yes, water withdrawn from the ocean, because water is everywhere and it cyclically circulates. Water in the ocean, in the air, in circulation, trapped, stagnant, and underground (Pielou 1998, p. 3). In the course of its circulation, it reaches the ocean, only to leave it, eventually becoming the water we drink. It is the hydrological cycle. Water circulating and cycling suggests a never-ending reservoir if it does not get lost, and it may even grow. However, it does so "not fast enough relief humanity growing water supply shortage problem" (Pielou 1998, p. 3). Fear for survival and projected conflicts are the consequences of less water than needed. The UN report on water in 2015 concluded by urging both individuals and policy makers to change their ways with respect to water usage. This phenomenon, and the entire phenomenon of climate change, explains the many images and stories of disappearing lakes and even creeks.

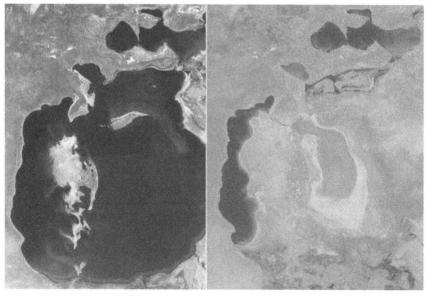

Figure 9.1.   Cachuna Lake: Left: July 1989. Right: October 2008. *Source:* NASA Earth Observatory

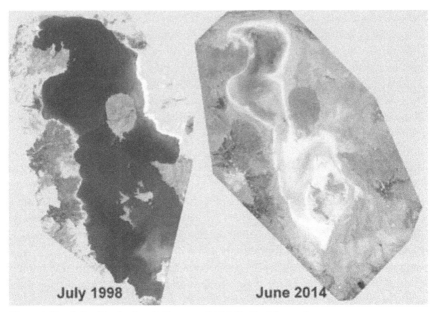

July 1998   June 2014

Figure 9.2.   Lake Urmia (Iran). *Source:* NASA Earth Observatory

For both renewable and nonrenewable natural resources, which contain as well biotic life (animals), depletion also means extinction. In both cases, depletion and extinction, the implication is reaching a point of no return. Once gone, they will be lost forever. The question then becomes how detrimental is the loss to both Earth and the viability of life on it.

Deforestation is "the process of clearing up land of forests to provide land for agriculture, fuel, cooking and heating, and construction materials" (World Resources Institute 2000, p. 6). It is another result of human activity and its effect on natural resources through exploitation of land and timber and through land development, as any road construction may cut through entire ecosystems, disrupting the habitat while removing key elements of the ecosystem and rendering species vulnerable, which accelerates their extinction process and affects biodiversity. Such an extinction of a species leads to complete reorganization of ecosystems (World Resources Institute 2000, p. 14). The same process of deforestation is part of the chain of events producing climate change, as it reduces the number of trees, therefore, compromising their useful role in cleaning the air and storing carbon, and ultimately contributes to additional emissions, as such activity and subsequent usage produce carbon emissions and increases the carbon footprint. Additional consequences are the disappearing other benefits associated with the existence of trees as protection against erosion and desertification. Furthermore, due to the extensive conversion of grasslands to agriculture and urban area ecosystems are becoming less able to provide goods and services related to biodiversity (World Resources Institute 2000, p. 130).

Overfishing disrupts underwater ecosystems, may produce extinction of species, and consequently impoverish biodiversity. Such extinction occurs "when an ecosystem is being fished at its biological limit or beyond" (World Resources Institute 2000, p. 16), causing disruption in the food chain, which produces either overpopulation or extinction, depending on the species.

In the end, the human activity of production and its reliance on natural resources ever growing assaults on such natural resources, relentlessly leaves their marks on the Earth and its ability, in a sustained manner, to remain hospitable to life.

These environmental consequences of human activity are in their very nature global issues. They are global issues simply because environmental issues are global by definition, as their impact is global, as nature does not know nor does it recognize human political borders, which constitute referential frames. A nuclear explosion in Fukushima, Japan, may become a problem for the US western coastal states. Pollution in Canada would not think twice before entering US space. These issues defy the notion of locale, location, or place. They are simply environmental issues. They are as well global issues because the environment is a global space. And they are issues that emerge as a result of human activity, which has the environment as a canvas; the environmental canvas is a global space, and their impact therefore is global.

Because environmental issues are global, they have emerged as a source of concern to the international community. Indeed, environmental issues have the potential of disrupting life itself. If nations spend time, money, energy, and resources to protect themselves from any disruption or potential danger to national security, environmental issues have such a potential of disrupting the security of a nation, as dramatically shown in the Hollywood film the *Day after Tomorrow*. National security is about nations, but there are no nations without humans. National security ought to ultimately be about humans. There is increasingly an awareness of this human dimension in national security, and many have argued that it is the kind of security that we ought to be more concerned with, as issues of national security are less and less alarming while those of human security are more and more so.

More than just disrupting national security or human security, environmental issues carry the potential of disrupting the security of the entire human race. Planet Earth is today the only planet that hosts human life. As long as that remains the reality, should we mess with the natural balance that has made life possible here in the first place, we risk rendering inhospitable the only planet that hosts human life. Should anything go wrong with the planet, it will be all of mankind that will go under with it. There may even be a planet Earth without humans, as its geophysical condition may still permit its existence but there may no longer be all the necessary conditions to allow life to blossom.

Now, there are those who have argued that the above-described scenario is nothing but alarmist and that we do not have to worry about nature. They argue that nature has its way of going through phases and cycles and that human beings are nothing but sheer extras; if as humans we have any role at all, it is minimal and negligible. This of course leads us to the contemporary environmental debate. The debate started to pick up steam in the last thirty years. Indeed, in the last thirty years, environmental pattern changes have become more and more noticeable. The melting glaciers, which may not have been noticed or neglected, will trigger interest if the melting is sustained. It is associated with changes in weather patterns and the frequency of hurricanes, tornadoes, and floods, to ring the bell of some environmentalists who argue that the climate is changing. Of course, with additional phenomena at hand their thesis was more or less understressed. Indeed, additional phenomena such as farmers in Denmark who could now grow grapes that produce red wine, a phenomenon that until then was possible only in southern Europe, was seen as a concrete example of climate change. Or when fishermen in Marseilles, France, started to see new kinds of fish, never before seen in the Mediterranean waters, were alarmed. They finally came to find out that they were now fishing some species that typically live in the warm waters of the southern tropics, around South Africa, but for whom, water in the Mediterranean was no longer too cold. Many other examples from the world of insects can be pointed to and their potential to carry new types of pathogens unknown in their new environments.

To many, these changes, because they imply deterioration of environmental conditions, were reasons to seek to understand their true causes. This need is more than a simple curiosity. It is justified by the risks that such changes bring. Soon enough three perspectives emerged. First, there were those who believed these changes were neither real nor structural; thus there was no need to explore the issue any deeper. Second, there were those who believed that the changes were indeed occurring but humans were not responsible for their occurrence. Finally, there are those who believe that not only are the changes there and that they are structural in nature but also that human beings are their true cause.

Of course, there is not much to follow up on from the perspective of those who deny any kind of deterioration of environmental conditions. There is as well a fatalistic attitude that seems to derive from the perspective of those who recognize some of the deterioration of environmental conditions but do not see in them as the consequence of human activity. But there are those who believe that these environmental changes are indeed real and happening, and they are essentially caused by human activity. There are those establishing the link between environmental conditions with such phenomena as the rising of sea levels; the frequency of floods, hurricanes, and tornadoes; the flying around of insects from familiar environments into new hospitable environments; changes in temperatures in ways until now unknown, etc. They argue, therefore, that these changes deserve our full attention.

Associations, political parties, think tanks, and small groups that were all beginning to be known as environmentalists had been sounding the alarm on potential disruptive effects to some of the acts we pose to the environment, and consequently to us, the inhabitants of planet Earth, since the 1970s, essentially in Western Europe. They have since not relented. Their movement has continued to grow. The awareness of potentially disruptive consequences of environmental changes was eventually taken seriously by relevant established international institutions.

This awareness justifies a number of initiatives that have emerged in the last forty years. The international community made the first step with the Earth Summit in Rio de Janeiro, Brazil, in 1992. The Earth Summit was a forum wherein discussions and exchanges could be carried out, and some educating of the participant public at large, for the most part, decision makers. From all the discussion and exchanges that took place, two key takeaways were achieved. The first was an agreement on sustainability and reforestation. The second was an agreement on protection of species, ecosystems, and biodiversity around the globe.

Three years later, as in Rio, one of the promises made was that such a summit was not going to be the only one. A second conference was going to be in Kyoto, Japan. The Kyoto Environment Summit had one focus: climate change. There, as well, Kyoto served as a locus for discussion, exchange, and education. Decisions to find a way to reduce carbon dioxide emissions into the atmosphere were expected, after a quasi-consensus emerged that there was such a phenomenon as the greenhouse gas effect and that we humans through production activities of our respective economies that essentially use fossil fuels to run engines and machines and ensure manufacturing output volumes were responsible. Any decision made was going to be about reducing emissions. reducing emissions requires either improving the environmental quality of the engines used, with for instance, catalytic converters, which requires new research and new investments, or simply using fewer such engines and machines that pollute the air and emit carbon dioxide, which simply means cutting down production. Cutting down production affects the bottom line of businesses. Many such businesses were those located in the Northern hemisphere, where we find the most advanced economies and therefore those that use the most machinery and emit the most emissions. Nations reflecting such features of advanced economies were asked to do more, which meant reduce emissions by 5 percent by 2025. The highest polluter, the United States was asked to reduce even more, by 7 percent. Levels of pollution of those in the developing world, because of the stature of their economies, namely, small, were deemed negligible. However, some nations in the same category of nations were developing fast, and consequently polluting in nonnegligible ways: China and India. They were as well exempted. The combination of reduced emissions by advanced economies, especially the United States, and the exemption of the largest growing economies from the developing nation's world was enough to cause resistance from the US delegation, which finally refrained from signing the final agreement document. The rest of the signatory nations agreed with its content, and it was known as the Kyoto Protocol. The efforts to reduce the amount of greenhouse gas emissions in the atmosphere has continued under the UN Framework Convention on Climate Change (UNFCCC).

Since the Kyoto Protocol and through the UNFCCC, the need to achieve reduction of greenhouse gases has produced flexible mechanisms, one of which was carbon credit issuance. The issuance of carbon credits creates a carbon market, which is both voluntary and regulatory to projects that align with the goal of carbon emission reduction. In the voluntary carbon market, carbon credits are generated through independent international standards (Verified Carbon Standards) to projects such as renewable energy, energy efficiency, forest regeneration, etc. Such projects earn the seal of Verified Emission Reduction (VER). The regulatory or compliance carbon market credits are generated through an approved mechanism, the Clean Development Mechanism, under the UNFCCC. Through the mechanism, projects earn credits based on approved quantity of greenhouse gases. In such a case, projects earn the seal of Certified Emissions Reduction (CERs).

In both carbon credit mechanisms, credits earned are stored in electronic registries, the market environmental registries. Carbon credits earned, mostly through the voluntary mechanism, can be through the Carbon Trade Exchange.

The awareness of environmental issues continues to rise. We have come to realize, as science continues to provide evidence and as environmental changes such as weather patterns increasingly catch our attention, that environmental issues are a matter of human security and that of preservation of the planet we have inherited. Such growing consciousness and the concern it dictates, although still not shared by many, can be witnessed and documented through the interest in environmental topics and discussion in various venues, from individuals to interest groups, from politicians and political parties to businesses, from scientists to religious organizations. This interest in environmental issues also explains the various gatherings and professional conferences discussing themes such as sustainable development, renewable energy, water resources, pollution, tourism, carbon footprint, chemistry and the environment, sustainable design and engineering, biodiversity, climate change, ozone layer, recycling, forests and rainforests, etc.

THE TRAGEDY OF THE COMMONS

Tragedy of the commons has been a phenomenon brought to the attention of the public at large by the American biologist Garrett Hardin in 1968.[2]

Hardin defined the notion of "tragedy of the commons" as the bad outcome emanating from the public access and use of resources open to the public, the commons. Such resources are goods that find utility among the public such as grass and pasture for herders and farmers with livestock, the air we breathe, the water in the oceans, public parks, etc. The commons are natural resources available and accessible to all. Such natural resources are finite and therefore depletable. And if they are stricken by tragedy it is because users and those with access to such resources tend to abuse them. The abuse comes in the form of pursuit of private gain, a remorseless pursuit of private gain, to use the terminology of Whitehead (1948), and which results in a tragedy, namely, the abuse, neglect, degradation, and harm, or simply the destruction, of the commons. The unhappy situation occurs because these commons are generally unowned, and therefore there is no one to control their use, to undermine their abuse, and to prevent their destruction. We have now reached a stage of near extinction of buffalos, bluefin tuna, and codfish off the coast of Newfoundland, Canada. We have polluted oceans (garbage gyre), created dead zones (the coast of Mexico) as a result of use of fertilizers, polluted the atmosphere, wasted groundwater, etc.

If there is a situation of near extinction of some fish species in the ocean, it is because of overfishing by some fishing companies that overfish to satisfy the demand of the market they supply without any concern or care in the long run for the "commons." Another example is the owner of a plant that makes any given product, such as tires, and uses machines that profusely emit carbon dioxide in the atmosphere, polluting the environment and even causing an increase in cases of asthma.

There is here a selfish behavior of the users, the fishing company and the plant owner, interested solely in their interest and gain. Such selfishness allows a private and personal gain. It leaves behind a loss of the commons that is public. The gain is 100 percent private. The loss from the abuser is a portion of the total loss incurred by the rest (1/N), and should the abused be called upon to participate in a collective effort of restoration of the commons, their loss may simply be a fraction (1/N) of the total cost. The loss is essentially public. It is a tragedy. Such tragedy, therefore, occurs because the commons are unowned.

The question that arises is whether to stand idly by and let the commons be abused, depleted, or destroyed. The second question that arises is whether to let the carelessness of some users destroy the commons that should be preserved for all. The third question is what should society do to prevent the unhappy situation expressed in the previous two questions from occurring? The answer to the first question is, of course, that we should not stand idly by and let the commons be abused. The abuse, depletion, and destruction of natural resources, the commons, raise in turn the issue of sustainability, which is of concern to all inhabitants of the planet and future generations. The issue is significant and important enough for society not to remain inactive. The answer to the second question is as well that we should not let the carelessness and the selfishness of some users undermine the commons for the rest of the users. And the answer to the third question is that we need to find solutions to prevent, protect, and safeguard the use of the commons. To achieve this goal, Hardin himself made a few suggestions. Among Hardin's suggestions to push back against the abuses of the commons is the closing or restricting of the use of the commons. The growing population and use of public parks undermines the benefits of a visit to a park and put pressure on sustained maintenance of the park. Such pressure calls for restrictions, Hardin argued. Among Hardin's suggestions, there is legislation on access and consumption of the commons and privatization of the commons. Hardin argued that one of the reasons for the abuses of the commons was because they were unowned by individuals or groups. As such, there was no incentive to care for them. His solution was to entrust the commons to the care of private owners who then will care for them, given the incentive they will have to do so. The incentive derives from the utility factor, as the commons can be commoditized. The fact that fish in the ocean are unowned makes them vulnerable to abuse. The fact that the air we breathe is unowned makes it vulnerable to abuse. The owners of the commons will protect them, as they benefit from their utility, and they will restrict, if need be, their access and abuse. In the process they preserve the commons for the rest of us and prevent their destruction. Finding a mechanism of transferring ownership of whales or salmon in the oceans to private individuals or groups may just be one way of ensuring their survival and avoiding their extinction, argues Hardin. These individuals or groups, who will see themselves given the proprietor title of these creatures, realizing their commodity value, will find in it an incentive to care for them and benefit from their fishing or whale tourism. They will regulate their uses or services for a more lasting ownership, and in the process ensuring by doing what is necessary that they stay around longer. By so doing they will save the species for generations to come, and we will all benefit.

Hardin's suggestion is in agreement with the notion of private property, as promoted in economic liberalism and Adam Smith. Adam Smith who argued for the benefit to society of self-interest, not selfishness, saw in private ownership the source of utilitarian care for the owner. As for self-interest, the owner cares for his/her property, thus, he/she increases its value. The care of private property is beneficial to society at large. As such a care may require the help of others, who all stand to benefit for the value of the commons. A concrete example of this liberal economic tenet is that the self-interest of Bill Gates to start Microsoft has led him to enlist the help and support of many others. As a private property that has utility (use of Windows), it provides incentive to care for, as it generates revenues for all workers. So Bill Gates's self-interest is beneficial for all those on board at Microsoft, but also beneficial to society that uses Windows. Bill Gates's self-interest is a positive force to dissociate from the selfishness of some other endeavors that often are remorseless and produce tragedy. It is the same reasoning at play here when Hardin suggests private ownership for the commons, as the owner will have the incentive to care for them, for his own self-interest, but in the process protection for all the commons from destruction.

There have been a number of criticisms formulated against Hardin's suggestions on how to curtail the abuses of the commons. Some have argued that his worry of the tragedy was historically not significantly observed. Others have pointed to the difficulties of privatizing international commons. Others again have argued that Hardin has a bit too strictly opposed private gain and public interest. They have argued that even those interested in private gain would recognize the need to protect public interest. Their private gain ultimately depends on the existence and health of the commons.

IMMIGRATION

Immigration is an age-old phenomenon. An argument can be made that it has been part of human history since *Homo erectus*. It is not historically linked to national territorial borders, as people have been migrating before the rise of the modern state. It was then simply called migration. The difference is early people in movement moved about in search for greener pastures. Today, they move about knowing where the greener pasture is. They emigrate with a migrant destination in mind. The entire phenomenon of emigrating from and migrating into is called immigration. The quest for greener pastures is a natural reflex for survival. That is what it was then. That is what it is now. Human beings seek places that accommodate life better. The Romans used to say *Ubi bene ibi patria* (home is where you prosper). This drive toward the location and place where one prospers undermines the romanticism of homeland, which, when translated in some languages such as Latin, wherein it is called *patria*, or German, wherein it is called *Vaterland*, connotes a certain sense of attachment to the land and culture of someone's upbringing. That sense of attachment to the land and culture of someone's upbringing becomes all too relatively less important in the face of the need for survival. So people easily leave their homeland when there is no longer green pasture to graze from. The phenomenon is driven by push and pull factors. Push factors are all those that compel individuals to leave their current environments. Pull factors are those that attract emigrating populations into certain migrating destinations. The notion of a push and pull factor is a tandem notion. Naturally, there is a correlation between push and pull factors. And so if economic hardship is a push factor in any given space, economic prosperity in another becomes a pull factor. If a political instability and insecurity is a push factor in any given space, political stability and security in another become a pull factor. And the same is valid for cultural intolerance opposed to cultural pluralism or religious intolerance opposed to religious freedom, etc.

Migratory processes in the modern era have been triggered by European expansion since the 1500s as a result of mercantilism, which has produced European colonization of regions outside Europe. Such colonization has been intensive in North and South America, Australia, and New Zealand, known as offshoots of the West. It has been less intensive in Africa with the exception of Southern Africa for climatic reasons, and Asia. The same migratory process has remained a recurrent phenomenon in the modern era. As the modern era unfolded, some regions and nations were faring better than others. Regions and nations faring better were those of the Northern hemisphere, Western nations and their offshoots with political and economic stability, cultural pluralism, and a high standard of living. Those struggling were the developing nations found in the Southern hemisphere and generally dealing with issues of political dictatorship, civil wars, lack of democracy, human rights abuses, cultural intolerance, struggling economically and therefore having employment markets unable to absorb the mass of able-bodied workers or provide adequate health care, etc. Under these circumstances, those nations faring better were displaying attractive factors that exerted a pull effect to those from the outside. The outside was the developing nations wherefrom the difficult conditions were presenting push factors, driving many to entertain the thought of escape and compelling them to seek a better life elsewhere. This situation constitutes one of the underlying causes of modern-day immigration issues. The issues of immigration seemed to grow as the push factors in the South grew and pull factors in the North became even more attractive. This described phenomenon reached its peak in the 1980s, the height of economic setbacks in the South due to SAPs, insolvency in some countries such as Mexico and Argentina, and debt crisis in others such as the majority of African countries, the many civil wars and political unrest, even famine. All these factors were push factors that explain the centrifugal force that led to the influx of immigrants seeking work from Latin America into North America. It led as well to the influx of African immigrants seeking asylum and economic relief in the North. It was as well the case for Asia, only Asia seemed to have found a remedy to escape what seemed to be the economic fate of southern nations. Malaysia, Singapore, South Korea, Taiwan, Hong Kong, and soon after even China started to develop redemptive policy measures of reform. Today, they increasingly look attractive. They exert a pull effect, as opposed to the push effect that explained, for instance, the large number of Chinese in the diaspora, in the history of the country.

The International Database of the US Census Bureau provides the following data: world population: 6,853,328,460, of which 215,738,321 are migrating. It is almost 216 million people or 3,15 percent of world population. Most of those migrating end up in Europe, which absorbs 3/6 of them, North America absorbs 2/6, and Asia absorbs 1/6. The data suggest that nations that are economically prosperous, politically stable, culturally pluralistic, and religiously tolerant attract more influx of migrant populations. The nations that assemble all these pull factors, the best, become as well the mecca for migrant populations. And so it is no wonder that in Europe, Germany is one such mecca, where most migrant populations in Europe end up. In the Western hemisphere, the United States is such a mecca (Table 9.1).

Emigrating populations have been those seeking better economic prosperity, those being displaced because of wars or natural disasters, or those seeking political asylum or refugee status as a result of political persecution. In the last category, in 2010, 16.3 million, or 8 percent, of international migrant populations were asylum seekers (Migration and Remittances Factbook 2011). The largest share, 64 percent, comes from the Middle East and North Africa, followed by Southeast Asia (20 percent), followed by Sub-Saharan Africa (17 percent) and East Asia and the Pacific region (8.8 percent).

The pathways linking emigrant countries to migrant destinations are known as migration corridors. Because there is a link between emigrant countries and migrant destinations, some migration corridors are more frequented than others. Such corridors can be those of proximity. They can also be distant.

Table 9.1.

Top Migrant Destinations	
United States: 42,788,029	United Kingdom: 6,955,738
Russian Federation: 12,270,388	Spain: 6,900,547
Germany: 10,758,061	France: 6,684,842
Saudi Arabia: 7,288,900	Australia: 5,522,408
Canada: 7,202,340	India: 5,436,012
Top Emigration Countries	
Mexico: 11,859,236	Bangladesh: 5,384,875
India: 11,360,823	Pakistan: 4,678,730
Russian Federation: 11,034,681	United Kingdom: 4,666,172
China: 8,344,726	Philippines: 4,275,612
Ukraine: 6,525,145	Turkey: 4,261,786

Source: Globalization101.org

Proximity corridors are those we see when a nation with predominantly a push factor is geographically located next to one with predominantly a pull factor. It is the case of the United States and Mexico. Distant corridors are those that show the route between emigrants of a given nation toward their preferred destination located far away. It is the case of Nigeria and Great Britain.

The most important migration corridors are those between Mexico and the United States, allowing the crossing of 11,635,995 emigrants; Russian Federation and Ukraine, allowing the crossing of 3,684,214; Bangladesh and India, allowing the crossing of 3,299,268; and Turkey and Germany, allowing the crossing of 2,733,109 (Migration and Remittances Factbook 2011).

The migratory process has been magnified by the complexity of contemporary life in the era of globalization. Under globalization there are widespread means of communication and transportation and a technology that facilitates access to needed information. They all provide support for a migratory process. The process is now driven by the need for global markets to achievethe needed synergy between availability of resources around the globe with investment financing and labor markets. The work that needs to be done needs to be linked with workers who can accomplish it. Resources that need to be tapped must be linked to corporations and the know-how that can exploit them. All this implies mobility of financial resources and workforce toward the immobility of natural resources and markets. Among the factors of production that are mobile is the workforce. This workforce is manpower, which means people. People are becoming more mobile or flexible, as they stand ready to go where labor is available. Current conditions of globalization have succeeded in getting nation-states to accommodate that need for a more mobile and flexible labor market. States, the recipients of the most influx of immigrating populations, have come up with legal paths to facilitate labor-based immigration. And where there is no viable and practical legal path, as is the case in the United States and elsewhere, there are illegal paths of immigration. There are those still willing to attempt entering nations with pull effects without proper documentation. And there are also those who have realized the existence of such need. They have organized to satisfy that need as it turns into a demand. It turns into a demand as those willing to travel are willing to spend money to embark on the journey away from nations with push factors to nations with pull factors. People and organized gangs specialized in facilitating the journey have different names in different countries, from "Schlepper" in Germany to "passeurs" in France or "coyotes" in the United States. Their policies differ. While the United States is sill politically divided on the issue of how to approach the existing and incoming flow of immigrants, Canada has found a way of targeting skilled workers with a start-up visa program. Since 2010, 21.3 percent of the population is foreign born. Japan, for instance, is one of the highest ethnically homogenous nations, with 97 percent Japanese, and has only 1.7 percent foreign population. Australia has been struggling to control the huge influx of asylum seekers and has resorted to a harsh policy through the Migration Act of 1958. The United Kingdom has managed to absorb a number as high as 7.5 million of migrant populations (UK Census).

The mobility that ensues is part of the contemporary immigration issue. It reveals as well the characteristics of today's immigration issue. The issue has two protagonists: the recipient nations on one hand and the emigrant nations on the other. Recipient nations are those with high per capita income, aging populations, investment potential, availability of funds, availability of multi-national corporations, with an economy essentially driven by the service sector, and IT technology and high minimum wage, leading to delocalization and outsourcing. The emigrant nations have a huge pool of cheap labor, young populations, natural resources, and skilled labor. The respective features of these protagonists in the immigration debate seem to display a complementary needs. Natural resources found in emigrant nations can use investments from corporations and financing from recipient nations. Cheap labor in the emigrant nations is attractive to corporations in the recipient nations. Young populations in the emigrant nations can compensate for the stagnating, even negative, birth rate in many recipient nations, etc. Today's immigration therefore seems to be simply economically responding to a natural law of recreating equilibrium, in this case, an economic or social equilibrium, where it needs to be. The only issue is how much influx of people from the emigrant nations can recipient nations take in. The proper number is critical, as too many can end up creating disequilibrium in the recipient nations. When the equilibrium seems threatened, voices are heard in recipient nations, expressing their concerns about a potential loss of identity, integration issues, stressed out labor market by the new immigrants' demand for labor, etc. There are political parties in Europe that have built a narrative around those themes and what they consider to be an overflow of new immigrants in their countries.

Despite a number of business opportunities in the South now emerging as a result of globalization, coveted corporations, and labor from the North, there are no worries of an overflow of immigration flow from the industrialized North into the South. The North remains the space of recipient nations, and the South, the space of emigrant populations. Hence, the debate becomes here again framed in a spatial context. We are here dealing with two spaces: the Northern hemisphere versus the Southern hemisphere. We are dealing with the North, countries of recipients of immigration, and the South, countries of emigrants.

The South has generally been a space wherein major push factors have been met, which explains the emigration dynamics. Conversely, the North has been a space wherein the pull factors have been met, and hence its immigration recipient status. This immigration process has a direction and a trajectory, which both point upward, northward. The space dimension here reveals that these respective spaces, North and South, are canvases wherein activity has been occurring. In this case, the activity is the economy. It is the thriving economic activity in one space and the struggling economic activity in the other space that are the root causes of the direction and trajectory of the migration. If the thriving economy had been occurring in the South and the North had been struggling, the direction and trajectory of immigration would be different. The debate on immigration, therefore, is often argued from the perspective of how to gain control in the recipient nations of the flow of immigrants from the emigrating nations.

The relevance of space in the immigration issue is that these spaces are places. And we have defined places as spaces with specific characters due to the kinds of activity to be found there. It is therefore logical to see the place we call Mexico as having a character, one of which is having an economy that does not absorb its workforce, and therefore the character of the place we call Mexico has produced an economic push factor. Conversely, the character of the place we call the United States has produced a pull factor due to the attractiveness of its economic activity. The trajectory and directions of immigration are the reflection the character of spaces involved in the immigration debate either as emigrant nations or as recipient nations.

GLOBAL HEALTH

Issues of health are naturally of utmost concern to human beings. Our health and that of our loved ones, and by extension, of all of humanity, is what we must have before having anything else. Consequently, the history of mankind has been paralleled by the history of medical science as we seek to ensure our survival, as the danger to humanity does not only come from wars, natural disasters, or famine. It comes as well from pathogens, microorganisms that cause diseases, or a medical condition. They have different statuses, contagious or not. They have many sources: humans, animals, agriculture, and the environment. They belong to different groups: virus, bacteria, fungi, actinomycetia, bacillus. And each has its family (subcategories), among them acinetobacter species, aspergilus species, streptococcus pyongenes, streptococcus pneumonia. They carry infectious diseases, some of which have the capacity to spread and bring death in huge numbers. Mankind has therefore constantly gained knowledge and degrees of control over health issues in order to be able to identify, prevent, contain, and ultimately cure diseases. It seems, however, that despite the successes of medical science, research, and practice, health issues seem illusive, as organisms causing diseases are not definitively all known. Moreover, new ones keep surfacing. And even those known can still morph and adapt and even figure out how to resist our best efforts to fight and eradicate them.

Highly populated cities have always been the most vulnerable, as both population density and sanitary conditions have helped spread the epidemic infections. It is no coincidence that known cases of plague in history have involved the large cities of their time, from Athens in 430–427 BC, to Milan in 1629–1631 AD, to London in 1665–1666, to Marseille in 1720–1722, to Moscow in 1771. It is as well no coincidence that such epidemic diseases have spread throughout larger territories that have been integrated by empire rule to become pandemics, as these larger territories offered good conditions for such spread. Such was the case of the Antonian Plague (165–180 AD) in the Roman Empire, during which time smallpox was brought back by empire legions from the Middle East, and the Justinian Plague across the Byzantine Empire, throughout the Mediterranean basin in the sixth century AD. China, a large and populous territory, was hit in 1860, and its experience with the plague lingered until 1894. In all these cases, historians count the death toll in the millions.

We have come to live in a globalized world with its high rate of integration, rendered concrete through, among other phenomenon, the immigration process, which implies travel and more exchange, and we communicate more extensively than ever before and ultimately increase our physical proximity globally. With such increased integration comes a risk of easy transfer and contamination of diseases, as sources and carriers of pathogens are less and less geographically restricted. The safety corridors provided by the isolation of tribal communities of the past have given way to the risk of fast-spreading pathogens due to the high proximity of people in megapolises and cosmopolitan spaces. Hence, the health of anyone in any given space is increasingly linked to the health of everyone anywhere else!

In addition to the increased mixing of people, animal trafficking also increases the potential of carrying pathogens formerly unknown to humans, such as the Ebola virus. Along with humans and animals as carriers of disease, there are goods and agricultural products that can carry microorganisms such as bacteria and other forms of pathogens that can cause illness and even death, such as "mad cow disease." And even the environment itself, its land, air, and water, can be a source and a carrier of pathogens such as pesticides and pollution particles, and bacteria-infected waters may cause harm to the general public in the form of allergies, asthma, dysentery, dermatitis, some forms of melanoma, etc.

Health issues hence are a concern to mankind in two complementary ways. The first is medical science and the second is public health. With medical science, we can go far back in history, not chronologically accounting for all contributions but only a few key ones, to the time of ancient Egypt in 2600 BC, when Imhotep was already diagnosing and treating hundreds of diseases. We must as well mention the Greek Hippocrates (460–380 BCE), if we consider the thorough observation and use of deductive logic to understand the cause of what happens when we get sick as the beginning of medical science. Since Hippocrates, there have been a number of contributions by a number of scientists, each focusing on a specific aspect of medicine that has helped advance the quest for identifying, preventing, containing, and curing diseases. These contributors have made discoveries, developed methodologies, deciphered mysteries of microorganisms (bacteria and viruses), found vaccines and cures, and invented instruments to advance their work. Among such contributing scientists we name just a few: Antonie van Leeuwenhoek (1622–1723), who observed microorganisms (bacteria) and discovered blood cells with a rudimentary microscope, which was invented in 1590 by Zacharius Janssen. Diocles in 300 BC authored the first anatomy manual. The Persian physician Rhazes identified smallpox in 910 AD. Avicenna authored *The Canon of Medicine*. René Laennec built the first stethoscope in 1816. Louis Pasteur (1822–1895) and Robert Koch (1843–1910) both focused on microbiology, precisely germs, and helped move the general knowledge away from the belief in the theory of spontaneous generation. Joseph Lister developed antiseptic surgical methods in 1867. Wilhelm Conrad Röntgen discovered in

1895 the X-ray, and Alexander Fleming developed penicillin in 1928. Along the way they got the upper hand on eradicating some epidemic diseases through the development of vaccines. Vaccines have been developed for the following diseases: cholera, anthrax, rabies, typhoid fever, plague, diphtheria, pertussis, tuberculosis, tetanus, yellow fever, typhus, influenza, measles, mumps, rubella, chickenpox, pneumonia, meningitis, and hepatitis B.

Today, more contributions to medical science continue to be made, from embryonic stem cell research to human genome decoding projects.

All these contributions, and many others not mentioned, have helped gain some degree of control over a few of the multitudes of agents and sources of infectious diseases that plague mankind. These contributions help infected individuals to treat or shake off their medical conditions. There is, however, a link between individual health and public health. In some cases, indeed, individuals can be sources or carriers of infectious diseases and contaminate others in a chain reaction to initiate public health plagues. Leprosy, sexually transmitted diseases, and body hygiene are some examples of how beginning with an individual, a disease may spread to become a matter of public health. In such cases, the individual's health becomes the cause of a possible public health issue. In other cases the outbreak of an infectious disease that develops into an epidemic and therefore becomes a public health issue may end up affecting the health of an individual. In such cases, the individual is a victim of public health.

Earlier references of public health awareness in the course of the history of mankind are found in one of the five books of the Torah, Leviticus in 500 BC, in which guidance is offered on body hygiene, sexual health, caution about awareness of contagious diseases, and the need to quarantine leprous populations. Another mention of issues pertaining to public health is in the Hammurabi Code, around 500 BC, wherein there is a text on a code of conduct for physicians and health practices as well as hints on medical drug prescriptions. Around 500 BC, it appears that the Babylonians, the Greeks, and the Romains were aware of the benefits of sanitary bathrooms and systems of water drainage to avoid the consequences of waterborne diseases. The genius of Roman engineering built aqueducts for water conservation and supply. The Romans are credited for having built the first hospitals. A book published in the fifth century by Hippocrates, titled *On Airs, Waters and Places*, reveals that not only was he a medical scientist but also one who pondered questions of human health and what might be referred to today as a holistic approach, insofar as he brought into consideration environmental factors in the quest for causes of imbalances of the human body that lead to ailments. Both the Greeks and the Romans were familiar with plague, as mentioned above.

Time went by, and issues of public health, like those of individual health, were not high on the agenda of communities around the world. Feudalism was the societal order. The peasants and serfs endured a laborious life. The aristocrats enjoyed the few societal benefits and perks that there were. Then the Middle Ages came. In Europe the Middle Ages were a space in time during which diseases were subject to superstitious reactions and speculations. Their mysterious origins made them a spiritual matter. They were entrusted to priests and the Church. Public health issues were not a matter of public health. Those who got ill went to pray and confess their sins. Hygienic conditions in Medieval Europe were poor. Such conditions were propitious for a rapid spread of infectious diseases. And an outbreak of any kind of disease would be a public health case. Indeed, the bubonic plague, caused by the bacterium *yersinia pestis*, and the other two kinds, septicemic and pneumonic plagues, broke out. They are thought to have ravaged (Black Death) the population of medieval Europe in 1348.

A new era, that of industrialization and exploration, brought about new social and environmental conditions in which which infectious diseases would continue to thrive. Early European mercantile activity produced outbreaks, among them yellow fever in the late sixteenth century from the colonies, smallpox that decimated Native American populations after their contact with the conquistadors, and malaria from tropical climates. The proximity of industrialized cities in Europe, with poor sanitary conditions, paved the way for the cholera outbreak in 1831–1832. Other outbreaks followed: lung diseases, phosphorus jaw necrosis, anthrax, rabies, tuberculosis, typhus, influenza, typhoid fever, hepatitis, and Lyme disease. Unlike in the Middle Ages, when there was little consciousness of public health, the nineteenth century was different. There were rapidly growing cities that attracted laborers from the rural areas, and their health issues could not be ignored. In 1854, the outbreak of cholera in Soho, England, gave to the physician John Snow the opportunity to find out its origin. It was the wells and the groundwater. A few precautions taken in light of that discovery and the ability of England to produce and supply electric power to light up public buildings and streets did plenty to improve public health conditions. Ever since, social demand for public health care grew. Epidemiology as a field of medical inquiry and interest would emerge. Public health issues were becoming political issues and continue to be so. Today, public health issues are a global political issue.

Recently, public health concerns have shown how global public health issues are today as demonstrated in the cases of swine flu (H1N1 influenza virus), SARS (severe acute respiratory syndrome), avian flu (H5N1), and a reemergence of tuberculosis.

They constitute a cause of global concern and therefore a global issue because they break out to become endemic, epidemic, and even pandemic. Breaking out is nothing but the expansion of the radius or space of reach of pathogens. This breakout is spatial. It justifies public health issues as a concern for all. It makes public health issues that have gone global truly a global issue.

Institutional Responses

The world has recognized the danger that fast-spreading infectious disease represents. And because the spread of infectious diseases is a recurrent phenomenon, there is a need for an institutionalized response to facing a potential outbreak. Such institutionalized responses focus on identifying potential cases of outbreaks, preventing them, containing them when there are already concrete cases, and possibly curing the disease itself.

There have been initiatives in Europe since the mid- and late nineteenth century dealing with the need to agree with quarantine procedures to prevent the spread of epidemic diseases, including a series of conferences to harmonize and standardize the treatment of infectious cases in the midst of flourishing international trade and its growing maritime activity. The flourishing maritime trade, indeed, has made port cities around the world vulnerable to infested steamships with rats onboard.

There have been the conferences in Paris in 1851 and 1859, Vienna in 1864, Washington in 1881, Rome in 1885, and Constantinople in 1866. In 1892 a treaty on cholera was signed. It was consolidated in 1902 covering plague and yellow fever. In the Americas, a Pan-American Health Organization (PAHO) was set in place in 1902 to deal with sanitary issues. In December 9, 1907, a conference in Rome established the Office International d'Hygiène Publique (OIHP) effectively constituted a year later the need to prevent internationally the spread of epidemic diseases in mind. After World War I, the Health Organization was established under the auspices of the League of Nations in 1923. The epidemic of typhus and relapsing fever and cholera in the 1920s only reinforced the consciousness of the need for an international public health focus. The Health Organization was designed to focus on epidemiological intelligence, standardization of antitoxic sera, agreement on amount of drugs required for medical purposes, international waterways, preventive medicine, and cooperation between the Health Organization and the public health authorities of various countries.

After World War II, the growing international dimension of public health led to the creation of the World Health Organization (WHO), in July 1946, and became effective April 7, 1948. Other UN agencies are linked to the work of the WHO. Such is the case of the World Food Organization and the United Nations International Children's Emergency Funds (UNICEF), now simply known as the United Nations Children's Fund.

The WHO's scope and breadth comprises 22 functions, covering almost all imaginable areas of health promotion. The organization describes health as "a state of complete physical, mental and social well-being and not merely the absence of diseases or infirmity." The organization sees the highest attainable standard of health as a fundamental human right. It has become, since the 1970s, more responsive to the needs of the developing nations. It underwent reforms in the 1980s and is still subject to adjustments as the field of public health copes with new challenges.

Among the daunting challenges of the WHO are the need to remain ready to face any outbreak in an ever more interdependent world. It must rely on a strategy in place to come to terms with such a challenge. It utilizes the strategy of emphasizing:

- Surveillance (programs in place to monitor disease)
- Pro Med-Mail
- GOARN: Global Outbreak Alert Response Network
- Diagnosis
- Response capabilities
- Prevention

The organization works with respective states and their own public health strategies. Indeed, every state has its own mechanisms in place to be deployed in case of suspicion or outbreak of a public health danger.

In the case of the United States, the Centers for Diseases Control and Prevention, established in 1946 and located in Atlanta, Georgia, is in charge of issues of concern to public health.

HUMAN TRAFFICKING

Human trafficking is another phenomenon we consider to be a global issue. It is an issue because of a number of problems it causes, and it is global because the conditions of globalization have amplified it to encompass different regions of the planet either as recipients or origins of trafficking. According to the US Department of Health and Human Services and the US Department of Justice, 800,000 people are trafficked each year, worldwide. Who are the people trafficked? Where are they from? Where do they go? What motivates the traffic itself?

Beginning with the last question, human trafficking is a phenomenon with a cause, with drivers or factors and stimuli. The causes may include the need for labor, sex, marriage, children, or organs. There is an intricate intertwining of these causes of human trafficking. Sex trafficking that is driven by sexual exploitation produces forced labor the in form of sex slavery and forced prostitution and marriages. The trafficking of young men and women for labor can rapidly morph into forced labor and forced sexual exploitation, and even into trafficking of organs. Trafficking of children is linked to the overall human trafficking phenomenon, as children can be utilized as labor force, sex subjects, organ donors, and just as a commodity.

If labor is a cause of trafficking, it answers the question of who are the humans trafficked. They are able-bodied young men and women. Fifty percent of trafficking victims are less than sixteen years old, and 20 percent are children. The same answer provides a clue as to where they come from. They come from the developing nations, where a predominantly youthful population is unemployed and willing to seek greener pastures elsewhere. It explains their involvement in the phenomenon of human trafficking, as they seek low-skilled labor in the hotel and hospitality industry, domestic servitude, peddling, restaurant work, and sweatshops. The often informal and illegal nature of trafficking has opened the door for forced labor. These young men and women in their quest for greener pastures, often with no resources of their own, in foreign environments and with improper documentation and supporting systems of their own, and unknowledgeable of the process, are often dependent on organized gangs of "coyotes." These gangs easily exploit such to produce forced labor. Under such circumstances, the notion of forced labor encompasses a number of constraints beyond labor itself. It encompasses restricted mobility due to housing confinement and due to lack of proper identification, restricted freedom, communication with the outside world at will, little to no payment, all of which are enforced with criminal fervor. Forced labor makes up to 18 percent of human trafficking victims, making it a second leading cause of human trafficking. Of the 18 percent, 20 percent are children. (Global Report on Trafficking in Persons, February 2009). Victims of labor trafficking around the world are primarily from Asia and the Pacific, followed by Latin America and the Caribbean, Sub-Saharan Africa, the Middle East, and the transition countries (Source: International Labor Organization). Victims of labor trafficking in the United States are Hispanic, 55 percent; White, 16 percent; Asian, 14.8 percent; Blacks, 9.8 percent; others, 18.0 percent (Source: The National Center for Victims of Crimes).

That sex is one of the causes of trafficking explains the high number of young women involved in human trafficking. Eighty percent of trafficking victims are women. They are involved for prostitution, forced or voluntary, and/or sex slavery purposes and arranged (forced) marriages. As a cause of human trafficking sex is the most significant as the UN Office of Drugs and Crimes suggests. According to this UN agency, it is estimated that there are between 800,000 and 4 million humans trapped in sex slavery around the world (Source: UNODC report published in 2012). Data (which is difficult to gather due to the clandestine nature of the phenomenon) from 155 countries reveals that 79 percent of trafficking is about sexual exploitation (Source: Global Report on Trafficking in Persons, February 2009). This makes sex the most important cause of human trafficking. As for marriages, they are a part of the phenomenon as far as they are organized in a clandestine manner with or without the consent of participants by illicit arrangements of organized underground networks simply because there is a demand that needs to be supplied. Such demand knows no borders. It is illicit because too many obstacles—visa, medical documentations, family approval, lack of own resources by participants, etc.—provide an opening for organizations willing to tap into the demand for such "goods" while avoiding the constraints of international regular border crossing requirements and procedures.

Children being a cause of trafficking answers the question of who are the humans involved in the traffic and the question of where they are trafficked. Indeed, children are in demand for labor (in sweatshops and even as soldiers in some regions torn by civil wars), for sex, for organs, and simply as a commodity, as they are coveted by childless couples. As a result children are victims of many of the facets of human trafficking violations, from sex to labor, to organs to commodity. The US State Department in 2006 estimated that 1 million children are exploited in global sex tourism. UNICEF has provided the figure of 55 million child victims of forced labor around the world. Children are naturally vulnerable. They lack force, knowledge, awareness, experience, etc. They are easy prey to predators and therefore in need of protection from society. Any crime perpetrated against children is a proof of lack of societal protection owed to them. And so their status as victims in human trafficking is a double betrayal by society, through both the predator and the society that allows predators to take advantage of them. The vulnerability of children has been the purpose of the existence of agencies such as UNICEF. It seeks to prevent, protect, and even prosecute those that prey on children. The agency lobbies governments to create laws or strengthen those that exist and enforce them against any crimes or abuses against children, among other things. Their task, however, is not simple. Children are part of given societies and specific families that may be stressed out and facing many other urgent difficulties, such as poverty, hunger, wars, disasters, or simply subject to cultural practices that do not define the needs of children as understood by UNICEF. These circumstances end up opening the door for the neglect of paying extra attention and protecting children. As a result, children from such societies become vulnerable to utilitarian forces that seek gain and pleasure from what children have to offer, as described above.

Human organs are one of the causes of trafficking because there is a demand for them. Human organs are seen as a commodity that donors can supply. Human organs in demand are often kidneys, livers, and hearts, but others as well even if to a lesser degree. Those on the demand side predominantly are patients in need of organ transplants in the economically advanced nations, where the list of those in need of organs is long, while the organs are scarce. There has been an effort to supplement the scarcity of available human organs through artificial ones, as in the case of artificial hearts. Research is under way to reproduce or create new organs from stem cells, or even to substitute failing human organs with animal organs, a transplant procedure known as xenotransplant. Indeed the medical community has reason to believe that some animals possess a genome coding and DNA structure germane to that of human beings. The pig has been cited as a potentially ideal animal suited for such transplants. However, we are not there yet, and the imbalance in the demand versus supply of human organs persists. It persists primarily because few people are willing to deal with the subject and willing to suggest their own organs, as they are forced to think about their own mortality. Many do not trust the system in place by hospitals. They suspect favoritism, which may discourage them to reveal themselves as donors at the end of their own existence. Even in concrete cases, many potential donors, when coming in question for a donation, are reluctant to submit their healthy bodies to surgery to donate, which they only consider in extreme cases such as the need of organs by a loved one. The scarcity of transplant-ready organs and the vital need they serve push those in need of organs to do all they can to save their lives, including considering alternative solutions or shortcuts to obtain the needed organ.

Where can these patients expect to get what they crave? Theoretically, they are those willing to declare themselves as donors while alive should anything happen to them such as an accident or just death in general, and their organs can be of utility for someone else. They constitute the ground for a legal organs market, domestic or international. This source of organ donors, however, presents its limits. Even though identified as donors, should anything happen to them, these potential donors still have to live in the meantime, which can be the time when their organ is needed by someone else. The scarcity persists. In the United States alone, there are 120,675 patients awaiting new organs. About eighteen people die every day waiting for a transplant. Every month there are 2,000 names added to the list of patients awaiting transplant (Source: US Department of Health and Human Services, cited by

US News and World Report). In Europe the situation is no better. In Spain, in 2013, there were thirty-five donors for 1 million patients; in France, twenty-four donors; and in Germany, twelve donors.

There is, however, another source of organ donors identified. It is donors of economically impoverished nations in dire need of money who may be willing and ready to consider relinquishing an organ without perishing for pecuniary remuneration. Kidneys are organs that fall under this category. Donors under this category are known to be from the South who agree to get their kidneys removed by organized organ trafficking gangs, to get paid anywhere between 700 and 2,500 dollars. These people are mostly poor peasants in Bangladesh, India, the Philippines, or Pakistan, to name just a few, who receive such sums. Organized trafficking gangs may pocket up to 100,000 dollars from desperate rich patients from the North (Bienstock, 2013).[3] The traffic organizing gangs pocket the lion's share, leaving crumbs to their victims and a more reasonable share to the surgeons performing the removal.

Others have been forced to relinquish some of their organs by criminal trafficking gangs, the criminal dimension of organ trafficking, making the entire phenomenon mostly illicit. The victims are lured in areas where they are more vulnerable than ever, like in the desert between Israel and Egypt, and often given sedatives or other means to induce their passivity and inertia. They wake up with huge scars and painkillers to lessen the pain. When they are lucky, they get some compensation. With the exception of the legal organs market, domestic or international, organs acquired through informal means, voluntarily or forcefully, are considered to be illegal. They still need to meet the potential recipients. As this is a transaction, it requires a marketplace. Things do get complicated here, as such a market can only be a black market. And if the market is illegal so will be transplants done with illegally acquired and trafficked organs. It is estimated (Bienstock 2013) that 10 to 15 percent of organ transplants are done through illegal channels.

The Ethical Dimension of Organ Trafficking

The entire need for human organs and the market it has produced has brought about a couple of ethical issues to grapple with. Those issues revolve around whether such a market is just any other where demand meets supply, considering that the product in question is human organs. In other words, should human organ parts be considered just like any other product? Because if they are, individual owners of such organs are the proprietors who now can bring them to the market any time they please. There are indeed those who argue in favor of a legalization of organ traffic and in favor of making it part of the open free market economic system. They argue that such openness will relieve the bottleneck situation that currently exists. It will provide incentives for donors to consider donating for monetary rewards and will minimize the risks of black markets and the medical hazards that come with it, as those active in the black market do not always perform the transplants under optimal conditions.

Individuals are in charge of other vulnerable individuals like infants in their care. The idea of selling organs may be tempting to those in dire straits to sacrifice these vulnerable beings. The ethical dimension here lies in the question whether we human beings are indeed the proprietors of our organs. After all, we have not created, produced, or earned them. We are entrusted with the responsibility of caring for them for our own good.

Moreover, others may be interested as well and criminally enter the business of supplying organs that might not have been acquired legitimately. Considering the scarcity of such organs and the willingness by those in need of them to pay makes any human being a carrier of needed goods and a potential victim of trafficking. The issue of availability of organs also presents an ethical dilemma for those tempted to sell as well as for those in need of buying. The temptation to sell organs has been felt in some developing nations where economic conditions have led some farmers and peasants in Bangladesh or the Philippines to consider selling a kidney to escape their harsh economic conditions. Three thousand dollars earned from a kidney donation may offer the possibility of a new economic beginning for such farmers and peasants. The dilemma here lies in the fact that on one hand they must resort to what amounts to a mutilation to earn the money, knowing that somehow the kidney they are giving is under their responsibility but not really theirs, and on the other hand the legitimate need to escape poverty. As for those in need of organs, they often know that it is the poverty of the donors that drives them to donate their organs. The buyer takes advantage of or exploits the poverty and the vulnerability of donors. Considering that in many cases those willing to buy organs at almost any price are often wealthy, the ethical question is should those already rich benefit even further from those already poor? The ethical dilemma for buyers is whether to buy from the poor because they are exploiting their poverty and risk dying. To many, this may not be a dilemma at all, as the principle of self-preservation would seem to trump any other consideration.

The Need for an International Regime on Persons and Organ Trafficking

To address and meet some of the questions raised by the issues of organ trafficking, there is, it seems, a need for an international regime on organ trafficking. International regimes are created in case of recurrent international issues that need rules, norms, and standardization of practices and a common pool of information and decision-making processes to regulate the behavior of participants. As partially unregulated, restrictive to a fault, and inefficient the international market for organs is, it calls for such a creation of an international regime. There have been various attempts to regulate or to restrict such organ trafficking. The UN Convention on the Rights of the Child in 1989 produced a document aiming at protecting the rights of children, called "Optional Protocol," on the sale of children, prostitution, and child pornography. There is an existing UN Protocol to Prevent, Suppress and Punish Trafficking in Persons, whose article 3 clearly includes trafficking for the purpose of removal of organs as a violation.

The WHO produced in 1991 a document called "The Guiding Principles on Human Organ Transplantation," in which it stated that the commercialization of human organs is "a violation of human rights and human dignity." In 2002, Europeans framed the prohibition of organs and tissue trafficking for financial gain in The European Convention on Human Rights and Biomedicine Concerning Transplantation of Organs and Tissues of Human Organs. Still missing is an overarching and binding international regime that oversees all issues pertaining to all areas raised by the different protocols and conventions.

Trafficking Movement and Trajectories

The question of where to leads us to explore the movement and trajectory of the trafficking. The exploration of the question reveals a phenomenon of close to home, domestic trafficking and intraregional trafficking movements (UNOD). This means that traffic organizing gangs are primarily local, domestic, and regional, and the phenomenon is essentially regional. This may simply be a case of calculated risks for organizing criminal gangs or the lack of sophistication and resources for high-scale worldwide operations. As far as regions are concerned, Asia is the continent with the most trafficking, with India with 23 million; Bangladesh with 200,000; Japan with 150,000, where we find mostly non-Japanese women as products of trafficking; and Malaysia with 142,000. In Eastern Europe, 200,000 people are involved in or victims of trafficking (Ukraine leading the way with 117,000, followed by Moldovia, Romania, 57,000; Belarus, 14,000; and Bulgaria, 9,800).

Besides the intraregional trafficking, each region or even state has its attractiveness (pull factors), which seems to particularly attract people from specific nations where push factors make them willing to leave. Organized trafficking gangs tap into that kind of willingness from people of a given

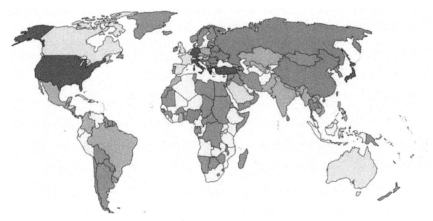

Figure 9.3.

region or state to move into a another specific other region or state. And so we have a tandem formation of trafficking, linking a source region with a recipient region or nation source nation with a recipient nation. Among such tandems we have the United States, which exerts a pull effect to people of Asia, and the United Kingdom, which exerts a pull effect to people of Nigeria or India, etc. The pull effect here can be such things as opportunity for factory labor, prostitution, domestic servitude, agriculture, and miscellaneous. As for the traffic in persons for the purpose of organ removal, the Organization for Security and Co-operation in Europe (OSCE)[4] has identified the following nations as locations of greater organ trafficking activity, whether as a locus of donors, recipients, or brokers. They include Brazil, Pakistan, India, China, the Philippines, Egypt, the Gulf States (Kuwait, Saudi Arabia, Bahrain, Oman, the United Arab Emirates), Israel, Turkey, Colombia, and Moldova.

This traffic of persons is justified by demand, which in turn explains the stimulus for supply. Those willing to supply humans for their labor, sex, marriage, and organs are the operating agents of the trafficking. Such trafficking, although regional in its dynamics, is a global phenomenon, as it encompasses all the regions of the globe.

NOTES

1. Soon, because although some estimates (e.g., Simmons 2005) speak of forty years or so, there are those who believe that there are still many reserves, known and unknown, and not yet tapped. In addition, Saudi Arabia, which currently is known to

possess the most reserves, has not allowed an inspection so a far more precise projection of such depletion can be made. The fact is that if the resource is depletable and it has been used without the possibility of being regenerated, it will someday disappear.

  2. Hardin 1968.
  3. Bienstock 2013.
  4. OSCE 2013.

Chapter Ten

The Role and Place of Nations in the Global Space

SHIFTING ROLES AND PLACES

Nation-states are global actors. They act through their leaders, their foreign policy and diplomats, their armies, their trade, and their people, who are scientists, entrepreneurs, philanthropists, etc. As actors they influence world affairs. They influence the course of history, which has produced this globalized world. They, indeed, are instrumental in creating the institutional infrastructure and superstructure that support and organize the functioning of the global society and tend to its various issues, some of which we have discussed here. The national participation of nations in organizing world affairs is referred to as global governance.

In this global society they have helped to foster, each one of the nation-state actors has not only a role to play but also a place it occupies. The notion of place can be understood both in its primary geographic sense, but also figuratively. In its geographic sense, as defined in chapter 1, it is a space with specific character. Among the elements conveying character to a place is its location and the geopolitical implications that come with it. In that sense, for instance, the place of Israel is in the Middle East, which has its own geopolitical implications. At the end of this chapter, in the section titled Geopolitical Codes, we explore such geopolitical implications of places. The term *place* can also be understood figuratively. Indeed, nations know their place, which figuratively reflects their respective capacity and its underlying capabilities, to influence world affairs, which we generally implies power, and their willingness to influence world affairs. And because such capacity and capabilities are asymmetrically distributed among them and have different degrees of willingness to influence, the role they play and the place they occupy differ. There is as a result some kind, of a hierarchy (determination of their place), not formal but de facto, of world nations based on the role they play and therefore the place they occupy in influencing world affairs. The hierarchy can be based on capabilities because there are empirical and therefore quantifiable and measurable factors determining their existence. They are empirical factors of power. Such empirical factors of power are economic resources, military capabilities (quality and reach of weaponry, logistics), effectiveness, technological know-how, demographic strength, location, etc.; they allow a hierarchy, their place among peers, of world powers in the following categories: superpower,great power, major power, middle power, regional power, small state, and dependencies.

The influencing role and place occupied by nations, where in these categories they stand, is neither static nor definitive. Because such a role and place depend on capabilities, and because such capabilities can morph, grow or shrink, the ability of nations to rise to such roles and position depend on the mastery of the factors of power. Those that rise all the way to the top influencing role and position are known as superpowers. And such a rise depends in turn on the ability of nations to successfully navigate the conditions of their times. Such conditions that have allowed the emergence of superpowers since the modern era have been mercantilism and the colonial era, the Industrial Revolution, and currently information technology and globalization. Under each one of these eras, some nations have successfully managed to surf on the waves of changes they brought and rose to the top of such hierarchy of world influencing powers. We have had, consequently, after Venice in the earliest stages of mercantilism, Portugal, the Dutch, Spain, Great Britain, and the United States. There are those whose rise did not get them to the top. There have been nations that ended up anywhere second or third in the hierarchy of world powers. They are known as challengers/contenders. Among them, have been the Dutch, Portugal, Spain, France, Great Britain, the Soviet Union, and the United States.

But any process that explains the process of rise must as well explain that of descent. Therefore, some nations that rose can descend or those that have descended can rise if and when they improve their capacity and capabilities. Such a dynamic of shifting of standing at the top of world economic or political powers justifies the existence of the theory of hegemonic transition. The theory explains the dynamics of ascent of some nations with a high and sustained growth rate versus stagnating or descending or just a low-rate growing nation.

As a result, the hierarchy of world powers has been changing, reflecting individual nation's abilities to cope with changing times. Leading powers of such a hierarchy, up until now have been Western, which explains that the bulk of world activity and world influencing decision making was occurring in the Western hemisphere, the Atlantic realm, between Europe and North

America, an affirmation of the Columbian Epoch. It explains as well the West's grip on decision-making mechanisms of world affairs.

Currently, changing times have been loosening the Western grip on influencing international affairs. Indeed, recent changes such as a globalized market system, mobility of production factors, new competitive edge and players, new technologies, new products, etc., have allowed some other nations to emerge. Among such emerging nations are China, India, Brazil, Russia, South Africa, South Korea, Malaysia, Singapore, Vietnam, Indonesia, Turkey, Saudi Arabia, and many others, known as the G20. The first four of these nations, Brazil, Russia, India, China (BRICS) which have caught the attention of the international business world since the publication of the investment report by Goldman in 2003, have economies that grew and continue to grow, at high or less rates but still have the potential of rising to unprecedented heights. They are huge territories, with huge populations, with access to the sea, natural resources, innovative economies, and available human resources, both cheap and high-skilled labor.

They are essentially non-Western. The currently changing times suggest another impending shift in the hierarchy of world powers. If and when it happens, given the fact that most, and the most dynamic thriving economies, are located in East Asia, growing activity is occurring in the realms of the Pacific and Indian Oceans (Barnett 2005; Kaplan 2009). If such activity is profitable, in so far as it is justified by commerce, the economic growth of nations in the region will produce prosperity and wealth. With wealth comes might, and with might, comes power. Following is how that happens: Nations that prosper improve their wealth class. Indeed, social economic class depends on income. In the world of politics as well it justifies the economic class of nations. With wealth, nations can affect the outcome of a number of issues, which confers them a greater role. Indeed, we tend to seek the help and ultimately take the advice of the most influential members of society. We ask those with influence to play prominent roles in any social construct, to get involved, to help decide, to contribute, and even to lead. And just as it is in society, where a higher social economic class brings along increased influence, so too in international politics. It is the greater role they play and the influence they acquire that confer to such nations power and ultimately the ability to influence even more. We define power here as the ability to get someone to do as you wish, or generally to have a voice to reckon with in their decision-making process. With increased influence comes as well an increase in political status. Nations with the most such influencing capacity acquire the status of superpowers. Wealth, class, influence, role, power, and status are often aggregately implied in the use of the expression political prestige.

Some of the nations with the most power have become imperial, using their power to expand it or subjugate lesser powers; others have become hegemonic, in the noble sense of the term, which means using their influence to lead the rest of the world's nations in matters of common purposes. The relevance of the establishment of a hegemonic power for global issues lies in the fact that it is entrusted to helping find solutions to some of the most pressing issues on the globe. Their status as hegemonic powers is the product of the greater role they play due to their capabilities.

The phenomenon of rising into such a leadership position is currently displayed with regard to China. China's economic clout has been growing as a result of its growth. The growth brings along wealth and the rise of China into the company or class of wealthy nations. As a result, China is in demand, as the last chapter describes. Its influence grows and it becomes a respectable and prestigious member of the international community of nations.

Indeed, China, the leading economy in East Asia, and increasingly in the world, is becoming the nation with the most opportunity of increasing its power status. It remains to be seen what will become of it. In the meantime, nations with growing capabilities attract many other nations with fewer capabilities. It explains why rich people have more "friends." This justifies the theory of alliance formation. In the case of China, it explains why the number of its partners and allies continues to grow. It also justifies the fact that each nation knows its place; it seeks to improve its standing, or at least its ability to survive in it. It is the phenomenon that underlies what Flint refers to as geopolitical codes.

GEOPOLITICAL CODES

The concept of geopolitical codes (Flint 2012, p. 55) describes the need for individual nations to find their safe place in the sea of many nations. This notion of geopolitical codes is simply about improving a state's security needs and minimizing its sense of insecurity. It is as well about increasing a state's change for more prosperity and decreasing its limitation for acquiring wealth. For the attainment of all these objectives, individual states in international politics rely on each other. They rely on allies. Geopolitical codes are an account of allies, potential and current, and of foes, potential and current, to ensure that sense of safe place. But because the political world is not static and is dynamic, and because the allies we have or do not have depend on individual state's interests but also on the interests of the other states for having us as an ally, and because such interests do change, as the world itself changes and induces a shift of interests, the game of keeping count of allies is flexible and dynamic as well. It becomes more so dynamic whenever changes are occurring, shifting back and forth, left and right, old against new interests, and in the process inducing the need for an adjustment, a refreshing of both what our current interests are and who are the current identified potential allies to help us obtain them.

We are currently at a junction in the political world where a number of changes have been inducing a shift in interests and therefore the need to reevaluate our count of allies, current or potential, and foes, current or potential. This segment, therefore, focuses on examining the mechanism of reevaluation of allies.

First, let us examine what Flint actually considers to be geopolitical codes. They consist of the following questions:

- Who are one's current allies?
- How can they be maintained and nurtured?
- Who is a potential ally?
- How can they be won over?
- How do we counter or minimize the nuisance of current and potential enemies?

Why does it matter to keep count of one's allies? It matters to know your allies, those whom one can count on as allies. Those that can be counted on, advance one's interests. Such interests are essentially one's security and prosperity. Allies can help improve our sense of security and are those one may count on when security is threatened. They can as well through cooperation and exchange contribute to one's economic prosperity.

Why does it count to maintain and nurture allies? It matters because any relationship needs maintenance and nurturing simply because life and its circumstances change and so does our basis for allegiance. Allies need reassurances. They need the reaffirmation of the allegiance. It matters because we have allies based on our interests. And because interests change, there is a need to adjust and update the identity of our allies. The allies we have as well their interest, justifying our status as allies to them. Their interests as well may shift and induce the need for an update and adjustment. Such an update and adjustment may affect or alter our status as an ally to them.

Why does it matter to identify potential new allies? It matters because political life, like life in general, is dynamic and interests change; even political changes of heart do happen. All of these changes open the door for the possibility of making new allies. About the dynamic political life, nations of the former Communist East Europe have become allies with other European Union member nations. Here, as well a political change of heart has taken place rendering possible the gaining of new allies—their interests are now in alignment. Menon (2007, p. 19), recognizing the need for realignment dictated by the changing times, although focusing solely on strategic alliances, which is about offensive and defensive goals, writes, "We are, I believe, in the early stages of what will prove to be a thoroughgoing redefinition in the means and ends of American statecraft: a total reordering of the way we deal with others and others with us." He continues, "I believe that we will witness a new turn in the American strategy—one that abandons cold war alliances and the military commitments associated with them." Strategic alliances change because the grounding circumstances that justify their creation change. Other nonstrategic alliances, known as partnerships under liberalism, are more open and engaging, as they are driven by a different rationale than that of security; they are based on expanding the pie of prosperity.

Why does it matter to win potential allies over? It matters because there is gain in having allies, because more allies means fewer foes and threatening parties out there; therefore, the more allies, the merrier. And, you win them over through diplomacy, through focus on common interests and through diffusing of potential or real areas of dispute.

Why does it matter to be able to counter or minimize the nuisance of current or potential enemies? It matters because nuisance is just that. It must be contained or removed. If it is potential it remains unsettling and must be preventively dealt with. How concretely this containing or removal of nuisance should look like depends on the options available and chosen by the nation concerned.

The nations asking these questions of the geopolitical codes are seekers. The questions are primarily driven by the interests of the seeker. The answers to those questions depend on who best can service the interests of the seeker. Whomever can best service the interests of the seeker is the purveyor. Because a state has more than one interest, it can have more than one purveyor. And because states depend on any given interest differently than they depend on any other interest, states do have different degrees of dependence on their interests. The importance of purveyors to any state depends therefore on the degree to which that state depends on the interest it gets serviced by the purveyor. Following is an example:

- The United Kingdom as a seeker vis-à-vis the United States, the European Union, NATO, and the Commonwealth as purveyors.
- The United Kingdom decides over the importance of its purveyors, based on its interests/circumstances.

Based on the logic above any state is a hierarchical list of purveyors, based on its interests and circumstances. This list however is not static, because interests are dynamic, as stated. Oil is still today inescapable as an energy source, as an interest, which makes it a valued interest and its purveyor equally highly valued. That, however, will change the day we find a more reliable, better, or even cheaper alternative energy source.

This dynamic of interests and purveyors also explains why today China has risen up high on the list of US economy purveyors, which was almost unimaginable thirty years ago.

There is a hierarchy of purveyors based on their capacity or ability to service interests. Generally, many interests are serviced through wealth. Those states with wealth are generally also seen as purveyors. As a result, the wealthiest states are the most valued purveyors. Wealthy nations can provide assistance to the developing nations. We have a purveyors versus seekers relation.

Nations with the most capabilities become purveyors with the most relations with seekers. This explains why the United States has the most seekers. But just as capabilities do increase, they can as well decrease. In the case of decrease, the purveyor may lose its status of having the most seekers, or if it still has seekers, these seekers evaluate and adjust their relations with the decreasing purveyor. Such reevaluation occurs to the detriment of the purveyor

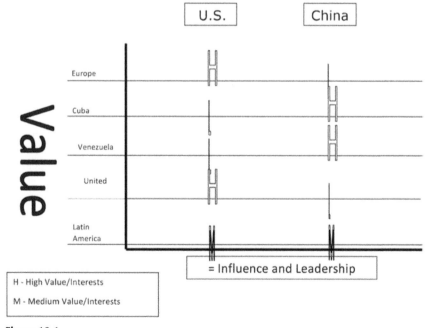

Figure 10.1.

losing its capabilities and in favor of the purveyor gaining capabilities. This process explains the rising number of seekers into China's corner as a purveyor and their reevaluation in favor of China as the most valued purveyor.

The dynamic nature of interests and the dynamic nature of capabilities to service them dictates the fluidity of geopolitical codes.

The following graph illustrates the changing geopolitical codes of the United States and China as purveyors of interests and the United Kingdom, Pakistan, Brazil, Israel, and Africa-Latin America as seekers of purveyors.

The end game: The purveyor with the most seekers has more influence, potentially leading to global leadership status.

RE-ORIENT

There was a time in history where the center of international commerce was located in Far East Asia, around the 1300s, until the European expansion. Indeed European expansion and ultimately colonization were triggered by the need to access the market in East Asia, where porcelain, silk, spices, etc., were found. A consensus has been emerging among contemporary economic historians suggesting that, before 1800, Europe had no real means (money and products) to respectably participate in that trade. A. G. Frank (1998, p. 5) writes, "the only real means that Europe had for participating in this world economy was its American money. If any regions were predominant in the world economy before 1800, they were in Asia. If any economy had a 'central' position and role in the world economy and its possible hierarchy of 'center,' it was China." East Asia has been thereafter the first international pole of commerce, which Europeans sought to join. But the Asian parochialism, documented by the Ming Dynasty retrieved from international exploration, the lack of a dynamism that later led Europe to capitalism, and a number of many other changes that have occurred since, the Industrial Revolution being the most impactful, have led East Asia to the loss of its pole position in international commerce.

Soon the core of international commerce was shifting to Europe, and its flourishing trade with North America ultimately made the Atlantic route the core of international commerce. That has remained the situation in international trade until recent changes. Recent changes are those brought about by the new paradigm of globalization. It seems indeed that East Asia has been regaining its once lost space of relevancy in international trade. And close by there is India's economic dynamism and the slow reemergence of Japan after a painful decade of the 1990s and early 2000s. The Orient is reemerging. But until it fully does, there is an emerging tandem of the old leading economy of the United States and the rising new economy of China, whose synergy stands to induce a new shift in the center of political gravity into the Pacific. The Pacific Ocean shared by both the United States and China would be the sphere of most trade and consequently of most political attention.

We will have then move from the focus on the Atlantic up until the World War II to the East-West confrontational geopolitical order, which was at the same time economically the time of the divide between North-South until 1991, the collapse of communism, and the beginning of global liberalism. The shift currently occurring is the one pointing toward the Pacific sphere (as illustrated below).

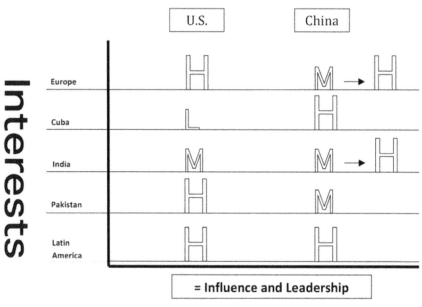

Figure 10.2.

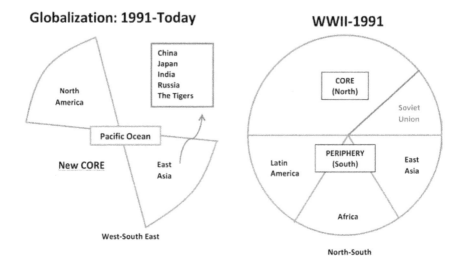

Globalization: 1991-Today

China
Japan
India
Russia
The Tigers

North
America

Pacific Ocean

New CORE

East
Asia

West-South East

WWII-1991

CORE
(North)

Soviet
Union

Latin
America

PERIPHERY
(South)

East
Asia

Africa

North-South

Post WWII/Cold War

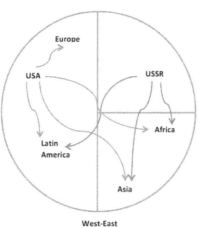

Europe

USA

USSR

Africa

Latin
America

Asia

West-East

Figure 10.3.

Chapter Eleven

The Cyber Space

A New Space and Its Issues

Next to ideas and trade, science and technology have been preeminent driving forces of history. As far as science and technology are concerned, they have produced since the 1980s an innovative invention, which we call digital technology, and we now almost inescapably use in the form of the Internet and its new software applications to run and facilitate our existence.

This innovative product of the Internet has provided society with a new kind of space. It is the virtual space. And as new technologies often do, they have the potential of impacting society in ways, minor or major and unforeseen. In the case of the technology that has rendered real the existence of the virtual space, the potential of that impact has turned out hardly to be exaggerated. The impact has been in fact major, if not colossal. Indeed so much so that it has heralded a new era: the digital era.

This digital technology and its invention of the cyber space have become part of the social and historical world, where their impact has been altering features of the existing reality. What reality? It is the reality of the liberal economic world and the reality of the political world. The impact of the new technology in the economic world recognized and endorsed by the political world has produced a synergy that has rendered possible the phenomenon we call globalization. The synergy has nothing but induced a new period of history, that of globalization.

The virtual space has allowed an array of activity in the globalized world to increase its scale (reach) from any given locality to be instantaneously global. Texts, images, words, and sounds can be instantaneously spread globally. That new reality has opened the door to an array of new possibilities in all spheres of human activity, professional and private. With these new possibilities comes an array of potential and real issues we need to see through.

We will proceed first by defining the notion of virtuality and by presenting its importance to the social and historical world. We will next explore the activity and the issues they raise. Finally we will look at the debate whether to regulate this space or not, since issues it raises carry concrete risks to any individual user, to society, and to the globe in general.

DEFINING THE VIRTUAL SPACE

The notion of virtuality has both a philosophical and a technological dimension. The philosophical dimension of the virtual lies in the fact that it is not necessarily the opposite of real, because the virtual is as well real. That which is virtual is the product of reality. The virtual is not as well necessarily the opposite of the factual, because fact can be induced in and from the virtual reality. The real can be experienced through our senses, seen, touched, felt, heard, and smelled. The factual can be evidenced. Both fact and reality are material and objective or rational. Where the virtual stands compared to the real and the factual is that the virtual is parallel or within the real. Although it exists, it is neither concrete nor real. The virtual is not material, not experienced, and therefore not objective. Although the virtual cannot be experienced because it is parallel or within the real, it can, however, be perceived by our consciousness. The perception of the virtual makes it an anti-empirical reality, meaning a reality that cannot be experienced, nevertheless existing. Any video games our youngsters play are virtual. Those playing the video games cannot enter into the space where the games are played. Racing car games give a player the satisfaction and the thrill of navigating the perils of a fast driving car but without the reality of driving the car. These are virtual realities that illustrate the parallelism of the material reality and the virtual reality. The material reality is the joystick of the virtual car racer, and the virtual reality is the danger the car faces while driving without the driver actually be in the car. The virtual reality is therefore reality, which, however, can be experienced in the world where it is the product of but not in the virtual space. We cannot simultaneously exist in both worlds, the real and the virtual. There is a dimension separating each. It seems sometimes that this separation is the basis of the fascination of many virtual games, attempting to project or at least to simulate our real presence in the virtual world. The closer they get, the more fascinated we become. A number of games are built from that premise. There will always be a threshold of immersion that will not be crossed. And should we cross that threshold into the virtual, the virtual would cease to be virtual but would become real.

Some virtual reality can even be experienced in the real world. Any simulation by NASA astronauts of an outer space journey is virtual but yet empirically real. The virtual is in fact the creation of our consciousness. If it is conscious it is the product of our perception. In the end, the virtual is nothing but that which has been consciously perceived. This opens the door for the possibility of that which is unconsciously perceived or not even perceived at all. Perception is our mechanism to cope with the complexity of the world, and our perception of the virtual world is a way of acknowledging that although we cannot experience the virtuality we somehow know that it is there.

The technological dimension of the virtual space is simply the fact that it is man-made. The cyber space is par excellence, one man-made technology-produced virtual world. As virtual, it is parallel to the real world. It exists in conjunction with the real world, which is the social world or historical world. This virtual world of the cyber space interacts with the social real. In this interaction with the real world, the virtual world relies on the use of software.

Cyber space has expanded our world; we now get to exist and navigate in and through two worlds simultaneously, the social world and the virtual world.

META-GEOGRAPHY

The cyber space has expanded our understanding of geography. It brought about a new space, beyond the physical geographic space. As a virtual space, as noted above, it is a new space that is real, however, not concrete. The realness conveys to that space its *geographic* credential, and the nonconcreteness conveys to that space its *meta* credentials. Together the virtual space therefore is a meta-geographic space. It is however a new meta-geographic space, different from other geographic concepts, constructs, or categories such as the *North* or the *South*, which are already meta-geographies, and inadequate at that, if one agrees with the geographers Martin W. Lewis and Karen Wigen (1997).[1]

This new meta-geography that is the virtual or cyber space brought about a parallel space, which we call meta-geography. This parallel geographic space is linked to the actual geographic space through software.

Through its various applications, the use of software has been allowing more and more transfer from the geographic world into the meta-geographic world. The more sophisticated the technology in software becomes, the more activity will be transferred from the horizontal geographic realm into the vertical meta-geographic space to the vertical realm. This means for instance no longer have to leave your house to go to the bank to transfer money to pay bills but simply using online banking for the same activity from your house. As a result, we buy, sell, play, bank, meet, learn, etc., in the cyber space.

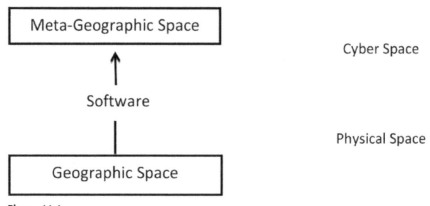

Figure 11.1.

Software allows the transfer of activity from the geographic space into the meta-geographic space.

Uploading photographs or films on YouTube or elsewhere and scanning a document to make it available into URL are all transfer activities.

Within the meta-geographic space, there is a great deal of horizontal transferring occurring, from one source to another address in the cyber space, as it is possible to upload a link or an attachment to an email or download a document from a web page into a different address in the cyber space or just into your files.

The more software applications allow us to do in the cyber space, the more horizontal exchanges in the geographic physical space will decrease. The

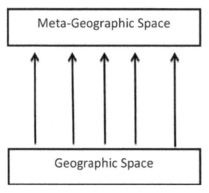

Figure 11.2.

Transfer

Activities are transferred from the geographic space (horizontal) into the Meta-geographic Space (vertical).

result is fewer physical interactions and communicational exchanges between acting individuals in the geographic physical world. Conversely, there will be an increase in vertical exchanges, from the geographic realm to the meta-geographic realm.

Today, more and more actions and communications depend on software. We depend less and less on entrenched traditional mechanisms of relationships, communications, and even power (Flint 2012, p. 158).

In the meantime, there is increasingly an effect of reverse transfer to be observed. Such a reverser transfer is primarily any activity whose origin is the cyber world and its effect in the physical world. Downloading a document to eventually printing it out is a reverse transfer, as it materializes virtual data. It is secondarily a phenomenon that occurs when any virtual reality, for instance, any imaginary activity, game, or fictitious occupation from the cyber space, comes with requirements, demands, or conditions, etc., that induce real consequences or have real repercussions in the real life of involved individuals. Imaginary and fictitious games, tools, or means may dictate new behavior or a change in behavior of meta-geographic users in their geographic space. The creation of a variety of imaginary or fictitious occupational games, tools, means of usages for leisure, utility, or entertainment has produced such an effect of reverse transfer.

This reverse of transfer concretely occurs when activity in the geographic physical space is initiated by, or depends on, a source in the cyber space. It is about any activity we may be involved in but in which we react to the directions, impetus, or even order from a source in the cyber space. It is a reality through sources in the cyber space may condition or even govern aspects of our existence in the geographic physical space. It can be anything such as printing out a document from the cyberspace. It can also be playing a game in the cyber space, whose rules and conditions affect our life in the physical space. As an example, there is the case of Second Life, a 3D virtual world created entirely by its users, who get to live a virtual life in the game, wherein something may happen, like losing a fictitious girlfriend, causing the player to get upset in the real world. There have been, as well, cases of people committing real crimes because of incidents in fictitious games online. There are fictitious cyber games requiring real money. There are those participating in a game in the cyber space whose name they print out on their T-shirts they wear in the real world, etc. All these are cases of reverse transfer, wherein activity from the cyber space is transferred down to have real effects in the geographic physical realm.

Interactive activities bring closely together the prerogatives of two spaces, namely the physical space and the cyber space, increasingly blurring the distinctiveness of each as some become emotionally invested in the consequences of their involvement in activity in the cyber space.

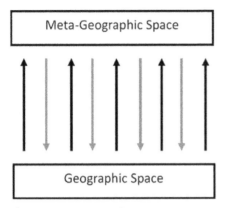

Reverse Transfer

Imagined, fictitious activity of the cyber space affecting real life in the geographic space.

Figure 11.3.

THE GLOBAL PUBLIC SPHERE

The era of globalization has been producing new phenomena already mentioned such as transnationality and transculturality. These notions imply increased flow of exchanges across national and cultural borders. Such exchanges are primarily facilitated by communication activity. We exchange sounds, images, and writing. The vehicle of such exchanges is the mass media. The mass media today is the sum of predigital communication technology tools, most of which have become digitalized, such as radio, paper, photography, and television, but also today actual digital technology tools, essentially the Internet and the various applications through software. Such digital mass media have a global scale, as their reach is global. They constitute a venue of exchange in the *public sphere*, to use the expression of Habermas (1989), or just the public space, to keep with the theme of this book. The public sphere goes beyond just cafés, bistros, restaurants, or stadiums, where people meet and exchange and form public opinions. Because of the global reach of digital media developing into a global mass media, the public sphere is morphing into a *global public sphere*. As the mass media develop into a global mass media, so will the public sphere develop into a global public sphere. If and when mass media help in the process of emerges of a public opinion, global mass media will constitute the vehicle through a global public opinion emerges. "Global media, if indeed they do exist, form the necessary material framework for any global public sphere that might exist or emerge" (Bennett and Entman 2001, p. 76). The process toward an emergence of global media that these authors express doubt about is under way. If the process continues, and there is no reason to think it will not, then not only are we on the verge of producing global media and a global public sphere but also subsequently a global culture.

There are indeed issues of common interest for all people around the world, such as the environment or global health, to name just a few, or for some category of people around the world, such as gender issues, same-sex marriage, etc. These issues justify the need to communicate extraterritorially. And such a need to communicate extraterritorially is not always and exclusively carried out by state actors in the age of cyber space. Cyber space users, who may form a community of like-minded, gather around issues of their interests. Some of these issues are purely social in their nature. They are about the need to communicate, to keep up with friends, to even just chat. Others may have a point to them. They may be about any area of interest to human existence, about which there may be some inadequacies, shortcomings, or injustice to decry, causing some people to develop a need to address or confront. These are the kinds of issues that serve as causes for the emergence of social movements. The cyber space has indeed become a platform for social movements, grassroot initiatives, nongovernmental organizations' activity, or individuals seeking exposure for their various causes. They can garner such support for their cause or at least inform the world about whatever idea, grievance, or solution they may have. They can use the technology to organize. They can, in the process, sway public opinion, both nationally and internationally, and ultimately influence governmental action in a world where global public opinion is increasingly becoming relevant. The relevancy of global public opinion is itself the result of the emerging global mass communication media. Mass communication media are becoming the battlefield where issues, as they emerge, locally can be uploaded and shared with the rest of the world, which may have a reaction. It is this reaction of the world that is becoming relevant, as it is the building of a consensus or at least a momentum for a cause, which we call the global opinion. Granted, there is strictly speaking no such thing as a global opinion, as opinions vary and a global consensus is almost unattainable. The idea of a global opinion is nothing but the emerging majority-shared views, sensibilities, or principles. It is this notion of global opinion that is often referred to in international politics in the expression "international community." There are ways through which to decipher such a global opinion. There are today international surveys being done. In the social media, it is increasingly easy to detect the mood, the opinion, and the sensitivities of most users. There are causes on YouTube or elsewhere that garner support in the millions, and they signal the process of adhesion or consent of those millions to the given cause. Taken from this perspective, global mass communicative media are increasingly the most relevant battlefield for exposing, arguing, competing, and contesting some issues. To this effect, H. G. Gadamer (2000)[2] argued that the mass media are today in fact the battlefield on which the fate of our future will be decided. The reason, he argued further, was that the mass media allow the formation of public opinion in a way that not even political power can contain or undermine. Such public opinion reaches political officials, making these public spheres the spheres in which citizens communicate with themselves and ultimately with government (Habermas 1989).

It is this dynamic that fuels current social movements and accounts for the successes of many. Among the social movements that were fueled by such a dynamic, we count the Egyptian uprising in spring 2012 and the "Arab Spring." The dynamic has been instrumental in galvanizing Saudi women in their quest for freedom to drive cars. The dynamic has facilitated the organization of the social-economic protest in Israel. The dynamic is the result of the global megaphone that global media offer, allowing social movements to spread their ideas to a global audience. The effect of such a megaphone can be observed in the case of the young Pakistani woman, Malala Yousafzai, mentioned earlier, or the kidnapping of 230 Nigeria schoolgirls by the terrorist organization known as Boko Haram and the "Bring Back Our Girls" movement that it generated. The digital space megaphone has been localizing global social movements and globalizing local social movements. Recently, the atrocities through the beheading of hostages perpetrated by an organization called the Islamic State in its quest to build a state in the Middle East have prompted the birth of a countermovement by moderate Muslims called "Not in My Name." The combination of the global platform that the cyber space offers and the many causes of concern emerging as a consequence of the flurry of activities in the globalized world justifies the continual births of new social movements. Indeed, recent cyber space–induced social movements have been driven by growing anxieties of many in the midst of a world in transformation and flux. Recently, around 2010, in both Europe and the United States, there has been an economic downturn, which in Europe sparked the policy of austerity, and in both Europe and the United States, the feeling that banks, corporations, interest groups, and international institutions have taken control of the political process, turning policy makers into tools who simply reflect the demands of such entities and in the process highjacking the democratic process. This perception has been at the origin of frustrations that led to the rise of social movements such as the Occupy movement and Anonymous. The Occupy movement expressed its frustration over the unprecedented influence and subservient attitude of political decision makers and decision making toward and in favor of the world of finance. Anonymous, which is essentially a community of anarchic hacktivists, has targeted institutions to cause digital vandalism or even worse, out of frustration, justifying their actions through their own sense of idealism against an unjust order. They justify their actions as going after those perceived to rig the system in their favor. They tend to disapprove of expressions of such a system such as the gathering in Davos, Switzerland, of the rich and powerful, the big banks and corporations, etc.

Elsewhere, there have been other causes of frustrations that provoke the rise of a community of dissenting voices. Such causes of frustrations can be anything from lack of political participation to lack of cultural recognition, from gender inequalities to poverty, etc. They produce causes around which dissenting voices galvanize, using the cyber space to communicate, allowing venting and possible actions to be taken against them.

Whenever taken to address the causes of their frustrations, such actions are empowering, as they can be initiated away from the influence and the restrictive effects of political power. And because these social movements, many of which, informal and noninstitutional, often challenge the status quo, the government and the elites, they benefit from their informality and the illusiveness of their noninstitutionality.

As long as there are issues of interest to be shared, spread, or exposed to the rest of the world, the digital media will serve as a venue of dissemination. They will serve as some kind of electronic graffiti canvas to share with the public at large any concern. This explains the successes of various service and social media providers, serving as links between communities of common interest, that we call users. The successes of these providers of digital platforms for communication have been phenomenal, from the blogosphere to YouTube, from Twitter to Instagram, from Facebook (1.3 billion users) to LinkedIn.

These providers facilitate the creation across national borders of emerging communities of connecting peoples through the public sphere of the cyber space. As they connect, so do their individual and cultural identities. In the end, the communicative public sphere of the cyber space not only is used to exchange images, sounds, and words but also to share stories of aspirations, sorrow, pain, joy, fate, etc. The result may very well go beyond the digital communities of users to communities of people emotionally linked and invested in each other's fate. If and when such communicative exchanges in the cyber space go beyond the communicative level to reach the emotional dimension of solidarity with the fate of others elsewhere on the planet, we will have built the bridge, the binding glue between communities across the planet that would justify the emergence of a global culture and evidence of a global public sphere.

THE CYBER WAR

Among the issues we face since the advent and the use of the cyber space through the Internet is a new kind of war. It is war because the cyber space just like any other space facilitates a host of activities, many of which have enhanced the quality of life and allowed for more productivity. It is a space that essentially facilitates the flow of information, and information is here taken as any exchange of words, ideas, knowledge, images, sounds, etc., as stated earlier, as each one of them can be codified in algorithms as we explain below. It is the reason we call the new technology information technology. The relevance of information is that it can be worth knowing and having, even by other than those it is produced for or destined for. Having information is generally a positive fact. Having information you can use is even better. And even best is having information you can use against a potential or actual competitor or adversary, simply because it gives you leverage. Hence, there is a need to acquire or access such information where you can, if one happens to be in a context that requires it. This need for acquisition of and access to such information explains the activity of spying. Such activity of seeking information for which one is not the intended recipient has now a new theater, namely the cyber space. And the abundance of information in this space is making it increasingly the privileged space of all kinds of illicit queries for information not intended for those seeking it. The cyber space has become a space where plenty of illicit activity, plenty of spying, is occurring. The intensity of such illicit quests for information has led to the notion of a cyber war, as it involves not only those illicitly seeking but also those targeted, as they need to protect themselves or even to retaliate or counterattack when deemed necessary. Hence, we have here a state of war, almost generalized, as long as there are no international mechanisms or procedures to contain or keep in check such illicit activity. But even if there were such mechanisms or procedures, they would not necessarily subdue illicit activity, just as the law does not keep thugs from engaging in thuggish behavior. Furthermore, those cyber space thugs with ill intentions to act illicitly may outperform any such mechanisms.

It is a different kind of war with respect to the battlefield, to actors, to means, to goals, and to expected outcomes. Any war presupposes a battlefield. The battlefield in the cyber war is virtual, not physical. The cyber space is therefore without boundaries. It is consequently a global battlefield. The virtuality of the cyber war has consequences for actors, means, goals, and outcomes. With respect to actors, the cyber space war is not the preserve of the army, formal military, and nation-states. In addition to nation-states and their armies, there are nonstate actors. Among nonstate actors we count individuals, corporations, and aggregated groups, with or without political motives. Such actors with political motives induce attacks we call cyber terrorism. Others, without political motives, justify their involvement in the cyber war through their own ideals. Among them we count Anonymous, for instance, and others get involved just for the "fun" of it, an act that resembles vandalism.

The multiplicity of actors means that such a war may involve state actors against state actors. It may involve state actors against nonstate actors. It may involve nonstate against nonstate actors. Cyber warriors can be just about anyone with the knowledge and the intention to engage in illicit activity in the cyber space and therefore become part of the cyber war. This means that some cyber war activity is political, some economical, and some may just be about nuisance. The blurring of civilian and soldier is here a reality. The same blurring explains the multiplicity of goals and outcomes, as each cyber warrior is motivated by his or her own interests. This diversity of interests makes it difficult for some actors to coordinate their defensive or preventive measures or activity. Such is the case with state actors, governments, nonstate actors, and businesses, as it can be demonstrated in the case of Google in China. The divergence of interests can come in the way of state actors and nonstate actors, even when they seem to be the targets of the same origins. This has been recently, around the end of 2014, in the United States the case of hacking of Sony Studios in Los Angeles and the difficulties for both the government and the studio to act in concert against the cyber attack.

With respect to the means, the fight in the cyber war does not involve tanks, aircraft carriers, bombs, or any other physical weaponry. It involves electronic bugs, viruses, worms, Trojan horses, etc. It involves activities or attacks such as breaking codes (hacking), sabotage, etc. And it is around the means utilized and the nature of the cyber space that cyber warfare is conducted.

CYBER WARFARE

The notion of warfare revolves around the conduct of the war. It is about tactics and strategies. It is about the means or weapons utilized and the ends for which they are employed. It is about understanding the enemy, their behavior, their ability, their capacity, their savvy. It is about knowing how to engage them in combat, only here the combat is a cyber combat.

The enemy may or may not be known. Because the technology allows cyber actors and perpetrators to hide the source of their malfeasant activity and therefore their identities, going even as far as using the identity of a third party as the origin and disguising their cyber footprint and forensic traces, it is not always possible to know who the cyber malfeasant or attacker is. And in a war where the battlefield is virtual, actors are not necessarily visible and physical death is not a factor, at least not directly. Actors do not physically show up to fight the cyber war but rather utilize "zombie armies" such as viruses (Trojan horses), worms (Conficker), and malevolent software code (Stuxnet). The weapons they use are not physical either but rather of a logical nature. And because their consequences may have the destructive potential of a bomb, they are called "logic bombs."[3]

The potential for destruction of cyber space weaponry is indeed devastating. This is due to the vulnerability of the World Wide Web. We have joined computers through the Internet in order to harness the power of communication. However, we have rendered anyone connected to using it susceptible of becoming a victim of cyber warfare. We are all vulnerable due to such World Wide Web interconnectedness. Two factors account for such a vulnerability. First, it is because of the scientific nature of computer science. It is based on a binary system, which uses ones (1s) and zeros (0s) in computational algorithms, a procedure that uses an initial condition of numbers and performs as determined the operation of combinatory sequencing to produce the expected result in data processing or in nonvalue judgment problem-solving cases. "Every number, every bit of data, every voice communication and every video can, in essence, be expressed as a string of 1s and 0s" (Rosenzweig 2013, p. 1). The structure of the string of 1s and 0s, etched in silicon chips integrated into circuits, makes their manipulation possible. It is the combinatory power of the string of 1s and 0s that led to "the explosion of computing power" (Rosenzweig 2013, p. 1). Such an explosion of computer power and the attractiveness of the applications it makes available to us justify the greater computer network sharing community. The availability of the scientific knowledge about algorithms allows those in possession of such knowledge to act malfeasantly (malfeasant actors). They are those that render vulnerable all other users.

Second, the growing pool of computer users has continued to grow and so did the variety of areas that rely on computational power. They are individuals, businesses, governments, nongovernment organizations, etc. This means that all of society's infrastructures and superstructures; telecommunication systems, satellites, and GPS; power plants; financial markets; drones; industrial plants (indeed, the Supervisory Control and Data Acquisition [SCADA] system, manufactured by the German company Siemens to oversee industrial production, has been linked as well to computer power), etc., are exposed infrastructures and superstructures.[4] If and when they are affected, one can see why the expression "logic bomb" has been used.

As a result, the need for cyber security is a feature of any of the infrastructures and superstructures we mentioned. They need to protect themselves. They have each come up with their own remedy. There are now what we call cyber defenses, cyber cops, etc., for that purpose. In the case of nation-state actors, they are developing entire units and command systems dedicated to just that, the defense of the cyber space. As examples, the United States now has a Cyber Command, a security team, and so does China, to name just two.

SHOULD THE CYBER SPACE BE REGULATED?

As a space, the cyber space is a canvas for activity. We now bank through the cyber space; we socialize through the cyber space; we make purchases through the cyber space, we communicate through the cyber space; we educate ourselves through the cyber space; we play and entertain ourselves through the cyber space. We exchange information, ideas, opinions, and knowledge, documents, images, etc.

Any space where there is a flurry of activity offers the potential for abuses, as not all activities are safe, legal, or honest. Not all users of the cyber space are well intentioned, with the interests of all in mind. Some may be malicious, ill driven, wicked, criminal, and even perverted. Among such criminal, risky, and dangerous outcomes of activity in the cyber space are child pornography, cyber bullying, terrorism, hate propaganda, piracy, hacking, identity theft, etc. This potential for abuses raises the question of risks associated with involvement in the cyber space. They are criminal and risky potential outcomes that endanger the welfare of individuals, society, and even the world. They compel the question on the safety and security of activity in the cyber space. They compel society to ponder the question of what to do to curtail such crimes and risks emanating from cyber activity.

There is a consensus on the potential and real crimes and risk from the cyber space. There is a realization of the need to find ways to gain some degree of control or at least oversight on what goes on in the cyber space. There is, however, less consensus and clarity on how to go about gaining control or oversight, or about how much control that will have to be.

On the control and regulation of the cyber space, two camps have emerged: those against any kind of control and those in favor of some control. Those against control are individuals who want, uninhibitedly, to surf and navigate the web at will. There are those who as a matter of principle do not want the government interfering with a space that is par excellence, a free space zone. Both argue on the ground of privacy, freedom of speech and expression, public access, and unfettered access to content.

Those in favor of some degree of regulation and control are businesses and corporations wary of counterfeit, hacking, piracy, individuals worried about infringement of intellectual property, and the government concerned with issues of national security. They argue on the ground of property rights, national security, and general well-being.

In the United States, the government has the duty and therefore the obligation to safeguard national security and promote the general well-being of the population. It has to do what it has to to live up to such an obligation. It is what absolutist theorists, such as Jean Bodin, referred to as *raison d'*état. It needs to have and therefore collect intelligence from any source, even the cyber space. Congress passed the CISPA (Cyber Intelligence Sharing and Protection Act). The Act is designed to allow the sharing of information between government-businesses and the technology companies for national security purposes.

Businesses in the United States have succeeded in getting lawmakers in the Republican majority House of Representatives to enact a few law propositions aimed at protecting their interests. Lawmakers have passed the Preventing Real Online Threats to Economic Creativity and Theft of Intellectual Property Act (PROTECT IP Act, or PIPA) and the Stop Online Piracy Act (SOPA), both of which are self-explanatory in their intent, namely, to protect copyright/intellectual property but also to protect against counterfeit products that cut into their profits and also ruin the legitimate manufacturers' good names.

These law initiatives essentially empower the Department of Justice to enforce the Acts. They empower the right holders to seek court orders to protect their products. These legislation initiatives have not been without resistance. The resistance came from different directions. Service providers have been those vehemently protesting these law initiatives. The burden and responsibility for abuses have been put on them. They stand to lose in the deal. Users of the Internet are among those also protesting the law initiatives. They argue that their freedom in the web will be compromised and that the interference will produce restrictions in their ability to surf around, which will ruin the entire Internet experience. They reject the notion of policing the web and the feeling of being watched while surfing through the Internet. Many other citizens with a libertarian vein just do not like the idea of government policing of the web. The difficulty has been to find a compromise between the legitimate need for national security protection and the freedom to surf about in the web without restrictions.

The issue around the need to regulate the Internet is not specific to the United States. Other nations have to deal with it. They deal with the issues differently. China is highly restrictive, while the Netherlands is not. And because the web technology is naturally global, issues of Internet regulation are naturally global. They necessitate therefore some degree of harmonization of rules or codes of conduct for users, providers, and governments, all of which have different interests.

The International Telecommunication Union (ITU) has been in existence since 1865, which predates the establishment of the UN. It has, since 1947, become a UN agency. The purpose of its creation was initially justified by the invention of the telegraph. Eventually the telephone and the invention of the Internet as a communication technology were part of that history. This agency has since 1988 been interested in the governance of the Internet and its content when it first issued new guidelines pertaining to the Internet. The same agency has deemed it necessary to get more involved, given the growing issues of access to the technology that makes it possible and access to the information and use of it and its social-political implications. The ITU recently (December 3–15, 2012) organized a World Conference on International Telecommunications in Dubai with the intent to come up with a new regulatory body of text or treaty that addresses all relevant concerns. Member states were urged to make suggestions. Some of the suggestions legitimately addressed issues of spam or cyber security. Some were restrictive in their nature, and some seek more control by governments and some degree of censorship. Although not all suggestions were either political or restrictive, the conference generated enough worry and concern that it was about to undermine the unprecedented benefit of this tool and space that the Internet is and in the process undermine its overall usefulness. Some nations, among them the United States, have shared that concern. Together with many others, up to eighty[5] countries ended up not signing the treaty that the many suggestions have produced. The treaty signed by the rest of member states will come into effect in January 2015, with consequences that are yet to be determined. The Dubai conference was not successful in the sense that many of the member states either did not sign or abstained. Some issues around governance or regulation of the Internet remain salient. The dilemma lies in the fact that there is a recognized need to have some degree of political control over the technology, but how much control should be made possible without undermining the very essence of the Internet. The issue remains delicate. Different nations, given the principle of national sovereignty, do possess the prerogative of interference into the Internet, as some do. Both nationally and internationally, there is a need for some form of regulatory framework, with some degree of political control. It is ultimately an issue of the geopolitics of the cyber space. It is about who controls the cyber space: the user, the provider, the businesses, or the government.

As a canvas for activity and because the activity has to be regulated to avoid chaos, all spaces induce the need for control of the activity therein. The cyber space is no different, but because it is virtual and unlike other spaces, it presents a number of challenges that society cannot afford not to consider.

NOTES

1. The authors deplore the inadequacies of such meta-geographies, which they consider reductionist and simplistic and therefore misleading and not useful.

2. Hans Georg Gadamer, TV series, 2000, by Rudiger Safranski, March 10, 2012. The German title is Gadamer erzaehlt die Geschichte der Philosophie 6/6.

3. *The Economist*, "War in the Fifth Domain," July 1, 2010.

4. A concrete case of such interference in the industrial production process of others has been documented with the example of the use of the Stuxnet worm. It has been used, although not officially confirmed, by the United States and supposedly Israel to infect a Microsoft Windows system from a thumb drive or a network share or directly across a corporate network if the network servers are not patched with the MS08–067. (US Computer Emergency Readiness Team 2009).

5. Among them were Australia, Canada, Chile, Costa Rica, Czech Republic, Denmark, Egypt, Finland, Greece, Italy, Japan, Kenya, the Netherlands, New Zealand, Poland, Portugal, Qatar, Sweden, and the United Kingdom. Some countries abstained.

Conclusion

Human beings, individually or collectively, negotiate their existence in a natural context involving time and space that is characterized by changing conditions. Life itself is changing, and human beings change along. In fact, Friedrich Hegel argued that the essence of existing is becoming. In the pursuit of becoming, we engage our environment, both sociological and ecological, in activities designed to facilitate, support, protect, and enhance the chances and the quality of existence. Therefore, we seek access to spaces that host our existence. We need to use them. We endeavor to organize them. We are compelled to control them. We have to protect them. We think to expand, etc. All this activity occurs not without issues simply because human existence is inherently negotiated through conflicts and therefore issues due to a variety of factors such as colliding interests. Global issues, from territorial disputes to cultural conflicts (ethnic conflicts, nationalism conflicts), from religious and civilizational (value systems tensions) to immigration, global health, human trafficking, and environmental issues, from cyber space issues to possibly future outer space issues, are nothing but the emerging challenges that we encounter, produce, or cause both in the sociological and ecological worlds.

Moreover, because all other human communities, ethnic to national, around the world are engaged in the same kinds of activities, we eventually cross paths. In addition, whatever activity we engage in as we cross paths brings about the emergence of issues with a cross-ethnic or national reach. Such issues are those that become global as communities continue to globally cross each other's paths. That has been exactly occurring exponentially as a result of the use of new technologies that defy time and space. Such technologies have even allowed the creation of a new space, the cyber space. Like any other space, this new space comes with the benefit of facilitating, supporting, and enhancing the quality of human existence and therefore attracting activity, but at the same time, comes with its own set of new issues.

The dynamics of human existence has now succeeded in expanding human activity from its initially umbilical centered ethnic community activity to the entire globe. The entire world is now the theater of all human beings. But it seems that the dynamic nature of human existence, which justifies the quest for new spaces, whether for the sake of accessing them to quench our curiosity or with the hope of finding new hosts with the potential of enhancing the quality of human existence, has not subsided with the global conquest. Indeed, the quest for expanding into new spaces is under way. Interest in the research by NASA about outer space, commercial interest in traveling to new planets and harnessing the riches of minerals found there, colonizing such spaces, and the interest of the masses in such endeavors are currently the evidence of such a quest. It may, therefore, be simply a matter of time before mankind starts a new adventure of its history. This one would be about colonizing new spaces, planets, outside of the one initially prepared to host human life and existence.

Such a quest is leading to the need to access outer space. Such a need, if or when achieved, will bring about the need to control it, organize it, and protect it, which in turn will lead to new sets of issues associated with such an outer space, issues not yet imaginable. History indeed is in perpetual motion and so are human activity and human issues.

Bibliography

Alexander, Jeffrey. *Twenty Lectures*. New York: Columbia University Press, 1987.

Aristotle. *The Nicomachean Ethics*. New York: Oxford University Press, 2009.

Associated Press. "UN Report 2015 for Water Day." New Delhi, India, Friday 19, 2015. The UN World Water Development Report 2015, "Water for a Sustainable World."

Barnett, P. M. Thomas. *Blueprint for Action: A Future Worth Creating*. New York: Penguin, 2005.

Baumeister, Roy. *Identity: Cultural Change and the Struggle for Self*. New York: Oxford University Press, 1986.

Baumeister, Roy, and Mark Muraden. "Identity as Adaptation to Social, Cultural, and Historical Context." *Journal of Adolescence*, 19, 406–418, 1996.

Benhabib, Seyla. *The Claims of Culture: Equality and Diversity in the Global Era*. Princeton, NJ: Princeton University Press, 2002.

Bennett, W. Lance, and Robert M. Entman. *Mediated Politics: Communication in the Future of Democracy*. New York: Cambridge University Press, 2001.

Bienstock, Ric Esther. Le don d'organes, 2013. future.arte.tv/fr/sujet/ledon-dorganes.

Bodin, Jean. *Six Books of the Commonwealth*. Oxford: Basil Blackwell, 1955.

Burke, Edmund. *Reflection on the Revolution in France, 1790*. New York: Penguin Books, 1986.

Callinicos, Alex. *Making History: Agency, Structure, and Change in Social Theory* (second edition). The Netherlands: Brill Academic Publishers, 2004.

Collins, Randall. "Civilizations as Zones of Prestige and Social Contact." In *Rethinking Civilizational Analysis*. Said Arjomand and Edward A. Tiryakian, eds. London and Thousand Oaks, CA: Sage, pp. 132–47, 2004.

David, Steven R. "Explaining Third World Alignment in World Politics." *World Politics*, 43 (2), 1991, pp. 233–56.

Davidson, Arnold I. *Michel Foucault: Security, Territory, Population: Lectures at the College de France, 1977–1978*. New York: Picador, 2004.

Donahue, John, and John Esposito, eds. *Islam in Transition: Muslim Perspectives* (second edition). New York: Oxford University Press, 2007.

Douglas, M. *Implicit Meanings*. London: Routledge, 1999.

Dahlerup, Drude. "Quotas—A Jump to Equality? The Need for International Comparison of the Use of Electoral Quotas to Obtain Equal Political Citizenship for Women." Paper prepared for workshop hosted by International Institute for Democracy and Electoral Assistance (IDEA) on September 25, 2002, in Jakarta, Indonesia. http://www.quotaproject.org/CS/CS_Comparative.pdf.

Du Gray, Paul, and Stuart Hall, eds. *Questions of Cultural Identity*. London and Thousand Oaks, CA: Sage, 2005.

Eisenstadt, S. N. "Multiple Modernities." *Dedalus*, 129, pp. 1–29, 2000.

Eriksen, Thomas Hylland. *Ethnicity and Nationalism: Anthropological Perspectives* (second edition). London: Pluto Press, 1993.

Esposito, John L., ed. *The Oxford History of Islam*. New York: Oxford University Press, 1999.

Flint, Colin. *Introduction to Geopolitics* (second edition). New York: Routledge, 2012.

Frank, Andre Gunder. *ReOrient: Global Economy in the Asian Age*. Berkley: University of California Press, 1998.

Friedman, Jonathan. *Being in the World: Globalization and Localization*. London and Thousand Oaks, CA: Sage, 1990.

Galtung, Johan. *Frieden mit friedlichen Mitteln: Friede und Konflikt, Entwicklung und Kultur*. Opladen, Germany: Leske + Busrich, 1998.

Gehlen, Arnold. *Der Mensch: Sein Natur und seine Stellung in der Welt* (*Man: His Nature and Place in the World*). New York: Columbia University Press, 1988.

Giddens, Anthony. *Constitution of Society*. Berkeley: University of California Press, 1984.

Glazer, Nathan, and Daniel P. Moynihan. *Beyond the Melting Pot: The Negroes, Puerto Ricans, Jews, Italians, and Irish of New York City* (second edition). Cambridge, MA: MIT Press, 1970.

Goodman, Jacqueline, ed. *Global Perspectives on Gender and Work: Reading and Interpretations* (second edition). Lanham, MD: Rowan & Littlefield, 2010.

Gramsci, Antonio. *Prison Notebooks* (volume 1). Joseph A. Buttigieg, ed. New York: Columbia University Press, 1975.

Griswold, Daniel. "The Blessing and Challenges of Globalization." Cato.org. September 1, 2000. http://www.cato.org/publications/commentary/blessings-challenges-globalization.

Hardin, Garett. "The Tragedy of the Commons." *Science*, 162 (3856), pp. 1243–48, December 13, 1968.

Hays, Sharon. "Structure and Agency: The Sticky Problem of Culture." *Sociological Theory*, 2 (1), pp. 57–72, March 1994.

Hegel, G. W. F. *The Philosophy of History*. Rockville, MD: Wildside Press, 2010.

———. *The Philosophy of History*. New York, Cosimo, 2007.

———. *Philosophy of Right*. Mineola, NY: Dover Publications, 2005.

———. *Science of Logic* (*Wissenschaft der Logik*). Nuremberg, Germany, 1816.

Hoodbhoy, Pervez Amirali. "Islam and Science Have Parted Ways." *Middle East Quarterly*, XVII (1), Winter 2010, pp. 69–74.

Horton, John, and Peter Kraft. *Cultural Geographies: An Introduction*. New York: Routledge, 2014.

Kaplan, Robert. "Center Stage for the 21st Century: Power Plays in the Indian Ocean." *Foreign Affairs*, March/April 2009, pp. 16–32. https://www.foreignaffairs.com/articles/east-asia/2009-03-01/center-stage-21st-century.

Katzenstein, Peter, ed. *Civilizations in World Politics: Plural and Pluralist Perspectives*. New York: Routledge, 2010.

Kessler, Suzanne. *Gender: An Anthropological Perspective*. Chicago: The University of Chicago University Press, 1978.Lazlo, Ervin. *Introduction to Systems Philosophy*. New York: Gordon and Breach, 1972.

Lewis, Martin W., and Karen Wigen. *The Myth of Continents: A Critique of Metageography*. Berkeley: University of California Press, 1997.

Mackinder, Halford J. "The Geographic Pivot of History." Article submitted to the Royal Geographical Society, 1904.

McNeill, William H. *The Rise of the West: A History of the Human Community*. Chicago: The University of Chicago Press, 1963.

Menon, Rajan. *The End of Alliances*. New York: Oxford University Press, 2007.

Moghadam, Valentine M. *Globalization and Social Movements*. Lanham, MD: Rowman & Littlefield, 2013.

Murphey, Rhoads. *East Asia: A New History* (third edition). New York: Pearson and Longman, 2004.

Nietzsche, Friedrich. *Thus Spoke Zarathustra*. New York: Algora Publishing, 2003.

O'Neil, Patrick H. *Essentials of Comparative Politics* (third edition). New York: W.W. Norton, 2010.

O'Neil, Patrick H. *Essentials of Comparative Politics* (fourth edition). New York: W.W. Norton, 2013.

Ong, Aihwa. *Flexible Citizenship: Cultural Logics of Transnationality*. Durham, NC: Duke University Press, 1999.

Organisation for Economic Co-operation and Development (OECD). Trade, Employment and Labour Standards. A Study of Core Workers' Rights and International Trade. Paris: OECD, 1996, pp. 12–13.

Organization for Security and Co-operation in Europe (OSCE). Office of the Special Representative and Co-ordinator for Combating Trafficking in Human Beings. "Trafficking in Human Beings for the Purpose of Organ Removal in the OSCE Region: Analysis and Findings." Occasional Paper Series no. 6, July 2013. http://www.osce.org/cthb/103393?download=true.

Parsons, Talcott. *The Structure of Social Action: A Study in Social Theory with Special Reference to a Group of Recent European Writers* (volume 1). New York: The Free Press, 1937.

Peterson, V. Spike, and Anne Sisson Runyan. *Global Gender Issues in the New Millennium* (third edition). Boulder: Westview, 2011.

Piccoli, Wolfgano. *Alliance Theory: The Case of Turkey and Israel.* Copenhagen Peace Research Institute, July-August 1999.

Pielou, E. C. *Fresh Water*. Chicago: The University of Chicago Press, 1998.

Plato. *The Republic* (Book 5). Mineola, NY: Dover Publications, 2000.

Popescu, Gabriel. *Bordering and Ordering the Twenty-first Century*. Lanham, MD: Rowman & Littlefield, 2012.

Popper, Karl. *The Misery of Historicism*. New York: Routledge, 2000.

Popper, Karl. *The Poverty of Historicism*. New York: Routledge, 1957.

Ravenhill, John. *Global Political Economy*. New York: Oxford University Press, 2011.

Reeler, Doug. "A Three-fold Theory of Social Change." Community Development Resource Association, 2007. http://www.cdra.org.za/articles/A Theory of Social Change by Doug Reeler.pdf.

Rosenzweig, Paul. *Cyber Warfare: How Conflicts in Cyber Space Are Challenging America and Changing the World*. Santa Barbara, CA: Praeger, 2013.

Rousseau, Jean Jacques. *Social Contract* (book I). New York: Penguin Books, 1968.

Samuels, David. *Comparative Politics*. Boston: Pearson, 2012.

Schmidt, Gavin, and Joshua Wolfe. *Climate Change: Picture the Science*. New York: W.W. Norton, 2009.

Simmons, Matthew. *Twilight in the Desert: The Upcoming Saudi Oil Shock and the World Economy*. Hoboken, NJ: Wiley, 2005.

Stavenhagen, Rudolfo. "Ethnic Conflicts and Their Impact on International Society." *International Social Science Journal*, 50 (157), September 1998, pp. 433–45.

Strange, Susan. "The Bondage of Liberal Economics." *SAIS Review*, 6 (1), Winter-Spring 1986, pp. 25–38.

Stubbs, Richard, and Geoffrey R. D. Underhill. *Political Economy and the Changing Global Order* (third edition). New York: Oxford University Press, 2005.

Thucydides. *The History of the Peloponnesian War*. New York: Barnes and Noble, 2006.

Tibi, Bassam. *Islam's Predicament with Modernity: Religious Reform and Cultural Change*. New York: Routledge, 2009.

US Computer Emergency Readiness Team. Alert TA09–088A: Conficker Worm Targets Microsoft Windows System, March 29, 2009. https://www.us-cert.gov/ncas/alerts/TA09-088A.

Walterstorff, Nicholas. *The Mighty and the Almighty: An Essay in Political Theology*. New York: Cambridge University Press, 2012.

"War in the Fifth Domain: Are the Mouse and Keyboard the New Weapons of Conflict?" *The Economist*, July 1, 2010.

Weber, Max. *Economy and Society*, New York: Routledge, 1989.

Weber, Max. *The Protestant Ethic and the Spirit of Capitalism* (1905). New York: Routledge, 1930.

Weinreich, Peter, and Wendy Saunderson, eds. *Analysing Identity: Cross Cultural, Societal and Clinical Contexts*. New York: Routledge, 1998.

Welsch, Wolfgang. "Transculturality: The Puzzling Form of Cultures Today." In *Spaces of Culture: City, Nation, World*. Mike Featherston and Scott Lash, eds. London: Sage, pp. 194–213, 1999.

Wilson, Sarah. *Melting Pot Modernism*. Ithaca, NY: Cornell University Press, 2010.

World Resources Institute. *World Resources 2000–2001: People and Ecosystems: The Fraying Web of Life*. Washington, DC: World Resources Institute, 2000.

About the Author

Jean Kachiga teaches at SUNY Brockport in New York. His courses include international relations, international political economy, and global issues. His research and scholarship focus on the dynamics of change in international relations. This focus justifies his most recent publication titled *China in Africa* and a forthcoming manuscript titled *The Rise to Super-power Status.*

Lightning Source UK Ltd.
Milton Keynes UK
UKHW011356230123
415820UK00016B/146